9+

H. L. Mencken and the Debunkers

# H.L. MENCKEN and the Debunkers

Edward A. Martin

The University of Georgia Press
Athens

Copyright © 1984 by the University of Georgia Press
Athens, Georgia 30602
All rights reserved

Designed by Sandra Strother Hudson
Set in Linotron 202 Times Roman

Printed in the United States of America

90  89  88  87  86  85  84    5  4  3  2  1

The paper in this book meets the guidelines for permanence
and durability of the Committee on Production Guidelines for
Book Longevity of the Council on Library Resources.

**Library of Congress Cataloging in Publication Data**

Martin, Edward A. (Edward Alexander), 1927–
  H. L. Mencken and the debunkers.

  Bibliography: p.
  Includes index.
    1. Mencken, H. L. (Henry Louis), 1880–1956—
Criticism and interpretation.    2. Satire, American—
History and criticism.    3. American literature—20th
century—History and criticism.    I. Title.
PS3525.E43Z675  1984    818'.5209    83-17874
ISBN 0-8203-0702-5

Portions of this book are based on the following previously
published articles by Edward Martin: "The Ordeal of H. L.
Mencken," *The South Atlantic Quarterly,* vol. 61, no. 3 (Summer 1962), copyright 1962 by Duke University Press; "H. L.
Mencken's Poetry," *Texas Studies in Literature and Language,*
vol. 6, no. 3 (Autumn 1964); "A Puritan's Satanic Flight: Don
Marquis, Archy, and Anarchy," *Sewanee Review,* vol. 83 (October–December 1975); and "H. L. Mencken and Equal
Rights for Women," *The Georgia Review,* vol. 35, no. 1
(Spring 1981). The author and the publisher gratefully ac-
knowledge permission to reprint the material here.

FOR PEG

# Contents

. . . in the hour of unusual affliction, minds
of a certain temperament find a strange, hysterical
relief in a wild, perverse humorousness, the more
alluring from its entire unsuitableness to the
occasion.

Herman Melville, Pierre, 1852

# Preface

My father, Alexander Tertius Martin, 1886–1968, belonged to the same generation as H. L. Mencken, Sinclair Lewis, Ring Lardner, Don Marquis, and the debunkers. Although there is another generation between theirs and mine, my interest in them is an interest in a matrix of time, place, and, especially, personality. They were men with both public and private selves: sometimes there was a duplicity to their lives that we, as a culture, no longer admire. Their point of view and their style have both puzzled and fascinated me. While I have sometimes found their humor more perverse than alluring, I have sought, like a dutiful grandchild, to understand it, because I feel, sometimes reluctantly, so intimately connected to them.

The quotation from Melville's *Pierre* that serves as the epigraph to this book struck my attention as I was reading Jay Martin's *Nathanael West: The Art of His Life*. While much of the humor of the debunkers *was* suitable to the occasion, its tendency, like that of some of the American writers both before and after them, was toward a wild perversity—what in our time we have called black humor.

It was Robert Gorham Davis who, years ago, in a graduate seminar at Columbia drew our attention to the wild, perverse humorousness of certain exchanges in *The Sun Also Rises* and used the word "debunking" to characterize them. I went on to study the satire of that period, with the help of Richard Chase and Donald Porter Geddes.

I have learned methods and emphases from many writers on American culture and literature. Where I can be explicit I have tried to acknowledge these writers in my text and notes. Walter Blair's books and Constance Rourke's book on American humor have been especially helpful for interpretations, sources, and methods. The early criticism of Van Wyck Brooks has provided special inspiration, as have the clairvoyant reviews and essays of Edmund Wilson. In a brief article in 1921 Wilson said what was essential about H. L. Mencken and no one has said it better since then.

There is a substantial body of biographical and critical writing about

Mencken. For information I have depended especially on Carl Bode, Charles A. Fecher, William Manchester, Douglas Stenerson, William H. Nolte, and Carl Dolmetsch. For interpretation I have found special support in Guy J. Forgue's encyclopedic book, which argues that Mencken is defined by his *"époque"*—by the *"climat culturel"* that gave rise to his work. I have tried to explore the relation between work and period, as well as the extent to which Mencken influenced that period.

I have avoided an elaborate theoretical apparatus about satire because I did not believe it necessary, and because I am unable to write one in any case, although I know I have been influenced by Freud's application of the theory of the unconscious to the analysis of wit. I use the terms *satire* and *debunking* interchangeably; by *debunking* I mean simply the satire of the period 1910 to 1930, which I hope to characterize in what I have written. There is, I believe, a special tension to the satire of this period, generated out of an ambivalence between destructive and affirmative impulses. The destructive is easier to detect than the affirmative. In writing about what is affirmative I have used the terms *comic* and *humorous* in very ordinary ways.

Not everyone's favorite writers appear in this book. Some of the omissions are arbitrary; I have not tried to write a survey of the satire of the period. I have tried to describe attitudes that were shared and expressed from, roughly, 1910 to 1930 by focusing on Mencken, Lewis, Marquis, Lardner, and a few others, because they seem to me to represent a generation of satirists, and, in a more limited sense, a generation of writers whose literary offspring is Nathanael West. I have tried to create a new perspective on what is in the main already familiar material, and Mencken is the crucial figure in my reassessment.

Earlier versions of parts of the chapters on Mencken were published as articles in the *South Atlantic Quarterly,* in *Texas Studies in Literature and Language,* and in the *Georgia Review.* A condensed version of the chapter on Don Marquis was published in the *Sewanee Review.*

A leave of absence and research grants awarded by the Faculty Research Committee at Middlebury College enabled me to prepare the final version of the book. My colleagues have helped me by looking critically at drafts of chapters: John Conron, Stephen Donadio, Robert Hill, David Littlefield, Robert Pack, David Price; John Bertolini stepped in with a crucial translation. The manuscript, as well as many penultimate drafts of chapters, was patiently and intelligently typed by Susan Coburn, Cynthia Ketcham, Carol Knaus, and Helen Reiff, who also prepared the index. Ian Martin helped with the list of works cited. Hilde Robinson edited the manuscript perceptively and meticulously.

# Introduction

In 1923 a symposium called *These United States* was published.[1] Another of many books examining American culture and history, this one gathered essays that had first appeared in the *Nation*, a periodical with a long reform tradition. The two volumes, borrowing subtitles from H. L. Mencken's six books entitled *Prejudices*, were called "First Series" and "Second Series." The essays, fifty-three in number, were written by different authors about each of the states, as well as the District of Columbia, Alaska, Puerto Rico, and Hawaii (New York City and New York State were given separate essays). In his preface the editor, Ernest Gruening, noted that in America a "period of flux" depending upon westward expansion and the unrestricted flow of immigration was over. "The transformation that is now taking place," he wrote, "is in many ways of a different character. Fundamental doctrines are being abandoned, or basically re-interpreted."

The first two essays established the ironic tone and the antiprovincial theme of the series. William Allen White led off by observing that "Kansans are marked by Puritanism," a condition resulting in repression of the sense of beauty and of the joy "that restores the soul of man." This condition, White concluded, is "tremendously American." Mencken followed with an essay called "Maryland: Apex of Normalcy." As White had done for Kansas, Mencken celebrated the natural beauty and physical abundance of Maryland, yet he saw Maryland as an index of American mediocrity:

> What is life like in arcadian Maryland? How does it feel to live amid scenes so idyllic, among a people so virtuous and so happy, on the hooks of statistics so magnificently meridional? I answer frankly and firstly: it is dull. I answer secondly: it is depressing. I answer thirdly: it steadily grows worse. Everywhere in the United States, indeed, there is that encroaching shadow of gloom. Regimentation in morals, in political theory, in every department of thought has brought with it a stiffening, almost a deadening in manners.

Although a few of the authors in *These United States* wrote celebratory essays, most established double perspectives like those of White and

Mencken: they criticized and sometimes ridiculed what they loved. Ridicule was expressed with rhetorical extravagance. For example, in "New Jersey" Edmund Wilson reported, "One finds oneself immersed in an atmosphere of tarnishment and mess. The cities are indifferent and dingy; the people are seedy and dull; a kind of sloppiness and mediocrity seems to have fallen on the fields themselves, as if Nature herself had turned slattern and could no longer keep herself dressed." But Princeton was an oasis of culture and beauty. Leonard Lanson Cline's essay was titled "Michigan: the Fordizing of a Pleasant Peninsula" and Iowa was represented as "A Mortgaged Eldorado" by Johan J. Smertenko. In his essay on Arkansas C. L. Edson noted the state's enduring natural splendor, which he saw threatened by its population of "proletarians with nothing in them except what has come out of them. And the result is a State that judged by the standards of the other forty-seven is zero in the world of ideas and cultural achievement, and a people so vulgar, ill-smelling, and outlandish as to shock the people of the other commonwealths when they behold them." Similarly extravagant simplification dominated what George Clifton Edwards wrote about Texans: "All of our present-day characteristics—our fondness for being fooled, our subjection to big business, our intolerance, our hatred, our preference for violent action, our prejudices against the Negro—have flowered in the Ku Klux Klan." Several years earlier (1917) in "The Sahara of the Bozart" Mencken had developed more fully the theme of the special cultural deprivation of the southern states.[2] That sense of barren provincialism in all the states ran through many of the essays in the two volumes of *These United States*. It was Mencken who reflected and in large measure influenced a style and perspective under which the reformer's concern survived. The focus for such concern was the attitude that the emerging American culture was ugly: "What we lack most keenly is a sense of beauty and the love of it."[3] Some of America's most distinguished writers were contributors to the two volumes: Sherwood Anderson wrote about Ohio, Willa Cather about Nebraska, Theodore Dreiser about Indiana, Sinclair Lewis about Minnesota. All of them celebrated the values of their regional landscapes. All noted the failure of the aesthetic sensibilities of most of the inhabitants of those landscapes. All deplored especially the manifestations of that failure in the banal aspects of popular culture, the prohibitions of Puritan morality, the glorification of provincial life, the blatant Americanism that had survived from the war years, and the pursuit of a meretricious prosperity. Many of them wrote with comic indignation or with lurid extravagance.

Concern about the ugliness they saw dominating America animated the satire of Mencken, Lewis, and Don Marquis—several writers among many who ridiculed the posturing and inflated rhetoric with which their culture valued itself. Because of their special outrage at the power of fraudulent language, they were debunkers (to use a word coined in the 1920s). Each at the beginning of his career especially valued language used traditionally: each sought enduring fame as a lyric poet, and created for himself a related romantic image of success as a writer of "serious" fiction, or drama, or social criticism, or linguistic analysis. But irony was the mode they all accepted for delineating the character of their world, because that is what their age expected, or, at times, demanded. Although none of the three created a radical analysis of American culture, all were shrewd assessors of it. Between, roughly, 1910 and 1930, they and others debunked elements of American life, generally aspects of middle-class life. There was in their satire, diverse as their methods were, a common element of style that entered the mainstream both of fiction and nonfiction in America. It will be my purpose in this book to describe the satire of this period, to characterize some of its creators, and to locate the element of style that is its legacy.

I have chosen Mencken, Lewis, and Marquis for close consideration because, males of the same generation, each can be seen as a mirror for the others, and there are important similarities in their backgrounds and literary sources. Their subjects and attitudes as debunkers were similar. They ridiculed American provincialism, puritanism, and the traditional, moral values of Americans: their practical idealism, their belief in progress, their belief in culture and learning—a basic triptych on the altar of American faith.[4] At the same time there was in their writings persistent love and nostalgia for aspects of what they ridiculed and for a simpler, rural way of life. Their nostalgia was a manifestation of the old allegorical dream of America as paradise or brave new world, with its origins in the puritanism of the Reformation, in pastoral tradition, and its other literary sources in the writings of Milton and Shakespeare. With the passing of the frontier, of the potential for the romanticized rural landscape, art replaced the garden-paradise in the allegory as a means of defining the self. The art of writing was the organizing mystery in the lives of all three, and their devotion was religious in its intensity. This was their immediate inheritance from the 1890s and part of their heritage from the romanticism of the nineteenth century. The lyric verse they all wrote (sometimes clandestinely) was uniformly mediocre, and each experienced frustration at his failure to be taken seriously as a poet.

But that frustration reflected a love of language used well. The abuse

of language indicated to them the deterioration not only of the art of writing but also the loss of authority of such institutions as family, church, government, and business. Language could be deliberately distorted and inflated, as it was in propaganda and advertising. Or it could pompously and wantonly celebrate the most transient and least worthy cultural manifestations. As writers they sought to be artists, in order to revitalize and purify their medium.

Each was in some sense a lacerated human being. Evidence of this laceration is to be found in their perceptions of the culture that surrounded them and that they created in their writings. Their common matrix was provincial middle-class life, not just the geographical circumstances of that life but its mythology, too. A pivotal event for their culture was the First World War, which all three experienced only indirectly, but perceived as a metaphor. The war in which they were involved was against the destructiveness and sometimes murderousness they discovered in modern life. They were lacerated men, wounded like soldiers. While they loved aspects of what they attacked, they were frustrated by their sense of powerlessness against the forces of the "enemy." They dealt with that frustration through satiric modification: the ironic tone was the only posture possible if they were to survive in what they thought was the no man's land of the modern world. Raking through the muck was the symbolic progressive action during the years of their young manhood. The figurative muck became the horrible excrement-fouled reality of trench warfare in France, a new symbol for the condition of their culture during their maturity.

One manifestation of the metaphorical warfare defining the conditions of their coming of age was the struggle of women to achieve new awareness of self, a struggle that reached one of its climaxes in the ratification of the Nineteenth Amendment in 1920. While superficially all three could sound like male chauvinists in satirizing militant aspects of the feminist movement, all of them had experienced needs like those of women to free themselves from the values and traditions of nineteenth-century, white, genteel middle-class life. All had been subjected to similar resistance and loving repression in their efforts to break away from the mercantile or professional expectations of their middle-class families. Each lived through the ordeal of the artist as a young man. The experience was not unlike that of women: what was at stake was the potential for individual, personal freedom.

As artists exploring means of expression in their time, they responded to influences like those working on the major modern writers. The styles of Mencken, Lewis, and Marquis had both European and American sources: the names recurring in the educations of all of them are H. G. Wells, George Bernard Shaw, and Mark Twain, with Nietzsche at least an indirect influence. Thoreau was their largely unacknowledged American progenitor, both in his romantic celebration of stylistic "extravagance" (which he defined as wandering beyond the limits of ordinary experience) and in his rearticulation of the American need to break with the past.

Sometimes topical references in their writings cannot be reanimated for us. But sometimes there is communication across the years—perhaps simply because the writers are our fathers or grandfathers. Each had facile mimetic skills, which could issue either in the form of parodies or as impressive characterizations. Their styles were hyperbolic, tending toward the extremity of nonsense and the hoax. Thus does the soldier deal with, in order not to succumb to, the horrors of war.

The maddest moments in their writings are not aberrations but deliberate constructions dramatizing for us their judgment of the sometimes frightening and sometimes funny disconcertedness and anarchy of modern life. While these perceptions were more profoundly rendered by the major modern writers (Conrad, Joyce, Yeats, Frost, Hemingway, Faulkner), it is in the writings of Lewis, Marquis, and Mencken that we also find early twentieth-century manifestations of attitudes with which we apprehend aspects of our own world. The banality they perceived in their time, and that is still with us, becomes tolerable because of the act of ridicule.

Mencken, Lewis, and Marquis wanted to be first of all artists and only secondarily satirists: form was more important to them than content. The tendency of their satire was to move away from those forms in which ridicule of objects or subjects is explicit and direct toward the inexplicit, the indirect, and finally to a resolution, a dead-end, in nonsense, which has no particular objects or subjects other than the logic and the order that are the necessary foundations of a civilized world. That tendency became manifest especially in the writings of their contemporary, Ring Lardner, and in Nathanael West, the oldest son, as it were, of this generation of debunkers.

# Chapter One

## Rejection of the Past:
## Foreground and Background

History is bunk.

Henry Ford,
1916

**M**encken, Lewis, Marquis, and other debunkers such as Lardner had what at first glance seems an unlikely ally in Henry Ford. On 25 May 1916 Ford expressed a criticial opinion that was publicized throughout the country. Interviewed by Charles N. Wheeler of the *Chicago Tribune,* he had been asked what he thought of Bismarck. Evading the question (it was not certain that he knew who Bismarck was) he was reported to have said: "History is more or less bunk. It is traditional. We don't want tradition. We want to live in the present, and the only history that is worth a tinker's dam is the history we make today."[1] That same year in an editorial the *Tribune* called Ford an anarchist. A good American, Ford sued for libel and three years later, when court proceedings were finally begun, Ford himself was, in effect, placed on trial. Throughout a long summer the *Tribune* attorney, Elliot G. Stevenson, sought to destroy the myth of Ford the great American industrialist and patriot. Stevenson succeeded: asked to explain his 1916 statement about history, Ford insisted he had only meant that most history was more or less bunk to him, that he did not need history himself and did not need to know about it. In 1922 Mencken quoted Ford's "history is bunk" in the *Smart Set.*[2] He was interested in Ford's easy, deflationary wit. He was also interested in the debunking attitude that sought to reexamine and reevaluate inflated descriptions of the American past and of the culture produced by that past.

In 1923 in a novel called *Bunk* William E. Woodward established minor fame for himself by coining the word *debunk*. In doing so he was giving a name to the satiric attitude recognized by Mencken and unwittingly exercised by Henry Ford. The title of Woodward's novel comprehensively described the cultural phenomenon with which it was concerned. Developed out of Woodward's experiences in journalism, publishing, advertising, and banking, *Bunk* was a nearly plotless novel of satiric commentary on the inflated language of these worlds. In a review Carl Van Doren wrote: "*Bunk* is satire seasoned with wisdom. It is, in its robust way, mellow and learned. And it comes at a happy moment, when bunk, long eminent, is being suspected as it has hardly been for a century."[3]

The hero of *Bunk* is a young man, Michael Webb, who believes that "our national consciousness has become as saturated with bunk and hypocrisy as a sponge is saturated with water." Webb finds that all he has to do to provide the catharsis people want and need is to clear their minds of the mental junk and "maxims" that have lingered on from the past. This process he calls "de-bunking"; it "means simply taking the bunk out of things. . . . An intellectual deflation. It's the science of reality." He teaches people "how to get along in the Age of Authoritative Mediocrity." Under this simple ironic tone Woodward was serious about the purpose if not the method of the science practiced by his hero. Michael Webb says: "You put new ideas over by making people laugh. All new ideas are looked upon as dangerous, and people fight them as they fight tigers. But all clowns are considered harmless. So you get a man laughing and before he knows it you've passed your idea on to him.[4]

Woodward wrote several other books, prose fictions that were not really novels at all, but were vehicles for ironic, humorous, often superficial commentary on many aspects of the contemporary scene. His attitudes and subjects were those of the other debunkers of his era. He ridiculed unsophisticated Americans and their puritanical way of life in the provincial regions of America—a ridicule exercised from the secure vantage point of New York City, with its geographical and cultural affinity to Europe. He deflated pretentious and false myths about America and American life. He mocked Philistine, middle-class attitudes towards art and literature. To Woodward the art of writing and the debunking urge were one and the same: "Writers always have to look down on things and people. If they look up at them—well, that's fatal. In schools where the art of literary creation is taught the very first lesson is an exercise on looking down on everybody."[5] *Bunk* was a novel that depended entirely for its effect on disconnected and dissociated commentary to which plot, characterization, delineation of manners, romance—any of the effects we ordinarily identify with the novel—were subordinated.

Woodward (who was born in 1874) belonged to the same generation as Mencken, Lewis, Marquis, and Lardner. Like them he made the journey from small-town life in the provinces to New York City. Like them his attitude toward that life helped create an American mythology, for he viewed his provincial origins with ambivalent feelings of love and contempt. A generation before, E. W. Howe and Hamlin Garland had taken realistic, semifictional looks at life in the Midwest, and their accounts had nostalgic overtones. They wrote of the Midwest as a backwash of the passing frontier. They remembered as background for their disillusionment those good old days so recently passed when men were men and masculine camaraderie was, somehow, the sustaining moral condition. Rarely in their accounts was there ridicule of a way of life that had become cramped, conformist, deadening. In 1919 Sherwood Anderson, in *Winesburg, Ohio,* continued in the tradition of reminiscent nostalgia. He was, in part, misread as another chronicler of an empty, sterile, morally and spiritually repressed midwestern world—misread because by 1919 contempt for life in the provinces was a fashionable attitude. Anderson was not a debunker and, in *Winesburg,* he was partly making use of and partly reacting against an attitude of contempt for the provincial that had become the point of departure for ridicule or criticism of many aspects of American life during the second decade of the twentieth century. Woodward inherited this ambivalence: his background was the same.

The epithet *debunker,* which was applied to Woodward early in his career, was an application he was soon to resent; he regretted ever having coined the word. Like Mencken, Lewis, Lardner, and Marquis, he dreamed of traditional success and recognition in the world of beautiful letters; Anderson was his model. In 1925 he abandoned fiction and worked on a biography which was published in 1926 as *George Washington: The Image and the Man.* People immediately said that now Woodward had debunked Washington. In a sense he had; there was a comic freshness about the way in which he addressed the Washington myth: "George Washington came of a family that must be called undistinguished"; "he was thoroughly undemocratic . . . and this, too, is typically American, for our country is the most undemocratic of all the great, free nations."[6] Reviewers noted that Woodward had reduced Washington from a god to a man. Allan Nevins wrote that "there does emerge despite many careless, blurred, or sometimes even inaccurate strokes, a vivid and faithful impression of Washington as a living man."[7] C. G. Bowers wrote: "Mr. Woodward does not criticize the man; he smashes myths."[8] In the same year the first volume of a three-volume life, *George Washington: The Human Being and the Hero,* by Rupert Hughes, was published. While it was a more thorough work than Woodward's, the two books were frequently reviewed together; they sold well, and certainly Woodward's reputation as a debunker helped the sales of both.

Henry Ford, however, remained one of the first and one of the best-known debunkers of history. He also, perhaps unwillingly, qualified as one of the first critics of Americanism, for by scoffing at history he was showing disrespect for a new American preoccupation. Some of the debunkers continued Ford's good work. Others, like Woodward, borrowed and popularized the findings of the new, "scientific" historians from perspectives very like those of the muckrakers. There was a liberating, cathartic effect in their iconoclasm, and they wrote out of the assumption that the truth about the past would renew American life in their time. In a profile of Lewis for the *New Yorker* Woodward characterized himself as well as Lewis when he wrote: "At the bottom Lewis is solidly bourgeois. He loves real estate and mortgages and bank accounts. Fundamentally he is a Rotarian, and in spite of his cynical writings about business and business people, he has an immense admiration for the superior executive type of businessman, for people who make money and succeed."[9] Woodward, like Lewis, made money and was a success. Although as a writer he will be remembered primarily by compilers of etymologies, he wrote with simple understanding that neither America nor life was perfect. He believed that the good in both could be conserved by isolating and ridiculing fraudulent and over-inflated language. He resented—but did not strenuously resist—the role of debunker thrust upon him by his readers. He filled this role while at the same time longing for recognition as a writer of serious fiction and history. His career was in the same pattern as those of other debunkers, and, like them, he was especially influenced by Mencken.

Woodward was partly justified in objecting to the application of the word he had coined to his own work and to himself. His novels, it is true, stand only as debunking novels: the occasional facetious commentary and satire in them are the whole of their effect. But as an historian he was quite serious about his common-sense approach to the past. He thought that most historical writing was "dull, insipid, and far too scholarly in style." His first aim as a writer was to attract popular interest; he was enough of a journalist to realize that one way to attract interest was through shattering myths and traditional patterns of beliefs. He would have been pleased with his obituary in the *New York Times*. In it he was credited with having "created a new technique of biographical writing."[10] Nowhere was he accused of having been a debunker.

Woodward's biographies and histories were not novel in technique or new in purpose, for along with other historians and debunkers he had the contemporary examples of Lytton Strachey's writings. Strachey's ironic examination of Victorian England, elegantly set down in *Eminent Victorians* (1918) and *Queen Victoria* (1921), paralleled a similar American interest in the nineteenth century and its genteel traditions. It remained for the cultural atmosphere which these new histories and biographies both shaped and reflected to add an expectation for satire; debunking became a generalized epithet for any exposure of pretentiousness or repressive myth. Perfectly serious and scholarly appraisals of the American past were read as deflationary attacks on tradition. It was a time of irreverence, of change, of breaking with the past. And it was a time when H. L. Mencken emerged as the single most influential and authoritative voice.

An urgent sense of resurgence and renewal in American cultural life began to be expressed early in the century. It was characterized by the revival of a romanticism that glorified revolt as the primary impetus to creative expression, a romanticism stressing the worth of the creative individual over the demands of family, society, church, and government.

These demands worked with special repressive effect upon the lives of women. The suffrage movement conceived of itself as both revolt and civil war. Women often wore uniforms and marched like soldiers in parades. When in 1917 Woodrow Wilson addressed the senate to urge ratification of the suffrage amendment, he developed an analogy between the war of the people for women's right to vote and the war against Germany.[11] The metaphorical revolt of women against some of the conditions of their lives was an important expression of the sense of resurgence in American life. Mencken was sensitive to the needs of women, as were some of the other debunkers.

The feeling of a general cultural revolution developed some of the effect of a movement when its leaders began to recognize one another. In 1915 Van Wyck Brooks outlined the forces that he felt were inhibiting America's coming of age. Mencken took note of Brooks's thesis from his position as editor of the *Smart Set;* he also was establishing himself as the enemy of puritanism whether in the provinces, the universities, or the government. Some of the spirit of revolt was dissipated into talk in the various Bohemian colonies; more permanent and sometimes related forums were the little magazines that appeared in twentieth-century America like mushrooms.[12] For example, in 1916 James Oppenheim and Waldo Frank started the *Seven Arts* magazine which proposed to be "an expression of artists for the community." In the first issue the editors wrote:

> It is our faith and the faith of many, that we are living in the first days of a renascent period, a time which means for America the coming of that national self-consciousness which is the beginning of greatness. In all such epochs the arts cease to be private matters; they become not only the expression of the national life but a means to its enhancement. . . . We have no tradition to continue; we have no school of style to build up. What we ask of the writer is simply self-expression.[13]

Preoccupied by the war against tradition that it was waging at home, the *Seven Arts* opposed the United States's entry into the First World War. As a result its financial backing was withdrawn in 1917. But other magazines, such as the *New Republic, Smart Set,* and *Dial* continued to affirm the sense of movement toward cultural freedom. Gradually a feeling of cohesion against the strongholds of tradition grew.

War in Europe did not entirely extinguish talk of a renascence in American life. In 1919 Frank wrote: "We must begin to generate within ourselves the energy which is love of life. For that energy, to whatever form the mind consigns it, is religious. Its act is creation. And in a dying world, creation is revolution."[14] Nevertheless, there was a growing sense of disillusionment and skepticism about the possibilities for American culture. The creative optimism of the prewar decade was remembered in the 1920s with cynicism and nostalgia, if at all. Contributing to what became a *carpe diem* reaction was the publication in 1917 of Henry Adams's *Education,* with its pessimistic sense of the meaning of history, and in 1920 the popular exposition of Albert Einstein's *Relativity,* with its baffling philosophical overtones.

There were, of course, dissenting voices running counter to the general atmosphere of revolt in American life. These voices identify and lend a perspective to the sense of metaphorical warfare that characterizes this period. There were religious traditionalists, prohibitionists, and Babbitts who could point to what they considered to be a growing lawlessness and loss of standards in America. In 1922 George Santayana wrote that "America's young radicals" "all proclaim their disgust at the present state of things in America, they denounce the Constitution of the United States, the churches, and above all they denounce the spirit that vivifies and unifies all these things, the spirit of Business. . . . I see what they are against—they are against everything—but what are they *for*? I have not been able to discover it."[15] Paul Elmer More's "The Modern Current in American Literature" attacked Dreiser, Anderson, Dos Passos, and Lewis as realists in the modern school. He wrote that they fail mainly because of "the theory that there are no moral laws governing life, or that, if such laws are, they have no jurisdiction in the artistic representation of life." Irving Babbitt felt that an emotional naturalism pervaded American life, a naturalism that had absorbed all the harmful excesses of romantic individualism and few of its virtues. He shared Mencken's distrust of the single-minded humanitarian impulse, but in "The Critic and American Life" he attacked Mencken's criticism as futile self-expression. Furthermore, he wrote, "the warfare that is being waged at the present time by Mr. Sinclair Lewis and others against a standardized Philistinism continues in the main the protest that has been made for several generations past. . . . This protest has been, and is likely to continue to be, ineffectual."[16]

The debunking manner was in another of its aspects an expression of the melioristic spirit shared by many of the spokesmen for the cultural resurgence which in America began to gather some of the force of a movement around 1910. Tradition was reexamined; much was rejected in the search for what Brooks called the usable past. In debunking there was also an attempt to rediscover and reassert a lost sense of vitality; it was a reaction away from sentimentality and gentility. Genteel manners and morals were debunked, especially sexual prudery and Puritan attitudes. Organized religions were attacked: special targets were fundamentalism, censorship, and Prohibition. The ethics of business and advertising, wartime propaganda, and Americanism were ridiculed. The campaign against sentimental effects and methods in literature was continued; the posturings of middle-class aesthetes were satirized. The image of the small town as the repository of the democratic virtues was frequently punctured. The cities in all their corruption had been exposed by the muckrakers; now the veil was removed from the small town. A tender, nostalgic image had lingered in many minds, in spite of realistic nineteenth-century descriptions by John W. DeForest, Harold Frederic, and Mark Twain. Most of the debunkers had themselves left small towns, lured by the more sophisticated environments of the big cities. But they never forgot those towns; the tension of their loving disaffection often is contained within their depictions of provincial life.

The attitudes, subjects, and methods of the debunkers had their sources in the American history that Ford had rejected as bunk. Elements of the satire of Mencken and the debunkers had parallels if not sources in some of the literary and journalistic responses to earlier American experience.

As we might expect, Puritan satire had existed in the service of the moral life, and that dimension survived in the debunkers to the extent that their underlying anguish about the condition of their culture was essentially moral. A more explicit survival was the satirical power of invective practiced by the Puritans either on the page or in the pulpit. Mencken's voice at times rose to the powerful extravagance of a similar invective. In the eighteenth century Ben Franklin's humor had functioned in the service of a moral system as defined, or derived, by Franklin himself; Mencken's prejudices also served him with all the authority of moral order and many debunkers imitated his aplomb.

Lewis P. Simpson, in writing about the early national wits of the eighteenth century, notes in their satire the expression of minds infused either with "millenialistic or utopian prospects" or with "fears of the imminence of a doomsday of social collapse."[17] That apocalyptic style of mind was another significant element in some of the debunkers of the twentieth century, and received clear expression in Nathanael West. According to George M. Roth, many American satirists of the late eighteenth and early nineteenth centuries had thought of themselves as modern practitioners of a respectable literary form. They could trace their ancestry back through Pope, Swift, and Dryden to Juvenal and Horace. They felt that their function was to keep America free of the vices of the old world. Satire was, in the view of these early Americans, "the mode of literature best calculated to sway people's minds and change their beliefs."[18]

Satire depended for its effect on the shock of exposure, on hostility released through the socially acceptable means of laughter. Traditional targets had been political corruption, pretentious elegance, and sentimentality. But American humor in the nineteenth century moved away from this tradition of formal satire toward burlesque characterized by an apocalyptic perspective. Although the fable and parody survived as satiric forms, burlesque had infused both to produce two different, more characteristically American satiric modes: the fable became the tall tale with its exuberant extravagance, and parody issued in the less formal, wildly nonsensical articulations of buncombe oratory. As James M. Cox has shown, the distinguishing tendency of the humor of the old Southwest (as manifest in the writing of Longstreet, Hooper, Baldwin, Thorpe, Lewis, Harris, and as an element of style in Mark Twain) was to "divorce pleasure from morality."[19] The buncombe orators parodied the declamatory language that glorified democratic institutions and heroes. Popular oratory of the 1830s and '40s, much of it political, borrowed the extravagance of the tall tale for its serious purposes. As Rourke indicates, burlesque of that inflated oratory seemed spontaneous and natural: "So far-reaching was the burlesque that it was often impossible to tell one from the other without a wide context of knowledge as to the subject and the speakers."[20]

The methods of the debunkers most often were the burlesque methods of the tall tale and of buncombe oratory. The buncombe orators, the confidence men of America, could be at once funny and vicious. Some of the Yankee humorists of the Civil War period—Brom Weber calls them "the misspellers"—had an element of style in common with the buncombe orators and with the southwestern humorists. According to Weber there was in them "an exuberant and often savage riot that went far beyond misspelling."[21] Many of the debunkers were in that tradition of parody, mimicry, and riot, in which pleasure and morality were unrelated.

An audience receptive to the questioning of the Protestant ethic and of the culture it had helped shape was not an audience unique to twentieth-century debunkers. Similar attitudes had developed earlier in America, most notably in the 1840s and 1850s. Rourke has written:

> American audiences enjoyed their own deflation; they liked the boldness of attack, the undisguised ridicule. . . . Even the nascent romantic picture of the American as builder and colonizer was punctured. . . . The distant must go, the past be forgotten, lofty notions deflated. Comedy was conspiring toward the removal of all alien traditions, out of delight in the pure destruction or as preparation for new growth. . . . If it punctured romantic feelings it kept a breathless comic emotion of its own.[22]

The debunking spirit, initially like the spirit of the 1840s, was a realistic spirit infused with comic emotion, although it was also a spirit more and more stricken with anguish as the events of the twentieth century unfolded.

The impulse toward satire animated some of the writings of the major American authors both in the renaissance of the 1850s and in the literary resurgence of the 1920s: the puncturing of sentimentally romantic feeling was as significant an aspect of the writing of Thoreau, Whitman, Hawthorne, and Melville, as it was of Hemingway, Faulkner, Fitzgerald, and Lewis. In each period there was a sense of conflict and tension in American life, a sense of warfare that issued literally (the realization of metaphor) in the Civil War, then in the World War. The aftermath of each of these wars was an eminently deflatable epoch: the Gilded Age on the one hand and the meretriciously materialistic 1920s on the other.

The rampant free enterprise which characterized American capitalism until the early 1930s had its beginnings in the acquisitiveness and corruption of the post–Civil War era, when Grant was president. Mark Twain and Charles Dudley Warner labeled it "the Gilded Age" and in the novel by that name (1874) presented the comic Colonel Beriah Sellers. Sellers is a dreamer, a schemer, and a clown. His fantastic acquisitive proposals are implemented through political manipulation. Although his exuberance is both funny and admirable, there is an underlying criticism in the book of a civilization that could produce such a character and that could provide a fruitful atmosphere for his ridiculous schemings.

A year later John William DeForest attacked the corrupt liaison between American politics and business with some of the debunker's cynical ridicule and much of the reformer's indignation. His novel, *Honest John Vane,* tells the story of a mediocre businessman who is elected as the Republican representative from Slowburgh, Maine. John Vane is described with incisive irony: "He was too ignorant to be a professor in the State University, or even a teacher in one of the city schools; but it was presumed that he would answer well enough as a law-giver for a complicated Republic containing forty millions of people." Incorruptible at first, in his stolid, dull way, he is soon changed by the social and political atmosphere in Washington. His vote is bought for support of a fraudulent scheme, the supposed construction of the "Great Subfluvial Tunnel Road," which is designed to connect Lake Superior with the Gulf of Mexico. There is an investigation, and Honest John clears himself with the investigating committee and with the public by pleading ignorance of the fraud. He is allowed to continue in the political life, his reputation for honesty enhanced. DeForest's comment is vitriolic, Juvenalian, indignant:

> The public,—the great, soft-hearted American public,—that public which has compassion on every species of scoundrel,—which tries murderers under jury restrictions warranted to save four-fifths of them,—which cannot see one condemned to death without pleading with tears for his noxious life,—that forgiving, milk-and-water public was as mild in its judgment as the committee: it magnified our dishonorable member for not lying, and exalted his name for not committing perjury.

Honest John, political leader and embryonic demagogue by virtue of his martyrdom before the committee, is portrayed as a bumbling, stupid, laughable character. The point of DeForest's satire is that honesty is a meaningless virtue in a public official whose dominant trait is stupidity. Finally, his ridicule is directed at "the public," a public which demands and responds to simplicity of mind in its leaders. DeForest wrote that "sadder spirits are asking which is the most alluring spectacle—a free America falling into squandering and bribery, or a monarchial Prussia ruled by economy and honesty."[23] He thought that behind the hypocrisy and corruption of his contemporaries lay the incompatibility of the respectable American's allegiance to a self-centered economic philosophy on the one hand and to a self-effacing, sentimental humanitarianism on the other. His scorn for what democratic process had become—although not for democracy itself—was very like Mencken's, forty years later.

DeForest, like Mencken and the debunkers, had explicitly satirized the middle class for its puritanism and gentility (as, for example, in the descriptions of "New Boston"—New Haven—in *Miss Ravenel's Conversion from Secession to Loyalty,* 1867). Although Mencken's attacks on Americanism—by which he meant distorted, dishonest language glorifying American democracy—were never organized into a systematic treatise, the collection of essays called *Notes on Democracy* (1926) was an effort in that direction. Mencken and DeForest were hostile to repressive forces wherever they operated. The most formidable agent of repression in America, both felt, was the middle class, with its self-satisfied, genteel pretensions and its pious, uncritical faith in democracy. The element in the middle class that they attacked was complacent and conformist. And, a more serious charge, this element insisted on its righteousness and attempted to force its Protestant ethic on everyone else. Its proselytizing issued in self-aggrandizing statements and in acts of censorship, and its moral hypocrisy created and tolerated corruption as an institution in political life.

There were other satirists of the Gilded Age's demagogues, leaders, and corruption. Henry Adams, for example, was like DeForest in his distrust of democratic procedure. In *Democracy* (1879) he satirized the climb of a fictional Senator Ratcliffe from provincial, mediocre beginnings to a position of power and prestige. But underlying his satire (which included the comedy of Washington's social atmosphere) was his aristocratic respect for political power. Like DeForest, and like Mencken, he disdained the simplicity which Americans demanded in their leaders.

Utopian literature of the nineteenth century was a source for some of the subjects and also the concealed idealism of the debunkers of the twentieth. This literature incorporated two tendencies, one destructive (the impulse to criticize and satirize the contemporary world), the other constructive and romantic (the impulse to imagine or dream a new world). For example, Edward Bellamy's *Looking Backward* (1888) contained criticism of the waste attendant on a freely competitive system.

But there was little intentional satire in Bellamy. He had great faith in America's capacity to evolve toward a socialistic, gadget-driven, undifferentiated paradise. William Dean Howells's conception of utopia ("Altruria," described in *A Traveller from Altruria,* 1894) was like Bellamy's in that it represented the achievement of American ideals; utopia was the final, inevitable product of social and economic evolution. Howells, however, was much more interested in social criticism and satire than in the depiction of the ultimate place.

Utopian literature was popular at the time, and Howells accepted the convention. There is much that is witty and sharply ironic in *A Traveller from Altruria.* Howells made extensive comic use of his setting, the summer hotel, as a social microcosm. His satire of American middle-class women is astringent and has the grace of wit, where Bellamy's treatment of women remains genteel and fanciful. Howells also made the ironic suggestion that utopia would be dull and boring. His Altrurian, a muscular, vigorous intellectual, must travel for diversion, and he lacks a sense of humor. There would be little to laugh at in the perfect state, with all hostilities, repressions, and anxieties removed. *Altruria* is a charming and amusing book. Howells is an expert delineator of middle-class manners; his ironies are subtle and convincing. The debunkers were like Howells in their assumption of an ironic method and tone, although rarely were they as subtle.

Jack London used the convention of the utopian novel for commentary, some of it satirical, on America, past, present and future, in its evolution toward the classless society. *The Iron Heel* (1907) tells of future events and assumes the "looking backward" vantage point. An ideological compound of Marx, Nietzsche, and social Darwinism, the book describes the class war in America. A gradual division of forces, which had begun in the nineteenth century, continues until the great mass of the proletariat (the unskilled laborers led by the socialists) are set off in revolutionary opposition to the "Oligarchy" (the organization of capitalists and skilled laborers). After seven centuries of class war the "Iron Heel" of the Oligarchy will be defeated. The text is mostly very serious, written with progressive fervor and indignation, but there is footnoted satiric commentary on the genteel manners and customs of the early twentieth century. People of the middle class were "inordinately proud of their genealogy," and in time the *Mayflower* "blood became so widely diffused that it ran in the veins of practically all Americans." These people were also "phrase slaves," for "vast populations grew frenzied over such phrases as 'an honest dollar' and 'a full dinner pail.' " They were fond of living rooms, filled with bric-a-brac, that resembled museums and required endless labor to keep clean; "the dust-demon was the lord of the household." This affluent society had the problem of disposing of the tremendous surpluses which were the constant accretion of the capitalist system. The Oligarchy for a long time solved the problem by building cities and vast road complexes, and by subsidizing art and science. Organized laborers, "the great labor castes," became placid and contented; they lived in "delightful cities of their own" and enjoyed short hours and long holidays.[24] London was, perhaps with ironic foresight, prophesying the surburban paradises which became realities in America around the middle of the twentieth century. But underlying this temporary era of luxury was the promise of eventual retribution, of bloodshed and primitive terror. "The roaring abysmal beasts"—the mob of unskilled laborers—could not be repressed forever. After centuries of warfare London foresaw their eventual triumph.

London was frequently an ironic commentator on the manners and ideology of the middle class of his day, and thus had something in common with the debunkers. His deflation of American "phrase slaves" was an early focus on the kind of fraudulent, inflated language that emerged as a central subject for the debunkers. His overt awareness of a division in American society, with the apprehension that the knowledge of this division engendered, was like the debunker's vaguer, more covert sense of disgust at America's tendency to evolve into a uniform culture. His impulse to examine America past and present was one he shared with the debunkers. He accepted the Marxist ideology and tried to apply it unreservedly to his later work, but his writings are struck through with Nietzschean attitudes and contradictions. The debunkers leaned toward Nietzschean individualism, too, but they were equally and acutely aware of the humanitarian traditions in their culture. They masked in comedy the hostility which Jack London had expressed more directly as propagandist, in *The Iron Heel.*

Satire is clearly and obviously a dimension in the development of the realistic novel both in America and in England, and in a general way the realistic tradition is background for the satirists of the early twentieth century. An equally important influence on the debunkers is the literature of the late nineteenth and early twentieth centuries in which heroes and heroines are defined by their rejection of the prevailing values and traditions of their worlds.[25] This rejection, with all the anguish and tension it entailed, is at the center of modern literature; its primary mythological expression culminates in James Joyce's *Portrait of the Artist as a Young Man.* Prevailing values and traditions were questioned in premodern literature but not rejected, and the satiric mode was as much a part of the impulse to question as it was to reject. Often the debunkers did not go as far as the major writers of the modern tradition in their assessment of the need for rejection, but they questioned either explicitly or implicitly.

Mark Twain's *Pudd'nhead Wilson* anticipates some of the debunking novels in that it contains satire of American small-town life in the 1880s. But the satire also has novelistic purposes. Each chapter is headed by a quotation or two from Pudd'nhead Wilson's Calendar; the result is a running set of ironic observations on manners and morals. This commentary is never specifically relevant to the plot of the novel, yet the effect is to provide an ironic and often pessimistic backdrop to the small-town ideology that forms the foreground of manners in the novel. Pudd'nhead Wilson himself is an American prototype for the debunkers. He is critical and skeptical, even cynical, about his society and environment, yet he is very much in it and of it. He longs for recognition and fame, he dreams of being a hero.

The debunkers, like other writers of the twentieth century, were profoundly affected by *Huckleberry Finn*. The enduring, compelling tension of that novel arose from its contrast between the genteel, civilized world of small-town life and the free, sensual world of life in natural surroundings. The implicit questioning of gentility is what readers disaffected with their culture found compelling, and its solution (Huck rebels by lighting out for the territories) they found as liberating as laughter. A special element of style distinguished *Huckleberry Finn;* it was a style derived and distilled by Mark Twain out of his experiences as a journalist-humorist in the Southwest. Cox describes the tension producing this style: "Between the knowledge and experience of Samuel Clemens and Mark Twain there is a gap, a vacuum, across which the very current of humor leaps. That vacuum has to do with desolation, nihilism, and the ultimate recognition that behind morals and religion there is nothing in the universe. The glory of humor is to convert that awareness into overt pleasure." After *Huckleberry Finn* Mark Twain moved more and more away from the overt pleasure of humor, its capacity for redemption from despair, toward the perception, as Cox tells us, that "always man would be a slave to the ruthless Moral Sense; always he would lie the old adult lie— the lie by means of which he conceals from himself the truth that cruelty is his deepest pleasure."[26] Some of the debunkers filled a similar sense of vacuum with the pleasure of humor; that was the significance of *Huckleberry Finn* to them.

Mencken observed in "Puritanism as a Literary Force" that American humor, traditional fountainhead of satire and irreverence, in the second half of the nineteenth century acquiesced to the genteel, feminine, Philistine atmosphere. An occasional exception in some of his writing, Mencken allowed, was Mark Twain. A consistent exception, and America's "one genuine wit," Mencken went on, was Ambrose Bierce.[27] Bierce's satires "after the method of Swift,"[28] his fables, fantasies, and polemics all prefigured the writings of the twentieth-century debunkers. He was like many of the debunkers in most respects except that he was born forty years too soon to be one of their number. He was a journalist; so were most of the debunkers. He aspired to more lasting literary fame via poetry and fiction; so did the debunkers. He was like them, too, in his vehement individualism. He shared with them a residue of the Puritan dualism—a sense that he was one of the elect among a majority of the damned—which pointed up his individualism while sharpening his indignation and asperity. Both Bierce and his followers drew extensively on the resources of American humor. Mencken, for one, wrote about Bierce with respect on several occasions, and Bierce lived just long enough (1914) to realize in Mencken a kindred spirit.

Bierce, like his twentieth-century offspring, reacted against what he considered to be a complacent, genteel, middle class in America. He shared the debunkers' contempt for life in the American provinces; from his citadels in San Francisco and later in New York and Washington he looked scornfully across the great midwestern desert. Like many of the debunkers he had been born and brought up in the Midwest (he was from Ohio). He attacked, as did his followers, those demagogues and men in high places—politicians, capitalists, and preachers—whose actions and pronouncements had gilded their era with a pervasive hypocrisy. He was especially offended by what Mencken later called the benign booziness: humanitarian sentimentality that produced reformers, prohibitionists, censors, and misguided philanthropists.

Baffled, oppressed, and offended by militant women in the political warfare surrounding suffrage, Bierce and the debunkers sometimes sounded like misogynists. But their behavior toward particular women was quixotic and Victorian in the extreme; they could be as sentimental and romantic as if themselves afflicted by the cult of the female and the religion of love. Bierce and the debunkers objected in general to what they considered to be the feminization of their culture. They were offended by what they felt was the attrition of their masculine individuality. Bierce was happiest when living the life of action, as a soldier during the Civil War and after the war as an inspector of far western lands and military outposts. His contemporary and competitor in the literary life, Mark Twain, had similarly been happiest on the frontier, or as a Mississippi riverboat pilot—worlds of activity from which the problems of treating women as equals were excluded. But Mencken and most of the debunkers realized that the equivalent of civil war had emerged in their time between male and female. Definitions of the role of women were changing, irrevocably, and the ratification of the Nineteenth Amendment in 1920 was only one manifestation of changes that were affecting every aspect of American life.

As journalists, Bierce, Mark Twain, and the twentieth-century debunkers lived in what was primarily a man's world. Journalism allowed them a convenient outlet for criticism and satire of the genteel, feminine culture which they found repressive to their individuality and to their larger aspirations as artists. There was a special tension here, for the world of beautiful letters was dominated by a feminine audience, and all of them sought status in that world.

Much of the writing by Bierce and by the debunkers was directed against the manners and morals of middle-class Americans and against works both in the graphic and verbal arts which glorified, flattered, and perpetuated those manners and morals. The debunkers continued to ridicule sentimentality in literature, as had Bierce. A special source of their contempt was the aesthete: that feminine or effeminate pursuer of the arts who might be disowned by the middle class, but who was nevertheless simply a member of the middle class afflicted by what Mencken called the divine afflatus. Bierce contended that ART was an icon that had been created by shifting a letter in the word RAT.[29]

Bierce was acutely sensitive to what he regarded as the absence of an overt satiric spirit in America. In an essay written in 1903 he tried to draw a sharp distinction between *wit* and *humor*—a distinction that he did not always observe in his own writing.[30] By *wit* he meant the satiric temperament; he wrote: "wit may make us smile, or make us wince, but laughter—that is the cheaper price that we pay for an inferior entertainment, namely, humor." He described wit as involving "an indictment of the whole human race; not altogether true and therefore not altogether dull, with just enough of audacity to startle and just enough of paradox to charm, profoundly wise . . . as admirable as a well-cut grave or the headsman's precision of stroke, and about as funny." He distinguished wit from humor:

> Humor (which is not inconsistent with pathos, so neatly allied are laughter and tears) is Charles Dickens; wit is Alexander Pope. Humor is Dogberry; wit is Mercutio. Humor is "Artemus Ward," "John Phoenix," "Josh Billings," "Petroleum V. Nasby," "Orpheus C. Kerr," "Bill Nye," "Mark Twain"— their name is legion; for wit we must brave the perils of the deep. . . . Humor

is tolerant, tender; its ridicule caresses. Wit stabs, begs pardon—and turns the weapon in the wound.

Bierce expressed contempt for local-color dialect writers and humorists. For example, he described James Whitcomb Riley, Mary Murfree, and Mary Wilkins Freeman as "the pignoramous crew of malinguists, cacaphonologists and apostrophographers who think they get close to nature by depicting the sterile lives and limited emotion of the gowks and sandhoppers."[31]

Bierce was objecting to the prevalence of humor in late nineteenth-century America that, to borrow a phrase from William Dean Howells, celebrated the smiling aspects of American life—humor reflecting the abundance, the color, the warmth, and the extravagant comic optimism of America. But this humor was also in a secondary and often unintentional way a humor which pandered to the tastes and repressions of the genteel, and only rarely offended or shocked, even when offensiveness and shock might have been healthful antidotes for overly complacent attitudes about American life. The irony and satire of Howells, as evidenced by *The Vacation of the Kelwyns* or *A Traveller from Altruria*, were, however, the instruments of a more profound commentary on the culture of the American middle class than anything Bierce accomplished.

To Bierce satire was a higher form of art because it was more direct and honest; it probed more deeply into the hostilities which smiling-aspects humor left untouched, or even flattered. The kind of satire he had in mind did not, he thought, exist in America in his own time (except, perhaps, in some of his own writings). In a dialogue between the "Melancholy Author" and the "Timorous Reporter" he wrote that satire had long been dead. As the Melancholy Author puts it, "Satire cannot co-exist with so foolish sentiments as 'the brotherhood of man,' 'the trusteeship of wealth,' moral irresponsibility, tolerance, Socialism and the rest of it. Who can 'lash the rascals through the world' in an age that holds crime to be a disease, and converts the prison into a sanitarium?" In fact, the Melancholy Author points out,

> The rascals go unlashed. Instead of ridicule we have solemn reprobation; for wit we have "humor"—with a slang word in the first line, two in the second and three in the third. . . . If we had today an Aristophanes, a Jonathan Swift or an Alexander Pope, he would indubitably be put in a comfortable prison with all sanitary advantages, fed upon yellow-legged pullets and ensainted by the Little Brothers of the Bad.[32]

America did not produce in the late nineteenth century the like of Aristophanes, Jonathan Swift, or Alexander Pope (although Mark

Twain belongs to that company, and Bierce would have been pleased to accept the Swiftian label himself). But during, roughly, the second and third decades of the twentieth century Mencken rose to a condition of spectacular Johnsonian fame, and there were in America a substantial number of articulate "wits," as Bierce would have called them.

Mencken was the most able and enduring of these wits, and to a major extent he nurtured the atmosphere in which the others flourished. Mencken shared, and perhaps borrowed, the Biercian attitude toward American humor, and that attitude of contempt was reflected by other debunkers, too.

As a lasher of rascals in the Biercian style, Mencken's first national vehicle was the *Smart Set* magazine, which was followed by the *American Mercury*. Most of his best-known books were reprints of essays and reviews from these two periodicals. Behind them, as one element, was the newspaper writing of the old Southwest, with its separation of morality from pleasure. Another element of influence was the late nineteenth-century emergence and brief survival of the esoteric "little" magazines, the *Lark* and *M'lle New York*. The *Smart Set* echoed some of the precious aestheticism of both. A similar aestheticism affected the early years of the *New Yorker*, which also absorbed much from Mencken's *American Mercury*, especially its debunking orientation and its concern for articulating a genuinely cultured point of view.

The *Lark*, mostly written and illustrated by Gelett Burgess, was published in San Francisco by William Doxey from 1895 to 1897. Burgess represented his magazine as being in the forefront of the revolt of the 1890s against the established literary journals. He recognized the Chicago *Chap Book* as another leader in the revolution. In the last issue of his magazine he wrote: "When the history of Nineteenth Century decadence is written, these tiny eruptions of revolt, these pamphleteering amateurs cannot remain unnoticed, for their outbreak was a symptom of the discontent of the times, a wide-felt protest of emancipation from the dictates of the old literary tribunals."[33] Burgess's methods as writer and cartoonist were primarily humorous: he used parody, satire, and nonsense to flout convention, tradition, and especially Philistine attitudes. His audience of necessity was limited to an elite, to those who shared a sense of regional and cultural superiority to the mass of Americans living between the Rocky and the Allegheny mountain ranges. Thus, in respect to method, subjects, and audiences, the *Lark* was a prefiguration of what the more successful and respectable *American Mercury* and *New Yorker* were to become later.

A more substantial magazine of humorous, sophisticated protest was

*M'lle New York*. Published in the 1890s in the *Mercury*'s and the *New Yorker*'s home town, it was edited by Vance Thompson and James Gibbon Huneker. Here again was pre-*Mercury* and *New Yorker* urbanity, although the *New Yorker* was much milder and more careful than either in its ridicule of middle-class sentiments. In size and format *M'lle New York* was similar to both. All of its articles were short, most of them less than two pages—a journalistic principle and aid to the humorous effect which the early *New Yorker* rigidly observed. The debunking pattern of *M'lle New York* was developed from an aristocratic, Nietzschean point of view. Thompson's editorial creed emerged especially in "Polite Letters," a section that was echoed later in the "Notes and Comments" and "Talk of the Town" sections of the *New Yorker*. His creed was "individuality at any cost,"[34] and individualism was persistently celebrated in his editorial commentary, with frequent references to Nietzsche. Thompson's method as editorial polemicist was similar to Bierce's and to the later Mencken's. A joyful and sometimes bitter extravagance infused his style. The subjects of his polemics forecast the later subjects of the debunkers, subjects which were also treated in more moderate fashion by the *New Yorker*.

Thompson commenced *M'lle New York* by damning the public. By the public he meant those who had "a sullen and irreconcilable hate for the extraordinary; who believe in philanthropy (the most selfish of vices) and in education (the most monstrous fetish of this thoughtless century)."[35] In short, the public was the complacent, respectable middle class, many of whom were "dull melancholiacs in the gray provinces (the lean pessimists of Kansas and the West, the neurotic criminals of the New England countryside)." Thompson, like the later debunkers, found that the transition from ridicule of middle-class provincials to ridicule of the America they had created and supported was easy and natural. He wrote in the same editorial that the "fat-witted and unviolent citizens" of the middle class were "fatted tradesmen . . . who build hospitals and posture in the churches," that America has a "cringing, gentility-mad civilization," that "this is a commercial nation. Its commerce is built upon roguery."

Like the debunkers, he found it natural to shift in the same editorial from the process of de-Americanization to a bitter condemnation of the culture produced and praised by middle-class America. He wrote that because "democracy has hated the individual," it has always "made it its business to castrate the thinkers." Professors and "little hairy poets," Thompson mocked, are "the crowned and laureled eunuchs of American literature."[36] The literary tastes of the middle class were debunked with extravagant, humorous aplomb: "That part of the middle class which reads the male blue-stocking, William Dean Howells, looks down upon that part of it which reads the female blue-stocking, Richard Harding Davis."[37] And: "I object to Mr. Richard Harding Davis because he is essentially bourgeois and ridiculous. His appeal is to the suburban mind—the commuter's intelligence. . . . He is a formidable imbecile."[38] Middle-class culture merged indistinguishably with mass culture; he wrote that the public "has debauched the stage to the level of Mr. Richard Watson Gilder's poetry and looks upon the drama merely as a help to digestion. . . . It has begun to 'popularize' science—your bartender has theories of the creation and your tailor argues the existence of God."[39] The *American Mercury* and the *New Yorker* in their commentary and departments on the theater, fashions, food, and literature assumed similar attitudes of mannered superiority, although the *New Yorker* was careful, by being less flagrantly aristocratic than *M'lle New York,* not to antagonize potential middle-class converts to sophistication.

Thompson's hostility toward militantly emancipated womanhood was another characteristic he shared with Bierce. He wrote that "the penultimate science of the average man is gynolatry." He thought that in the United States the worship of women had been "carried to ludicrous lengths." His argument about woman's cultural, intellectual, and physical inferiority followed his interpretation of Nietzsche closely. The woman, Thompson wrote, has only a limited reproductive function. She is fine "for fondling joys and disquieting nights," but it is "monstrous" to worship her.[40] Much of the cover art and many of the illustrations in *M'lle New York* echoed Thompson's sense of the woman's function, as well as his contempt for what he called gynolatry. There were many decorative line drawings which, scattered informally alongside the columns of type, depicted ladies who, in varied stages of undress, were living the orgiastic life. One macabre cover (September 1895) showed a buxom courtesan type who was being embraced by a lascivious, grinning skeleton. Another (November 1895) showed a lady with tentaclelike hair ensnaring a fat man who carried a heart-shaped bag of money. Perhaps the most incisive antifeminist cartoon cover (December 1895) was of a naked woman who was drawn in the act of genuflecting before a grotesque sphinx crowned with the pawnbroker's three-ball cluster. Here, in *M'lle New York,* were graphic representations of the composite middle-class female whom Thomas Beer in *The Mauve Decade* (1926) called "the Titaness," and whose influence on American culture both Beer and Thompson considered to be repressive and deadening. Both the *Mercury* and the *New Yorker* drastically modified this antifeminist attitude; the *New Yorker* was careful to single out "the old lady in Dubuque" for its ridicule. Young ladies in Dubuque were potential sophisticates and subscribers; along with the young and many of the older ladies in and around New York they made up most of the readership of the *New Yorker,* and they read the advertisements.

Thompson and Huneker, as well as Percival Pollard, turned up next on the staff of the *Smart Set,* which began in 1900. Published so as to please the four hundred families of the Social Register and those who wished to be like them, it tried to be "a magazine of cleverness" providing "lively entertainment for minds that are not primitive." The line of descent to the early *New Yorker* and its somewhat similar initial conception of audience includes the addition to its staff of Mencken in 1908 and George Jean Nathan in 1909, as book reviewer and drama critic respectively, then both as editors from 1914 through 1923.

There was in the *Smart Set* an editorial statement that articulated the resurgence of American culture. This statement was not written by Mencken but by Willard Huntington Wright, who was editor for one year, in 1913. Wright in his brief tenure changed the direction of the *Smart Set* and placed it more in the mainstream of the feeling of renewal that was animating many aspects of American life. He wrote:

> I believe that this is a day of enlightenment on the part of magazine readers. Men and women have grown tired of effeminacy and the falsities of current fiction, essays, and poetry. A widespread critical awakening has come, and with it a demand for better literary material. The demand for pious uplift, for stultification, and for the fictional avoidance of the facts of life has diminished. The reader of today demands truth.[41]

Mencken and Nathan had already (in 1912) begun to laugh at pious uplift and stultification in the column called "Pertinent & Impertinent," and Mencken had undertaken similar ridicule in his monthly book reviews for the magazine. When Mencken and Nathan took over as editors a year later, they may have been helped by this articulation of direction and purpose. In any case, their version of the *Smart Set* contained some of what Wright described, and that same policy also defined Mencken's concept of the *Mercury.* The early *New Yorker* sought a more flippant version of what Wright called "truth," and its eventual success depended on its ability to find "better literary material," but the Wright prospectus implicitly functioned there, too.

One other late-nineteenth-century development is an important part of the background. After the Civil War, when abolition had (at least officially) succeeded, many dissenting ideas and energies in America were absorbed in philanthropic activities or in the varied attitudes of what became the progressive movement. The dissenters nearest to the debunkers in time were the Bohemians and muckrakers of the late nineteenth and early twentieth centuries. The Bohemians, who clustered in New York, San Francisco, and later, Chicago, differed from their muckraking brothers and sisters mainly in respectability; they were alike in that both had found outlets for dissenting energies. In a sense the debunkers were cultural muckrakers. Where the interests of the muckrakers had been limited primarily to reform through the exposure of social, political, and economic injustices, the debunkers expanded the scope of their subjects to include manners and morals. They ridiculed the language in which the manners and morals of Americans were glorified and perpetuated. There was sometimes in their writings a muckraking sense of horror and fastidiousness, although generally indignation was modulated or concealed by their comic tone.

Like the muckrakers, the debunkers viewed their world with a double vision. Both measured their realistic description of their surroundings according to a traditional Protestant sensibility. The debunkers were not primarily interested in changing their world, although their moral attitude, usually implied rather than expressed, was an important aspect of what they wrote. They sought to point out in a comic way both the contrast and the relation between the world they observed and the world as it might be. Their pleasure and purpose were primarily in the act of articulation and in self-expression. As comic writers the creative act—the manner of articulation—remained their first concern. What impressed them most about muckraking was its style: they borrowed its rhetorical energy and its posture of authoritative indignation, which they could both evoke and parody.

"Mr. Dooley," the creation of Finley Peter Dunne, was a popular comic character whose satiric comments had sources in the progressive attitudes of his creator. He also was for the debunkers a link to the earlier newspaper wits, in the deceptive innocence of his dialect as well as his unbridled indignation. Like many of the muckrakers the debunkers wanted to write well in a new way.[42] Thus the use of a dialect narrator as the vehicle for progressive ideology was especially appealing, as was the indignant, sensational extravagance of much of the muckraking literature, which reached a large audience. In contrast stood the much more limited public reached by the extreme moral fervor of a social critic like John Jay Chapman, with his sources in a tradition of New England reform, and the scholarly, careful style of magazines like the *Century* and the *Nation*. The reform orientation of these magazines and their traditions of moral integrity were impeccable. They were rarely extravagant or sensational. The debunkers responded more to those progressive writers who sought to influence readers through sometimes lurid appeals to their emotions, and who tried to charm them through the play of language.

Muckraking journalism was a high vocation, a form of missionary work with noble purposes suddenly enhanced by technological advances that made it possible to spread the word throughout the country almost instantly. The muckrakers worked from assumptions about the basic goodness of the American people: you had only to report to them on the shortcomings that had developed in the ways their institutions were administered. Their righteous knowledge would somehow right these wrongs, leaving the sound institutions of American life intact. During their formative years, the debunkers inherited such assumptions from the muckrakers, but they also inherited the muckrakers' legacy of failure. For the muckrakers had discovered that their progressive idealism was not enough in their warfare with evil in America. Their immediate followers were left with an almost obvious task: to examine the institutions that the muckrakers had assumed were sound, and especially the mythological underpinnings of those institutions. Their tone or style shifted from exposition or even polemic to satire and ridicule, because satire was a way of dealing with their feelings of bitterness and disillusionment as they discovered the inadequacies of some of the ideals upon which American life had been based. They also adapted to their satire, at least initially, an assumption of the muckrakers: show intelligent, responsive Americans the ridiculousness in how certain American institutions are valued and they will do something about them. But even this belief in the desire and power of Americans to change American life for the better became disillusioned.

By 1912 muckraking as a significant movement had to some extent been defeated—or absorbed—by reactionary attitudes and there was a shift of focus from its goals and methods. In analyzing the decline of "the progressive impulse," Richard Hofstadter has emphasized the extent to which the muckrakers became aware that their function was largely psychic, a function that "their work was performing for themselves and their public, quite apart from any legislative consequences or material gains." The reform literature was, therefore, "a kind of symbolic action" in which the muckrakers "provided a large part of the American people with a necessary and (as they would have said) wholesome catharsis."[43] As cultural muckrakers the debunkers were responding to a continuing need of the American middle class for wholesome or even not-so-wholesome catharsis. Laughter was the most aerobic and cleansing of psychic responses.

As the muckraking period came to a close, interest in social, economic, and political reform within existing democratic institutions lessened. Many of the dissenting and idealistic young turned toward the world of art. It is from this group that many of the debunkers came. They partly disguised their sense of idealism, of purpose and mission, behind comic masks. They turned to diffuse and sometimes oblique reactions against the entrenched interests and attitudes that were inhibiting America's coming of age. Debunkers needed comic masks for their satire in order to manipulate and obliquely to express subversive, hostile feelings in a socially acceptable way, while at the same time gaining the approval of their audience and the comforts of success. Yet the release of these feelings was a motive secondary to their attempts to find in satiric writing a satisfying and significant manner of creative self-expression. They seemed to question the Protestant ethic, and the values of middle-class lives dedicated to its realization in a modern world, that appeared to be moving toward meaningless complexity, relativism, and even chaos. But this questioning was not overt. Their explicit subject was the inflated or pompous language in which the ethic and its values were glorified.

Nevertheless, that ethic continued to lie under the attitudes of the debunkers. Like satirists of any era they looked back to an indefinable Golden Age, to the good old days when life, somehow, had been better. Many of them were from provincial America, and most were at least third-generation middle-class Americans. While they debunked the life they had left behind them in the provinces, at the same time they nostalgically remembered aspects of that life with twinges of regret for its loss. While they seemed subversive in that they attacked the self-glorification of the American middle class, they remained entirely American and determinedly bourgeois in their irate individualism.

Typically, the debunkers never completely purged themselves of their middle-class origins. There was an ineradicable tinge of Philistinism in their loudest strictures. Yet they resisted with the weapons of burlesque and parody the movement of their culture toward a complacent condition in which the values of genteel life were expressed in unashamedly celebratory language. For a time their comic articulations seemed to contribute to the creative optimism of America's cultural resurgence after 1910. It was a deceptive contribution, for the debunkers more often looked backward than forward. Satire was the natural means for the free expression of their disaffection. And satire was the sophisticated instrument for cultural criticism.

The principal stronghold of sophistication was New York. Many of the debunkers were attracted there by the reputation of Mencken, a commuter from Baltimore, whose magazine essays, reviews, and books were well known by 1915 and practically notorious by 1920. It was in the writings of Mencken that the debunkers found some of their methods, a prophetic voice and leadership in the warfare against repressive Puritan traditions.

# Chapter Two

## The Ordeal of H. L. Mencken

The true objection to the modern dances
is not moral, but aesthetic. They are evil because
they are ugly.

"The Free Lance," *Baltimore Sun*, 15 July 1915

Although Mencken died in 1956, in one sense his life ended in 1930, for the tendency from the 1930s until after the Second World War was to denigrate his importance and sometimes to ridicule him. Since then he has been regarded more affectionately as one of the last of the articulate and stylish American individualists. He is remembered usually as an iconoclast who transcended time and place, an image of him projected in the reverent nostalgia surrounding the 1980 celebration of the centennial of his birth. However, he was very much of a time and of a place. His glorified hostilities are postures out of the past; he was like a lay analyst who helped free our culture from its repressions. He was a stylist, a propagandist, a popularizer of important late nineteenth- and early twentieth-century ideas. He made a public spectacle of our genteel traditions and attitudes, yet it was characteristic of his Puritan individualism that his own gentility informed what he called his prejudices. Because of the turmoil produced by the spectacle, we sometimes forget that he was twenty years old in 1900, and that his early training as a journalist was during the period when the progressive attitudes of the muckrakers flourished. In a review of the centennial outpouring of books and articles, Murray Kempton reminds us of the "social outrage" that was always characteristic of Mencken's rhetoric. We sense, and should not forget, in Mencken the same characteristics that he early celebrated in the writing of Theodore Dreiser: his "pity," "awe," and "profound sense of wonder."[1]

As a nineteenth-century American who reached his prime early in this century, Mencken embodied the contradictions in his middle-class culture, which is why he is valuable to us; it is also why he has often been misunderstood. He was successful in creating the image that we remember him by: he wore the armor of the picaresque iconoclast most of his life, thus covering the Puritan weeds underneath. He wanted us to think of him as a gay (that is, variegated, colorful, jovial) fellow: "The liberation of the human mind . . . has been furthered by gay fellows who heaved dead cats into sanctuaries and then went roistering down the highways of the world. . . . One horse-laugh is worth ten thousand syllogisms."[2] The invariable sanctuary into which he heaved his many dead cats was the front parlor of the genteel, middle-class American home. All of his polemics and joyful bellicosities had in common the same posture of hostility toward the respectable American of middle means, abilities, and ambitions. But he himself belonged to the class whose way of life he ridiculed: most of his animadversions were touched with love and affection. He was an obedient son in a prosperous family, and seemed satisfied to obey dutifully his father's wish that he work in the family cigar-manufacturing business, right after his graduation from school. But all the while he was clandestinely scribbling away at poems and short stories, and planning his escape.

His father's sudden death in 1898 released him from the paternal expectation, and almost immediately Mencken sought employment with the *Baltimore Herald*.[3] He seemed to be effecting a compromise between literature and respectable middle-class life by beginning a career as a journalist; he continued in private to write poetry and fiction, and when he sought publication he sometimes used pseudonyms. His training in reporting the miscellany of Baltimore life was extensive and rigorous. His work for the *Herald* and for the *Sun* was a trying-out of style, and over the years (until he began his own column in 1911) formed a collage of character sketches, poetry, jokes, reviews, reporting, and muckraking—an impressionistic image of the reality of that time and place. Exaggeration was a perfectly natural element of style; in raking through some of the mucky activities of Baltimore's City Council, he invented news when he could not get it by other means.[4] Early, as an extension of this inventiveness, he developed skills at parody and mimicry. When he had to give up the journalist's convention of anonymity as writer for the *Smart Set* and other national magazines, he made the transition by using many pseudonyms. He could invent characters, mimic many styles, and create "facts" with all the skill of a writer of fiction.

Mencken's national exposure as a debunker began in 1908 when he became book reviewer for the *Smart Set,* and was extended in 1911 when he began to write "The Free Lance," a column for the *Baltimore Evening Sun.* For the *Sun* he was told to write on any subjects he chose, as long as he was entertaining and readable. Thus his iconoclasm was not simply tolerated by editors and owners, it was sought out and prized as a good editorial investment in response to a public demand. Behind this editorial policy there was the muckraking tradition, as well as a respectable nineteenth-century tradition of newspaper satirists and wits. The only subject forbidden Mencken in 1911 was the Christian church, but this restriction was soon lifted.[5] Another sounding board was established in the *Smart Set,* especially in 1914 and the decade following, when Mencken and Nathan were editors. A major vehicle for his debunking was his monthly book review column; he reviewed at least a hundred books each year for fifteen years. Others were the *Smart Set* departments called "Pertinent and Impertinent," "Répétition Générale," and "Americana," started in 1912, 1919, and 1923, respectively. A frequent pseudonym used by Mencken, Nathan, and Wright was "Owen Hatteras," not only as the fictitious author of "Pertinent and Impertinent" but of many other stories, articles, comments, aphorisms, epigrams, and purported American creeds as well. In addition Mencken invented an astonishing number of pseudonyms that multiplied his monthly writing for the magazine to amazing levels. The *American Mercury* continued much of what Mencken and Nathan had started in the *Smart Set.* The *Mercury* then became the main vehicle for Mencken's reputation as America's foremost critic and satirist, at least until 1927.[6]

Mencken's main critical resource as an editor for poetry and fiction was the resource of a journalist: the topical, the interesting, the realistic attracted his attention. As a reviewer, especially as he grew older, he paid less and less attention to poetry and fiction. As a critic he was at his best when evaluating a whole culture in terms of his favorite thesis about the pernicious influence of puritanism. He was quick to identify and report on the cultural resurgence in twentieth-century America. There were intimations of the resurgence in his book on Shaw (1905); he was one of the first to recognize the importance of Dreiser; he approved of the young Van Wyck Brooks as a prophet in the Emerson and Whitman tradition; he recognized in the undercurrent of revolt a healthy element of skepticism.

All of Mencken's best-known subjects appeared in the years before the First World War; the next twenty years were years of selection and repetition for the benefit of a new audience which grew steadily until about 1930, when it began to lose interest. What he selected and re-peated touched upon three phenomena of American life. One was the unsophisticated, provincial, Anglo-Saxon American, usually of the middle class and usually from the vast desert of the Midwest or South. The second was the national institutions created and perpetuated by the middle-class citizen, whose ideology, Mencken thought, was based on a devitalized, dissipated version of the Puritan tradition; the major ob-jects of satire in this area were the Puritan tradition itself, democracy, pretentious myths about America, religion and the doctrine of service, Prohibition, censorship, demagoguery, and fundamentalism. Menck-en's third area of deflationary activity was the Philistinism of the gen-teel, middle-class world. As a book reviewer he attacked not only the sentimental, moral literature of the middle class, but also the literature of the newly liberated aesthetes, whom he saw as products of that same class.

Mencken was a complex man whose public self was sometimes in conflict with a private self.[7] We see abundantly a public figure, the gay heaver of dead cats into the parlors of the genteel. We also see a man passionately devoted to the aesthetic values of the art of writing. His devotion was religious; it transcended or sometimes conflicted with the social, moral, political, and economic values of the middle-class world in which he was brought up and in which he lived. A portrait of the artist as a young man emerges from his earliest writings (1898–1910) and be-comes fully limned in the transitional period roughly from 1911 to the beginning of the war. These were the years of his developing conscious-ness of the Puritan characteristics of his middle-class world, a world that he loved deeply. At the same time he came to realize that this world disapproved of his passionate commitment to the art and act of writing. Philip Wagner, who knew Mencken personally and who followed him as editor of the *Baltimore Evening Sun,* has indicated that Mencken's father's insistence that he learn the family business "was the cause of some friction between father and son."[8] From our perspective the myth of the artist's ordeal as a young man was best described by James Joyce, who was of the same generation. But both *Dubliners* and *Portrait of the Artist as a Young Man* were published too late (1914 and 1916) to do more than confirm for this generation a sense of common experience. And their sense of the role of artists in a hostile middle-class world was prefigured by writers during the 1890s, especially Stephen Crane, Har-old Frederic, Kate Chopin, Jack London.

Mencken was a younger member of a generation of middle-class men and women who felt that they had lost power and status to a new elite of business magnates and political bosses. As Hofstadter describes it, they felt that their traditional authority and effect as owners of businesses, as lawyers, editors, doctors, ministers, and teachers had been displaced.[9] Their response was to expose, always from an indignantly moral posture, the corruption they observed in the world controlled by the new class of businessmen and political bosses. Mencken as a young journalist in his twenties shared these concerns, sometimes without the moral posture, and the evidence for his participation can be found abundantly in the articles, the editorials, and the columns he wrote for the Baltimore papers and for the *Smart Set* during his formative years as a writer.

While Mencken was living the ordeal of the young, middle-class aspiring writer, he was also assimilating the attitudes—he called them prejudices—for which in the 1920s he would become famous. These prejudices can be sifted down to a very few ideas, which recur in Menckeniana like a litany. These ideas were behind many of the subjects of his writing, and most were expressed by other debunkers. Part of this correspondence is due, of course, to Mencken's widespread impact between 1920 and 1930. But some of Mencken's assertions and some of his subjects were shared with other late nineteenth-century and early twentieth-century writers. The resemblance of Mencken's attitudes to those of other debunkers depended in part on Mencken's shrewdness as a journalist: irreverence and satire were especially in demand. Mencken met the demand.

The main acknowledged intellectual influences on Mencken's personal ideology were Shaw, Darwin, Huxley, and Nietzsche. In Shaw he saw many of the characteristics that he was to nurture and propagandize in himself, even when his admiration had turned to rancor: in 1919 he described Shaw as the "Ulster Polonius." The playwright was the object of Mencken's strident hyperbole, yet his admiration and self-projection were conveyed again and again even through his rhetorical hostility. He wrote: "Practically all of the sagacity of George Bernard Shaw consisted of bellowing vociferously what everyone knows." "It is his life work to announce the obvious in terms of the scandalous." "He has a large and extremely uncommon capacity for provocative utterance; he knows how to get a touch of bellicosity into the most banal of doctrines." He is "cocksure and bilious"; he completely lacks aesthetic sensibility: "Beauty is a lewdness, redeemable only in the service of morality."[10] Vociferousness, hyperbole, bellicosity, arrogance, and lack of aesthetic sensibility were also characteristics assumed by the Juvenalian narrator Mencken created as his spokesman.

Mencken's earlier (1905) book on Shaw and his plays was less superficial, but just as self-revelatory. His announced purpose was "to exhibit the Shaw plays as dramas rather than as transcendental treatises." However, dramatic analysis was only incidentally his purpose in the introduction and exegeses that followed. The Shaw who interested him most was not primarily Shaw the dramatist, but Shaw the sham-smasher and satirist, the exemplary Shaw for the young Henry Mencken. He wrote in the introduction that "the accident that made him what he is was one of time. He saw the light after, instead of before Charles Darwin." Then, in familiar Menckenese: "From him [Darwin], through Huxley, we have appendicitis, the seedless orange, and our affable indifference to hell." It was Darwin, Mencken wrote, who in the *Origin of Species* brought irrefutable scientific evidence to bear in the fight against orthodoxy, custom, and authority; "the practical result of this [Darwinism] was that seekers after the truth, growing bold with success, began attacking virtues as well as vices." Darwinism produced a conflict "between the faithful and the scoffers," and Shaw, Mencken thought, was an exemplar in this conflict. Mencken joined the battle with a crusader's zeal; he felt he was like Shaw because his mission in life had been determined by an accident in time. It was to Shaw the sham-smasher that he responded; he thought dramatic conflict had arisen both in the theater and in life between "old notions of conduct and new ones." The old notions of conduct were those held by the middle class, "the self-satisfied businessman and taxpayer."[11] Mencken discovered in Shaw powerful reinforcement for his own posture of hostility toward the provincial, middle-class American and toward the lower classes ("the yokels") who followed the institutional and cultural leadership of the middle class with democratic docility.

Mencken's admiration for Thomas Henry Huxley began early and remained consistent. He admired the clarity of his "devastating agnosticism" and his defense of Darwin against the outrage of the religious establishment. He admired Huxley's "nearly perfect English prose."[12] Mencken was to take on for himself a role as champion of enlightened thought against the many manifestations of puritanism in American life.

Nietzsche's influence on the young Mencken gave his writing much of its insistent dogmatism.[13] Mencken discovered Nietzsche sometime after 1905 and wrote a book about him in 1908. He used the same approach in the book that he had used for Shaw: he analyzed the life and works of Nietzsche for their exemplary content; Nietzsche was a hero and prophet to Mencken. He saw a vigorous individualism in the man which had grown out of his reaction away from the moral, Christian, conservative,

Philistine culture of his time. Mencken stressed Nietzsche's sense of self: his pride and individualism, his intellectual separateness and his courage as a sham-smasher. Nietzsche was a hero because he had shaken himself free of the dominant thought of his time.

The Nietzschean creed, Mencken wrote, "may be called a counter-blast to sentimentality." That creed was based on a dualism which ran all through Nietzsche's thought and work. Mencken traced the dualism from its expression in Nietzsche's first book, *The Birth of Tragedy* (1872). Greek tragedy had depended upon the conflict between worship of the gods Apollo and Dionysus. Apollo was the god of art, of life recorded and preserved, of life at second hand; Dionysus was the god of life at first hand, the god of vitality and action, Mencken wrote. The Apollonian-Dionysian dichotomy applied to modern life meant that "men were still torn between the apollonian impulse to conform and moralize and the dionysian impulse to exploit and explore." Nietzsche, Mencken reported, thought of the Dionysian class as the master class: its members were aristocratic, iconoclastic, immoral; the Apollonian class was the slave class: its members were servile, religious, moral. The ideal society would be the result of a balance between these two forces. But Mencken distorted Nietzsche, for Nietzsche never glorified the Dionysian at the expense of the Apollonian. The Christian doctrine of service, Mencken continued, had violated the natural division between inferior and superior beings by preaching that the strong should give of their strength to help the weak. The doctrine of service had violated the principle of natural selection; it constituted an interference with the processes by which the fittest survived. Any form of self-sacrifice (as Mencken interpreted Nietzsche) was against the law of nature, and therefore would weaken humanity in the struggle to evolve the superior individual.

There was at this point in the Nietzschean theory (according to Mencken) disagreement with Darwin, and Mencken emphasized the point of difference. Darwin had believed that civilization constituted a modification of the law of natural selection, and that although civilization had interfered with the natural processes of the survival of the fittest, human beings would nevertheless, through their intelligence, prevail. Mencken noted the point of difference—two of his intellectual heroes disagreed—but he never resolved it. The dualism that underlay his reading of the Nietzschean theory was both to inspire and confound Mencken all his life: the dualism between Dionysian individualism on the one hand and Apollonian humanitarianism on the other. Mencken responded to Nietzsche as a crusader for nothing less than the truth. To

Mencken one principle of truth applicable in America was that the individual was being smothered by the humanitarian elements in his culture. He found in the Nietzschean theory the basis of "a mighty crusade against all those ethical ideas which teach a man to sacrifice himself for the theoretical good of his inferiors." Like Nietzsche, Mencken saw himself as part of a culture dominated by moral, Christian, conservative, and Philistine elements.[14] At the same time he had inherited the humanistic attitudes of his culture, attitudes that reached new heights of eloquent expression during the years of Mencken's young manhood, in the activities of the progressives. By the beginning of the First World War the resulting tension began to appear in his writing.

Other writers who appear in the lifelong litany of Mencken's admiration were Edgar Allan Poe and James Gibbon Huneker. Although Mencken found Poe's poetry artificial, his stories juvenile, and his style elaborate and ornate, his criticism was "direct and clear." Mencken saw him as an artist unrecognized in his own time, an artist who had freed American letters from the dominance of English taste.[15] Mencken sought in the clarity of his own prose to liberate American letters and life from the dominance of puritanism and its moral perspectives. He was drawn to these writers because they held that the import of art was aesthetic, not moral. William H. Nolte has observed that together Huneker and Mencken "led American criticism out of the wilderness of academic stultification,"[16] but Huneker seems less significant than Mencken.

The only other nineteenth-century American writer of the Mark Twain–William Dean Howells–Henry James generation upon whom Mencken looked with special respect was Bierce. In his famous essay "Puritanism as Literary Force," Mencken recognized Bierce as one of the few outspoken condemners of puritanical Philistinism, as one of the few in his time who did not capitulate to genteel civilization.[17] In other words, he was a hero in the Nietzschean tradition. Bierce was, Mencken wrote in another essay, "the first American to lay about him with complete gusto, charging and battering the frauds who ranged the country."[18] In many ways Mencken was Bierce reincarnated in a period friendlier to his ideas and methods. Both were journalists who published much of their journalism in book form. Both revolted against hypocrisy in humanitarian movements and against the dominance of the Puritan ethic in America. They publicly and loudly professed distrust of the rule of the common people. Neither was ever deterred from vehement opinion or pronouncement by either ignorance or knowledge. Both sought more lasting recognition as writers than their reputations as journalists had given them. They were alike in their Rabelaisian geniality; both noisily escaped into masculine camaraderie from the feminine world of home and family, and happily returned. Both were loud in their rhetorical indictment of respectable bourgeois life: they ridiculed its preachers, its aggressively emancipated women, its politicians, and its affected artists. The program which Bierce laid out for himself in his prospectus for *The Lantern* (published in London, 1874) might easily have been written by Mencken forty years later. Bierce called for the "disapproval of human institutions in general, including all forms of government, most laws and customs, and all contemporary literature . . . unruffled disbelief in the exaggerated claims of reformers and philanthropists."[19] Mencken was more selective in his prejudices, especially with respect to contemporary literature; nevertheless exaggeration for comic effect was central to the methods of both.

Although they had met briefly in 1911 at Percival Pollard's funeral, the meeting had not made any special impression on Bierce. It was not until 1913 that he began a correspondence with Mencken. In this correspondence Bierce apologized for having just "discovered" Mencken and expressed his appreciation for the Menckenian style and point of view. He wrote in one letter to Mencken that "your remarks are more than cleverly made—they charm" and in another that "the *manner* of your fighting is altogether admirable." He was pleased especially by what Mencken had written about socialists, although he thought that Mencken's attack had been altogether too courteous. "I have never met one who was not in open and candid sympathy with crime. . . . Moreover, he is a cry-baby and a 'fraid-cat.' Furthermore, he is commonly devoid of decency, and his female is that way, too. . . . Socialism is going to get our goat."[20]

Sometimes what may have appeared to be humorous observations in Mencken's writing were indistinguishable from attitudes drawn out of the depths of his half-knowledge, ignorance, and carelessness: these were prejudices in the most ordinary sense. Frequently he could carry off bigotry and inaccuracy with aplomb; when his rhetoric was at its thumping best, the reader was inclined to accept exaggeration and to overlook misinterpretation. He always favored the startling, dramatic illustration to the strictly factual one, depending upon the overriding satiric effect of the Juvenalian voice in his writing. Nevertheless, many of his *obiter dicta* on cultural and literary matters, in spite of the extravagant pose, were flagrantly, although often consciously, uninformed. Sometimes he tried for comic profundity by invoking racial theories which seemed the careless products of his Nietzschean individualism.

One of his comic extravagances led him to explain the genius of Jack London by suggesting that London might have had Jewish blood.[21] He applied racial notions to other American writers, trying to show that those who rose above the common level of mediocrity had blood other than Anglo-Saxon in their veins: "Whitman was half Dutch, Harte was half Jew, Poe was partly German, James had an Irish grandfather, Howells was largely Irish and German, Dreiser is German and Hergesheimer is Pennsylvania Dutch."[22] And he wrote that most of the leaders of America's twentieth-century cultural resurgence were the products of crosses from non-Anglo-Saxon strains (he did not, on this occasion, name any of these leaders).[23]

Such statements were one of the ways through which he tried to shock—and amuse—his middle-class readers, for it was one of the sacred tenets of Americanism that the middle class had a stolidly Anglo-Saxon heritage. He further twitted hyper-American patriots when he used a racial theory to explain the preponderence of boobs and yokels in America: most Americans came from inferior immigrant stock. The Anglo-Saxon majority came from second-rate Englishmen; the Italians had brought "no more of the essential culture of Italy with them than so many horned cattle. . . . So with the Germans, the Scandinavians, and even the Jews and the Irish."[24] He thought that the reason for America's comparatively arid, uncivilized cultural climate was that America lacked "a civilized aristocracy, secure in its position, animated by an intelligent curiosity, skeptical of all facile generalizations, superior to the sentimentality of the mob."[25] His insistence on individualism and his desire for a genuine aristocracy of the intellect were inseparable articles of his faith. Still, when he wrote about Jews and blacks, his attitudes sometimes seemed the ordinary ones of a narrow-minded, Anglo-Saxon Protestant, and reflected the typical bourgeois social values and careless ethnic witticisms of his upbringing.[26]

His affectation of racism could be both deliberate and ambiguous, deliberate to the extent that he sometimes burlesqued racial attitudes in order to satirize them, and ambiguous in that he was sometimes willing to let racists among his readers believe he was advocating, not ridiculing, their position. That ambiguity extended into the value system of Mencken's middle-class world. For example, an early article of his (20 November 1904), published by the *Baltimore Sunday Herald,* was entitled "The Race Problem and Politics—A Southerner's Plan for Benevolently Obliterating the Nigger." In it the southerner was extravagantly praised as an idealist and individualist. Or at least so it might have seemed to racists among his readers. Mencken created an ambiguous effect, for sympathetic liberals would inevitably have read this article as a burlesque, a piece of writing parodying racial attitudes. At several points in his signed "Free Lance" columns (1911–1915), he reflected stereotypically "southern" views of race problems. He wrote frequently about the high disease and death rates in Baltimore, which he attributed to the living conditions of Negroes. His argument was racist in its fastidiousness, but it was also practical: clean up the habitat of the Negroes, he said, and educate them in hygiene in order to prevent the spread of disease to whites. If Mencken had humanitarian concerns other than for the eradication of disease, they were not expressed. But he was writing both *at* and *to* racist elements in his audience. Most enlightened readers would have assumed his tone was extravagant. Sara Mayfield, who was a close friend of Mencken's wife, has written that Mencken "was one of the earliest champions of civil rights for black and white alike," although she does not support this claim.[27]

Carl Dolmetsch writes that Mencken was "often unjustly accused of harboring racist sentiments, probably because of his outspoken and decidedly un-euphemistic style in discussing racial matters." He was "un-euphemistic" in that he frequently used the most blatantly racist and offensive terminology for discussing racial attitudes and problems. He used such language because it came from the ordinary speech patterns of southern racists, and was inappropriate to the liberal views he was expressing: the effect was to ridicule racists among his readers. In one *Smart Set* review, the black is referred to variously as the "niggero," the "Ethiop," the "coon," the "blackamoor":

> What, ladies and gentlemen, in hell or out of it, are we to do with the Ethiop? Who shall answer the thunderous demands of the emerging coon? For emerging he is, both quantitatively and qualitatively, and there will come a morn, believe me or not, when those with ears to hear and hides to feel will discover that he is to be boohed and put off no longer—that he has at last got the power to exact a square answer, and that the days of his docile service as minstrel, torch and goat are done. . . . Not only is the coon not come to equilibrium; he is jumping up and rocking the boat more and more.

The context for this language was Mencken's argument that the black "in all that is essential and lasting . . . has shown better progress than the Southern whites."[28] In that progress Mencken saw the potential for the emergence of the South from its dismal condition, what he referred to elsewhere as a cultural Sahara. In another review his intention was social criticism rather than ridicule of racist attitudes. He used the racially neutral "Negroes" to describe the need for realistic assessments of blacks in the South: "But the fact remains that the Southern whites have to deal with the actual Negroes before them, and not with a theoretical race of African kings. These actual Negroes show defects that are very real and very serious. The leaders of the race, engrossed by the almost unbearable injustices that it faces, are apt to forget them."[29] He referred to the deficiencies of the "emerging Negro" by enumerating "his lack of self-restraint, his savage passion, his almost Jewish impudence and obnoxiousness."[30] A reference to "Jewish impudence" in this context may have struck some of Mencken's readers as offensive, and some as comical. The same ambiguity of effect (of which Mencken must have been at least partly aware) was again present. As in some of his observations about Negroes there is a startling disjunction between language and context.

Many of Mencken's best friends and associates were Jewish. Usually racist ridicule was clearly directed at Jews whom Mencken saw as militant promoters of Jewish group or class rights. He was equally acerbic when he talked about vice crusaders, Puritans, New Dealers, militant feminists, or any group that in promoting itself seemed to interfere with or ignore the rights of individuals. Again and again he wrote about Jews as if they had tribal identity: "Jews as a class are generally impolite." "The Jewish rabbis as a class seem to be very foolish fellows." "Jewry as an organized body is almost unqualifiedly unpleasant." But also: "The most outrageous of all the Nazi doctrines is the war to the general effect that Jews have no civil rights." Here he was consistent with his defense of individual civil rights elsewhere and with his views that *any* militant group is bound to infringe on the rights of others. Nevertheless, some of his statements may have been due to the kind of ignorance shared by other members of his class: "If the Jews were exposed to one-tenth the disadvantages that oppress the Negroes they'd be howling all the time." That observation, like the other examples above, was made in 1939, when Mencken was trying to put together a book of miscellany to be called "Advice to Young Men." Later, in 1948, he culled out these statements as he was editing the manuscript for publication; it was not published until after his death, under the title *Minority Report.*[31] At least by 1948 he was sensitive to some of the offensiveness of such views. And much earlier, in 1922, he had written from Munich to a friend about the "confusing and astounding spectacle in Germany": "Every intelligent man looks for a catastrophe. If it comes there will be a colossal massacre of Jews."[32] The paradox between Mencken's pragmatic understanding of the dilemma of racism and the bigoted extravagance of some of his statements cannot be clearly resolved. But his extravagance can be explained as sometimes mimicking or parodying the casual, usually privately expressed racism of his class and time. That racism was no less ugly and offensive because it was so casual; still, it was often contradicted by the public, political, and personal behavior of Mencken and his genteel peers, who in the privacy of their parlors somehow found it amusing to talk about "coons" and "kikes." Militant feminists were frequently included in the joking. Guy Forgue has argued that the evidence usually cited for Mencken's racism was really "inside jokes culled here and there in his writings," and that these jokes were "designed to tease his friends."[33] In another place Forgue identifies what he calls Mencken's "instinctive racism," but such an attitude is not borne out by the evidence of Mencken's concerns, for example, about the condition of blacks in America. Charles Scruggs has shown that Mencken's empathy for blacks and black writers was consistent and significant, and that in the early 1920s he was an important influence on the writers of the Harlem renaissance.[34] Nevertheless, he could both parody and pander to the racism, the antisemitism and the antifeminism of his WASP friends.

In the 1930s the contempt Mencken expressed for Roosevelt and the New Deal was an extreme version of what was as much a commonplace of middle- and upper-middle-class American life as were inhumane jokes about Jews.[35] By the 1930s he had lost most of his audience and his attitudes sounded more and more conservative and dogmatic. As Mencken both loved and ridiculed the attitudes of his class and the seemingly permanent world it had created, his work was bound to reflect his conflicting feelings. This conflict animated his best writing, but faded, in his worst, into a querulousness indistinguishable from bigotry.

Mencken's ambivalence about the middle class of which he was such a comfortable member was central to his development. The pose of hostility toward that class in his writing was tempered by nostalgic memories that he expressed overtly late in his life. In his important book on Mencken, Forgue describes the Baltimore where Mencken was born and lived all his life as "a complex of contraries: security and freedom, north and south, city and country."[36] As a boy Mencken was puzzled and frustrated by a loss of masculine vitality in his time. The figure of the authoritative patriarch, whether his own father, or the pioneer at the center of the struggle for survival, or the Puritan who had rigidly controlled the New England environment, was gone. His sense of the loss received poignant attention in his reminiscences of childhood life in Baltimore. His childhood Baltimore was like a small town, and every summer the family moved outside the city to a rural setting. His upbringing was thoroughly middle-class and provincial. Mencken did not reject this life, although much of his rhetoric condemned provincial values. His recollections in tranquility were extravagantly nostalgic and idyllic. It was a pastoral world, not quite real when remembered from the distance of age, but free, at any rate in memory, from the evils and complications of the city.[37] Of special relevance are his contradictory memories of his father.

He wrote in the preface to *Happy Days* (which was published in 1939 and covered the years 1880–1892) that his father "was always at the center of his small world." The important word is *small,* for it is precisely the smallness of this bourgeois world which emerged in the anecdotes that followed, and that echoed in its casual racist language. Mencken, at least in the nostalgia of maturity, had no quarrel with the smallness; he wrote that he had been "encapsulated in affection," that he had been "a larva of the comfortable and complacent bourgeoisie." His father was a cigar manufacturer, rigidly reactionary and benevolent in all his capitalistic and labor practices. Mencken described his daily routine as "no doubt quite typical of that of hundreds of other Baltimore employees of the period." He would arise very early and immediately after breakfast go to his office at the cigar factory; then he would read his mail, which consisted of checks, orders, and reports from and about his salesmen. A half hour would be spent in a perfunctory inspection of cigars manufactured the day before. "The rest of the morning he devoted to a furious and largely useless figuring"; elaborate cost-sheets were kept which no one ever consulted. At one o'clock he would rush out to lunch, either at a saloon, or, if the family was in town, at home. After lunch, he took a nap from which he would guiltily awake after a half hour or so; then he would rush off again to his office: "To the casual eye he seemed to be in haste, but when he got to his office there was really next to nothing for him to do." He spent the afternoon reading the newspaper or gossiping with anyone who happened to drop in. He went to the baseball game if there was one in town, or followed the scores of out-of-town games at an oysterhouse. In winter he frequently spent the afternoon entertaining a customer at the saloon next door. A great deal of his energy was expended in concocting practical jokes. The father Mencken described was rarely an authoritarian figure (except when his own routine was violated); he was simply a big brother, the oldest child in the family.[38]

As the oldest child, Mencken's father, like Mencken himself, was subject to the all-embracing authority of the home. In these early reminiscences Mencken rarely mentioned his mother; he re-created a childhood idyll with all its antisocial pleasures and irresponsibilities. Yet his sense of home and of his mother was pervasively present as the background of everything he recollected. His mother was the stable center of the genteel way of life against which Mencken later directed some of his rhetoric. One aspect was the mercantile routine that his father followed and that Mencken was expected to follow. The vast pretense necessary to hide the purposelessness of this way of life must have become apparent to him when he was quite young. For a boy who dreamed early of being a chemist, then of being a poet, cigar-making could have held little promise of enchantment. Mencken worked, as his father in his affection and firmness wished, in the cigar factory until immediately after his father's death. Then he left the factory to begin his career as a writer.

Mencken wrote (in an unpublished autobiographical fragment) that "for a man whose life has been mainly given over to letters I grew up in an amazingly unliterary environment."[39] Unlike other artist-writers seeking to emerge from their middle-class worlds, he did not make disaffection with family life a subject of his writing. As "a larva of the comfortable and complacent bourgeoisie," he became aware of its complacency when he began "to read indignant books," as he wrote in his autobiography. One early reading experience (at, he reported, the age of nine) was *Huckleberry Finn,* and this experience contributed to his sense of the pleasantly concealed futility and emasculated nature of the way of life he knew and loved as a boy. He credited *Huckleberry Finn* with having been nothing less than the most important single influence on him. From it, for one thing, he gained the excitement over literature that led him to read omnivorously all his life. But he gained something more: *Huckleberry Finn* expressed for him vague and covert feelings about his own condition in nineteenth-century America. Huck Finn is idle and lawless and free; he struggles against the moral codes that were the product of nineteenth-century genteel civilization, the product of puritanism proselytized and devitalized. His struggle is just as much a struggle for survival, is just as vital, as a more primitive struggle against natural forces would have been. Thus, as Leslie Fiedler has written, *Huckleberry Finn* is truly a subversive book.[40] The young Henry Mencken responded to the subversion of genteel values: to the awakening the book provided he added his awareness that his father, whom he loved and admired, had the real status in his family of only another child, and that his whole way of life was highly rationalized, excessively pointless, and futile. In a sense, the young Mencken was himself a Huck Finn to his father's grown-up Tom Sawyer. But he was finally unlike Huck Finn and more like Mark Twain himself in that he was never able to reject or move away from the warmth and security of the female-centered domestic world that had nurtured him.

Our nostalgic image of Mencken's individualism is derived from our memories of him in the 1920s, when the full force of his rhetoric in the *American Mercury* and in his *Prejudices* was a phenomenon of national significance. Appraisals of his development (from 1900, when he was twenty years old, until 1920) have isolated out of the copious writings the attitudes and ideas that we best remember him by. These attitudes and ideas were produced by a complex background. His early writings show diversity, contradiction, sometimes confusion; they often suggest an underlying tension. While it rarely shows explicitly, we sense that Mencken was living through an ordeal experienced by other aspiring middle-class writers of his time and of his generation. Mencken emerged as a leader of the satirist-debunkers whose focused concern was to expose and ridicule the abuse of language, the fabrication of bunk: the distortion or obliteration of reality and truth. Mencken was the first of the cultural muckrakers because his operating assumption was that exposure of fraudulent expression and language through ridicule could bring about changes in manners and morals. He derived some of his attitudes and aspects of his style from the muckrakers whose writing dominated the journals during his apprentice years as a writer. Mencken wrote upon many aspects of social and political reform, partly in response to the interests of his audience, and partly as the expression of his own humane and sometimes sentimental sympathies. The writings of his formative years render a rather different figure from the flamboyant, individualistic, antiprogressive iconoclast we so affectionately remember. We will see, as I hope to show in Chapter Four, a young man who shared many of the humanistic attitudes and assumptions of the progressive philosophy that was the dominant, middle-class, liberal orientation of his developmental years. His explicit, public rejection of that philosophy emerged fully around 1914 and 1915, just as the First World War was beginning.

His love of the art of writing was the organizing passion of his life. He had to find ways of expressing that passion in a genteel world that relegated concern about art to women.

# Chapter Three

## H. L. Mencken and Equal Rights for Women

[Women] . . . are oppressed by man-made laws, man-made
social customs, masculine egoism, the delusion of masculine superiority.

"Appendix on a Tender Theme," 1920

One of Mencken's declarations about sex roles in transition in American life occurred in a review of *Women in Modern Society,* by Earl Barnes, published in 1912, which was a crucial period for the formation of Mencken's attitudes about women. In the review Mencken objected to militant aspects of the women's movement that obliterated sex differences. Then he concluded:

> The ideal of the years to come is a woman emancipated from convention
> and superstition, a free agent in human society, the full equal of her man—not
> a grotesque parody of that man, arrayed absurdly in his *toga virilis,* smoking
> his bad cigars, monkeying with his labors and vices, but a creature standing
> squarely on her own rotund legs, not a pseudo-man but an authentic woman,
> not a grotesque blend of angel and grafter, but a free equal.[1]

Although he was a cigar-smoker, Mencken had much in common with his ideal woman: rotund of leg as well as torso, he was a free agent emancipated at least from superstition, and he too was neither angel nor grafter. Above all, he was clear and unreserved in his affirmation of political and social equality for women. The immediate context for this view was the intense feminist activity leading up to the ratification of the Nineteenth Amendment in 1920, when the right to vote was extended to women.

Nevertheless, Mencken could describe women in ways that reflect the more ordinary male orientation of his time and place; a few years later in a series of portraits of Americans, Mencken wrote that the "flapper" is

> a charming young creature. There is something trim and . . . confident about her. She is easy in her manners. She bears herself with dignity in all societies. She is graceful, rosy, healthy, appetizing. It is a delight to see her sink her pearly teeth into a chocolate, a macaroon, even a potato. There is music in her laugh. She is youth, she is hope, she is romance—she is wisdom.[2]

To Mencken there was no conflict between these views: a flapper could also be a "free agent" and "an authentic woman" (although if "rotund" of leg she would, presumably, have to rouge her knees). But the emergence of the flapper was not usually regarded as a political phenomenon. Mencken's tone in this description is both celebratory and exuberantly ironic, like the portraits of flappers by F. Scott Fitzgerald and John Held. In his rather genteel way, Mencken celebrated the process by which women were freeing themselves from Victorian attitudes. But at the same time it is clear that to him a woman's charm depended on conventional notions of femininity. Mencken also tolerated and sometimes fostered a public image of himself as a Victorian gentleman who knew that a woman's place was in the home. He noisily defended the condition of bachelorhood with what we would call chauvinistic assertions about the wiles of women in the battle of the sexes. In 1930, when he married for the first and only time at the age of fifty, it was a national joke that at the height of his career and fame the male-chauvinist Mencken had surrendered his freedom happily and complacently.

Therefore, it is not surprising that Mencken's sympathetic attitudes toward women have often been misunderstood, misrepresented or ignored. Carl Bode, in his Mencken biography, indexes his discussion of *In Defense of Women* under "anti-feminism." Although *In Defense of Women* burlesques aspects of militant feminism, it is not antifeminist. William Manchester, in an earlier biography, *Disturber of the Peace* (1950), wrote that "*In Defense of Women,* as is generally known, was anything but a defense; it was instead a delightful lampooning of the more ridiculous aspects of the relationships between the sexes, and was inspired, Mencken told his friends, by thoughts which came to him while lying abed with cuties."[3] Mencken probably never lay abed with cuties (although he liked to talk about such fantasies for the benefit of some of his male friends), and his book is basically serious, which is not to say that it is witless or solemn. Douglas Stenerson in a critical study has written: "H. L. Mencken opposed women's suffrage and often directed his satire against women who embarked on public careers."[4] But Mencken consistently supported suffrage for women and he both respected and admired women who were intelligent, independent, and successful at public careers. He objected to the most militant of the suffragettes not because they were women but because of their single-minded and simple-minded moral obsession; he objected to the reformer mentality in male or female because of its willing potential to abuse the freedoms of those who were less vehemently or less irrationally committed.

He sometimes posed as an antifeminist, thereby provoking the most serious-minded and strident feminists, while simultaneously mocking the male chauvinists among his readers (who missed the irony and were reassured that he was still one of them). Alistair Cooke, writing about the "private" Mencken in a memoir of his friendship, noted that "a good deal of what had seemed heavy or windy in Mencken began to appear as a parody of just such heaviness and pomp."[5] The public image projected by this complex man was often misleading.

Mencken sympathized with those advocates for the women's movement who were beginning to question assumptions about what women could and could not do. Similarly, assumptions as to what a man-child could do had constricted his own early life. As the eldest son in a middle-class family he could not make an open and unashamed commitment to what Mencken called beautiful letters without rebelling against strictures as to what professions were appropriate for a man-child in America at the turn of the century. Women in his time were publicly and painfully also experiencing conflicts between roles imposed on them by a genteel culture and their needs to create more diverse and fulfilling careers. Ironically, the world of letters was traditionally and automatically open to them, where for Mencken it was not.

Manifestations of his interest in the cause of women's suffrage and concern about the status of women are extensive: he wrote often in support of the women's movement during his prolific years with the *Baltimore Sun* papers. As a reviewer for the *Smart Set*, from 1908 to 1923, he selected for extensive essay-reviews books about cultural emancipation for women by writers whose views were progressive and liberal. Even in his early nonjournalistic writing, the attitude that became consistent in his later years emerged. In 1908, in his book on Nietzsche, he recorded at length Nietzsche's ideas that woman's instinct was for reproduction, that women were not equal to men in physical strength and therefore were unequal in the struggle for superiority. Hence, their tactics were subversive: they were "to deceive, influence, sway and please men."[6] While this is not a promising beginning for even a clandestinely sympathetic feminist, part of Mencken's fascination with this aspect of Nietzsche was his instinct that writers must employ similar tactics to influence, sway, please, and even to deceive. In the politics of the male-female relationship, women, according to Mencken's interpretation of Nietzsche, compensated for their physical inferiority; they used sentiment, modesty, humility, fidelity, self-sacrifice, as their weapons. Here was a theoretical basis for Mencken's feeling that American culture was female-manipulated. The "feminine" values of sentiment, humility, and self-sacrifice were highly celebrated by the middle class of Mencken's day: these values motivated the progressive activists. Mencken overtly, in good "male" fashion, reacted against such feminization, which he later identified with the militant aspects of the women's movement.

He seemed to want to reassert the masculine, aristocratic, iconoclastic characteristics of Nietzsche's superman. His interpretation of Nietzsche provided for him a theoretical extension of the individualism which he thought was being threatened, violated, or simply harried to death by the female-dominated middle class of which he was a member. Conflict and confusion exist here, for he knew that women also were individuals. And he knew, as he began his career early in the century, that the literary world to which he aspired was relegated by the middle class of his day to women.

Mencken was conscious that his own artistic potential was considered feminine. To begin to express that potential, he had to leave the conventional male world of his father's cigar-manufacturing business (although he maintained symbolic connection to it by smoking, or chewing, cigars all his life). Immediately following his father's death, Mencken began his literary career by biting hard on his cigar, by thumping out tough journalism on his typewriter, and by glorifying Nietzsche's Dionysus at the expense of Nietzsche's Apollo. Meanwhile he secretly wrote bad poetry and romantic short stories, publishing them often under pseudonyms; he must have dreamed of entering fully the world of beautiful letters while still retaining his muscular male orientation. Mencken's dilemma was not unique. But his solution was unique in that he created for himself in his maturity highly successful roles as cultural critic and as historian of the American language—roles definable by neither masculine nor feminine stereotypes.

In the process of working out a sense of an effective, participating self as writer-journalist, Mencken sympathized with the humanistic and aesthetic values of the women's movement—with the concerns of women to achieve self-expression and to do no less than change the quality of life in America—but not with the moral concerns of what he considered to be the lunatic fringe of militant suffragists. He could be vehement and venomous in his ridicule of those whose orientation was simple or single-directional, whether male or female/But he was especially sensitive to the ordeal of intelligent women and to their plight in freeing themselves from social traditions that limited their intellectual development: their ordeal and plight were his, too. "Women," he wrote, "always excel men in that sort of wisdom which comes from experience; to be a woman is in itself a terrible experience."[7] The manifestations of this ordeal were both public and private, political and personal. Consciousness about the quality of relationships between women and men affected many aspects of American life. Ann Douglas, in *The Feminization of American Culture,* has described the situation into which Mencken was born: "The tragedy of nineteenth-century north-eastern society is not the demise of Calvinist patriarchal structures, but rather the failure of a viable, sexually diversified culture to replace them."[8] As a cultural critic, Mencken was to lead the attack on "Calvinist patriarchal structures"; at the same time, he evoked the need for "a viable, sexually diversified culture." Forgue sees him as expressing the preoccupations of an entire generation, and lists the condition of emancipated women as one of its concerns.[9]

Although he was brought up at a time when Victorian definitions of sex roles were beginning to lose authority, the authority of the matriarchal figure remained constant in his life. In the first sentence of his book of reminiscences, originally published in the *New Yorker,* Mencken wrote: "At the instant I first became aware of the cosmos we all infest I was sitting in my mother's lap and blinking at a great burst of lights."[10] The image of the mother emerging from his autobiographical writings is indistinct, and her figure is not much amplified by the one letter to her that has survived and been published. Yet the feeling for her implicit in the reminiscences is of a strong, loving woman of firm, supportive character who, because she was the center of the emotional life of the family, was the arbiter of everything of importance in that life. The circumstantial evidence is striking: Mencken was three years old when the family moved to a comfortable brick house at 1524 Hollins Street in Baltimore. He was to live there for the rest of his life, with the exception of the five years of his marriage. After the death of his father, when Mencken was eighteen, he continued to live in the family home with his mother and sister, then, after his mother's death in 1925, with his brother, August. Mencken's strong home-orientation suggests that the pattern of his attitudes about women may have been established in his childhood relationship with his mother. In his biography Bode has gathered and analyzed the available evidence, some of it from Mencken's unpublished private notes.[11] As Bode reports, in the Mencken family the "central figure was certainly Henry's mother," and Mencken's feelings for her "showed a beguiling combination of tenderness, whimsical appreciation for her crochets, and respect."[12] She provided for all his domestic needs, and she supported him, as his father had not, in his literary aspirations.

Five years after his mother's death Mencken married and this superficial pattern was repeated: there was again the catering to physical comfort, and the dominant feelings were tenderness and respect. Sara Haardt was thirty-two when they were married. Mencken had known her since her college days, and his affection for her had grown steadily as he helped her with the development of her own literary talents. After five years the marriage ended with her death, following a long illness with tuberculosis. She was a witty, intelligent, and attractive person. She provided a comfortable, rather Victorian environment for Mencken to work in, but she also had her own work, and Mencken respected her as a writer and helped her professionally. Their relationship was idyllic. For Mencken it was the blissful convergence in his life of domestic care and intellectual interests.[13]

There were many relationships with women before his marriage. Bode reports that those women closest to him were "pert, trim, and bright," contrary to Mencken's boisterous assertions that "his ideal was a buxom German waitress, apple-cheeked, amiable, and eager to attend to his wants." Anita Loos was one of the pert, trim, and bright ladies; her *Gentlemen Prefer Blondes* was written with Mencken in mind. She describes her attraction to Mencken in *A Girl Like I,* where she also indicates that Mencken married Sara Haardt because she was a motherly figure to him.[14]

Marion Bloom was the woman he came closest to marrying before he met Sara Haardt; their friendship extended for ten years, ending with her sudden marriage. She was an independent person whom Mencken tried to encourage as a writer, and their relationship had a range of complex emotions. Mencken seems to have tried to mold her in Pygmalion fashion; she felt that at times he dominated her, and she especially resented his failure, or inability, to verbalize a tenderness for her which she felt was concealed under his sometimes cruel behavior.[15] Perhaps while Mencken admired her for her attractive independence, another part of his affection sought to shape her into the comfortable Victorian pattern of the relationship between his mother and himself.

Other women in his life were independent and professionally self-reliant. Beatrice Wilson, a journalist, shared his prankster, hoax-making sense of humor, and he encouraged her work, sometimes sounding in his letters more like Polonius than Pygmalion. His most spectacular woman friend was Aileen Pringle, the actress. There were other actresses and artisans: for example, Adele Astaire (the dancer), Gretchen Hood (an opera singer), and Anita Loos. During the 1920s Mencken was an active bachelor, attractive to intelligent women because of his reputation and the range of his conversation, rather than his physical appearance: he was lumpish in shape and indifferently old-fashioned in his dress. There may indeed also have been buxom German waitresses among his intimate women friends, but if there were, this part of his life remained well concealed. What is clear is that the noisy rhetoric of male locker-room camaraderie he used occasionally to describe an ideally complaisant female is quite belied by his preferred associations. Like much of his public rhetoric, the tone is extravagant, ironic, deceptive.

Mencken's interest in reviewing depictions of modern women in fiction led him to seek out books that characterized women according to his preferred criteria. For example, in 1910 the featured novel in his *Smart Set* review for February was *Ann Veronica*, by H. G. Wells. He had already admired Wells extravagantly when *Tono-Bungay* appeared. Now he celebrated the publication of *Ann Veronica* because it dealt with "the modern woman and her war upon the laws moral and social." He found a vivid portrait of a young woman who sought intellectual fulfillment but who was born into a middle-class family whose "fireside god is respectability." A similar conflict had occurred in Mencken's own family experience, and Ann Veronica's father, like Mencken's, regarded the pursuit of knowledge as "sacrilegious and indecent." She tries to escape the narrowness of family prejudices by going to London. Ironically, she "encounters orthodoxy here as well as at home," and discovers that both "her woman's skirts and her woman's pruderies handicap her in her struggle for existence." Mencken closed his review by noting the cultural significance of Wells's novel: "It is not a mere idle romance fashioned for fools, but a careful study of a type [of woman] whose aspirations and demands will soon be making a loud noise in our philosophical groves and sanhedrins."[16]

A few months earlier a similar perception was expressed by Mencken in a featured review of *The Hungry Heart* by David Graham Phillips. Mencken noted that the novel tells the story of Ibsen's *Doll's House* over again, with the addition of a fourth act—it is a further exploration of the story of the middle-class woman who becomes dissatisfied with

family life and leaves home. Mencken wrote that it is a novel of "asser-
tive and unmistakeable merits." Its heroine, Nora, is as real as Dreiser's
Sister Carrie: "She represents, in brief, exactly that combination of
formerless aspiration and vague discontent which marks the average
American woman of the middle class. As she says herself, she has been
educated too much and too little—too much to make her the complacent toy of a man, and too little to make her his free equal."[17] She is a
prototype for Lewis's Carol Kennicott, heroine of *Main Street,* a novel
Mencken praised with even greater enthusiasm when he reviewed it in
1921.

In 1911, Mencken called Phillips "the leading American novelist"
because of his "earnestness" and "intelligence."[18] (Phillips had recently
died, shot by a madman who had been offended by one of his books.) In
an editorial for the *Baltimore Sun,* in spite of disapproval of his "preposterous muckraking for the uplift magazines," Mencken praised Phillips
because "he ceased to be a mere story-teller and made shift to be a
social philosopher," and because he dramatized feminine discontent,
restlessness, and aspiration accurately.

Mencken's response to Theodore Dreiser's *Sister Carrie* and *Jennie
Gerhardt* has become part of literary folklore. In 1911 he reviewed
*Jennie Gerhardt* and immediately wrote his praise in a letter to Dreiser.
He saw that both Carrie and Jennie were more than realistic portraits;
they were human types, emerging from poverty, ignorance, and dumb
helplessness to an "essential gentleness," and "innate, inward beauty."
And these novels were both "a criticism and an interpretation of life,"
depicting "the life we Americans are living with extreme accuracy."[19]
Part of his critical celebration was due to his awareness that in his time
women were special victims of the conventions and values of American
culture. As he put it in a 1916 essay-review comparing Conrad's and
Dreiser's heroes and heroines: "They are essentially tragic figures, and
in their tragedy, despite its superficial sordidness, there is a deep and
ghostly poetry."[20] He found that tragic aura in the repressive circumstances of American life and called Dreiser's evocation of it poetic
precisely because his central characters were women whose significance
was typical and symbolic.

Mencken was as generous—if not as quick—in praising Lewis as he
had been in recognizing Dreiser. Of *Main Street* he wrote: "Here is the
essential tragedy of American life, and if not the tragedy, then at least
the sardonic farce: the disparate cultural development of male and female, the great strangeness that lies between husband and wife when
they begin to function as members of society." Given his awareness of

the centrality of problems of sex roles in America, he saw Carol Kennicott as a symbolic character to whom life is "complex and challenging.
She has become aware of forces that her husband is wholly unable to
comprehend, and that she herself can comprehend only in a dim and
muddled way."[21] The virtue of the book lay, Mencken wrote, in its
trueness to the realities of American life and idiom.

One of those realities for Mencken was the growing tension in relations between men and women. But by the time *Main Street* was published he had already articulated in a book of his own—part serious and
part burlesque—his views of what was happening between the sexes.

*In Defense of Women* was Mencken's book about sexual politics in
America. It gathered together and expanded short essays and pieces
about woman's suffrage culled from his journalism over the years.[22] His
treatment was sympathetic, a practical amplification of the essay-
reviews in which he featured books about women. *In Defense of Women*
was put together and published in 1918; it was republished in a new,
revised edition in 1922, during the early years of Mencken's rise to
spectacular fame.[23] Between the two editions had come the adoption of
the Nineteenth Amendment. For the 1922 edition Mencken added some
short sections, created a new structure, and wrote an introduction, in
which he explained (with the comic extravagance so familiar to readers
in the 1920s) that in 1918 he had, because of the war, chosen women as
subject for a book because they were "neutral." His audience, typically
American, he wrote, had "an extraordinary antipathy to ideas." Later,
in a bibliographical note, he explained: "I was unable to print my view
of Wilson and his warlocks, which was a very low one, and I refused to
engage in patriotic whooping."[24]

*In Defense of Women* is not a neutral book at all, for it is in a sense
about a civil war for the emancipation of women from the bonds of
convention and superstition; it is in the pattern of much of Mencken's
writing, which had the liberation of the individual as a goal. Mencken's
admiration for intelligent, independent women was expressed throughout the book. While he ridiculed women of the suffragette mentality for
their extravagant, militantly moral preoccupations, he also ridiculed and
deliberately tried to shock the sensibilities of American men of middle
intelligence, middle values, and middle aspirations: male members of
that class he called the "booboisie." Much of the book is directed at this
audience, abusing its "antipathy for ideas" by offering what it would take
to be outrageous assertions about the superiority of women. But there
were elements of deep seriousness behind his deliberate extravagances.

He began his book by extolling the perceptiveness of women in understanding that the family patriarchal figure, while appearing to be "a hero, a magnifico, a demigod," was in substance "a poor mountebank." And "the whole bag of tricks of the average business man, or even of the average professional man, is inordinately childish." Mencken had gone through a similar process of discovery in his own life. He wrote: "In brief, women rebel—often unconsciously, sometimes even submitting all the while—against the dull, mechanical tricks of the trade that the present organization of society compels them to practice for a living, and that rebellion testifies to their intelligence." But like that of many women, Mencken's own rebellion had never been overt, for he had dutifully begun work in his father's factory while all his aspirations had been toward literature and writing. He was fully sympathetic when he wrote:

> To be a woman under our Christian civilization, indeed, means to live a life that is heavy with repression and dissimulation, and this repression and dissimulation, in the long run, cannot fail to produce effects that are indistinguishable from disease. . . . Women suffer from a suppressed revolt against the inhibitions forced upon them by our artificial culture, and this suppressed revolt, by well known Freudian means, produces a complex of mental symptoms that is familiar to all of us.[25]

Their best defense, and relief, he concluded, was in their capacity for "cynical humor." He might have been writing about himself.

The most notorious addition to *In Defense of Women* for the 1922 printing was an entire penultimate section called "The Eternal Romance." It is in part a fantasy, in part the burlesque of a Victorian male-female relationship, and it reflects what is often typical in Mencken: his willingness to ridicule his own deepest prejudices. In order to illustrate what he calls a state of "perfect peace and contentment" in a relationship with a woman, he projects an image of himself as a Victorian gentleman. In the fantasy he is lounging late in the afternoon on a sofa, after a "busy and vexatious day" and after a cocktail or two. Contentedly half-asleep, he listens to a lovely but mature ("not too young") woman who entertains him with clear, intelligent, picturesque talk of "all the things that women talk of: books, music, the play, men, other women. No politics. No business. No religion. No metaphysics." The language is nostalgically Victorian as he burlesques the fantasy of a tired businessman. But he also represents a more serious longing: the "feminine" world of talk about "books, music, the play, men, other women" was of as much interest to Mencken as were politics, business, religion, and metaphysics. It was a world which a male brought up in the traditions of genteel, middle-class, American mercantile life could enter only by asserting his sexual identity, as in this fantasy of a verbal massage in a Victorian parlor. The fantasy is terminated "when the girl grows prettily miffed" and throws him out; he returns to the "challenging and vexatious" world both "purged and glorified." The male fantasy is completed when the woman becomes an unsatisfied girl-nymph and the male withdraws, his pleasure fulfilled, the Victorian male-female sex roles confirmed. The tone here is a complex of whimsical playfulness and burlesque. Under it lies Mencken's serious perception that the relationship between woman and man in American life is defined by the stereotyped sexual identity each assumes.[26]

The complexity of tone in most of *In Defense of Women* depended upon the responses of Mencken's readers: Mencken expected his ideal reader to understand that his observations about the superiority of the female would only seem to be exaggerations to chauvinistic males for whom extravagant joking about a woman was a commonplace. These males, and some females, too, read *In Defense of Women* as simple ironic extravagance through which Mencken seemed to mean the opposite of what he wrote. But, for once, he meant much of what he wrote, and one of his purposes was to ridicule and deceive readers who thought he was joking. Because the evidence of his sympathy and empathy for the condition of intelligent women is so extensive, the observations in *In Defense of Women* cannot be fabrications, and the tone of the book cannot be explained as exaggeration rising out of Mencken's own misogyny. Mencken knew he would be misread by some of his readers, and he enjoyed such hoax-making enormously.[27]

In the 1922 edition Mencken imposed a clearer structure by organizing a single long discursive sequence of numbered sections into chapters entitled "The Feminine Mind," "The War between the Sexes," "Marriage," "Woman Suffrage," and "The New Age." His sense of organization, of purpose, and even of polemic were clarified. In the opening part of the last section his sense of history was clear, too. He called it "The Transvaluation of Values," and he began: "The gradual emancipation of women that has been going on for the last century has still a long way to proceed before they are wholly delivered from their traditional burdens and so stand clear of the oppressions of men." Underlying his sympathy was the idea that a mixture of feminine and masculine elements was necessary to the development of individual creativity: "The truth is that neither sex, without some fortifying with the complementary characters of the other, is capable of its highest reaches of human endeavor."[28] The liberated individual, male or female, would combine what he called the "divine innocence" of the male with the female's capacity for cynical realism. (His notion of sexual stereotypes here seems to derive from a complex, perhaps Miltonic, version of puritanism in which an innocent male Adam has his life transformed by the imaginative intelligence of Eve.)

But his sense of individualism is sexless, for his awareness that women were individuals, too, was crucial to his own development. When his attitudes seem contradictory, it is because he was too greatly involved in what he attacked to risk antagonizing drastically the source of the approval, love, and prosperity that he needed in his life. As a satirist and iconoclast, he used comic methods: the tone of burlesque infused his style, or seemed to infuse his style. Humor was in part a mask for feelings that he did not wish to express overtly. The laughter he evoked was a sign of approval and affection.

Mencken was rigidly Victorian in his own sexual behavior toward women. His personal ideal was genteel, austere, and chaste, in spite of, or perhaps because of, his noisy eye-rolling expressions of lust for buxom waitresses. To keep an ideal mother-image untrammelled, he preserved in his sexual behavior the double standard toward women that was being broken down in his own time. In his public writings he never used explicitness about sex as a weapon in the war against genteel values. He supported other writers in their demands for greater freedom to write realistically, but he primly believed that there was such a thing as going too far. He observed the convention that sex was an improper topic of discussion; by the 1920s he felt that the American writer was quite as free as he or she needed to be. This propriety about sex, except perhaps before masculine audiences, was a sign of the genteel side of his nature. It was also an indication of his respect for the human dignity of women.[29]

Mencken's attitudes about women were at the center of his complex nature. His ideal was a society of individuals "emancipated from convention and superstition," and women were to be equals to men as individuals in such a society. In those vital years of awareness just before the war, he assimilated and often wrote about the views of those who saw that a version of civil war between male and female was taking place in American life. For example, Walter Lippmann articulated a humanistic argument that touched Mencken deeply: both women and men must be placed at the center of politics, as measures for all aspects of society. In *A Preface to Politics* (1913) Lippmann had written that women want "a readjustment of their relations to the home, to work, to children, to men, to the interests of civilized life." Mencken, when he reviewed *A Preface to Politics,* recognized this desire as a need for individual identity; he also sensed that it was a need shared by other men, and by himself. As he had put it in 1912, the liberated woman "will not submit to tyranny, whether gross or petty. She will not live with her man ten days after she has ceased wanting to live with him. But who but a scoundrel or a cry baby, on that brighter and better tomorrow, will ever ask her to do so?"[30]

The ordeal of women in American society was like the ordeal of artists, and Mencken both sensed and experienced the similarity. The resulting sensibility was characterized by Rebecca West when she observed that Mencken was "perfectly charming but appallingly feminine. Feminine, that is, in the old abusive sense. He prefers to exploit his personality instead of doing the hard thinking he is capable of."[31] He used or borrowed or distorted the hard thinking of others as his determination to exploit his personality emerged during his apprentice years early in the century—when the subjects and attitudes of the progressive journalists dominated the media.

# Chapter Four
## The Progressive H. L. Mencken

At this point enters, at a hard gallop,
spattered with mud, H. L. Mencken, high in oath.

> Stuart Sherman, *New York Times,*
> 7 December 1919

In the years after the First World War, Stuart Sherman, a Harvard-trained literary critic, New Humanist, and super-patriotic defender of the American Puritan tradition, quarrelled publicly with Mencken, and thereby helped establish Mencken's reputation as a feisty iconoclast. In one attack (the year was 1919) Sherman evoked memories of Teddy Roosevelt and the prewar muckrakers when, in a review of Mencken's *Prejudices: First Series,* he wrote the sentence that heads this chapter.[1] By creating the figure of the gallant, mud-spattered cowboy-muckraker he was associating Mencken with a period and spirit that Mencken had begun to assess with his most extravagant ridicule. But, ridicule notwithstanding, Mencken had been vitally and lastingly influenced by the muckrakers' progressive attitudes and styles—as Sherman had noted—although much of the writing of his most popular years (the 1920s) openly and vehemently satirized the moral obsessions of reformers.

What Roosevelt dubbed muckraking was often successful journalism because of its sensational or extravagant nature. Poverty, social conditions, the abuses of power in government and business, graft—these were some of the subjects about which the muckraking journalists wrote with fervor and often with great skill. Their operating assumption and optimistic belief was that somehow reforms would follow exposure. While Mencken's beliefs were less optimistic and perhaps less naive, he shared in the concerns of the muckrakers and wrote some of the muckraking literature himself. It is important to recognize this aspect of his development, because we often remember him as an antireform, anti-progressive, and conservative individualist. This was the popular, public Mencken of the 1920s, a Mencken not simply piping according to his inner muse but responsive to what his age demanded, and to the ample rewards for satisfying that demand.

Mencken's apprentice years as a journalist from 1898 until the beginning of World War I had been years dominated in the news media by the subjects, attitudes, and style of the muckrakers. Mencken shared in the popular optimism of the time about the efficacy of muckraking: the journal was an instrument of progress through reform, it had a purpose and destiny. When muckraking was discredited at the beginning of the war, Mencken, high in oath, reflected that attitude too, and in fact exploited and advertised the shift of interest from political, economic, and social concerns toward cultural and aesthetic ones.

However, Mencken's public assessment of himself as a capricious debunker of the muckrakers has prevailed in our memories. For example, Bode, one of Mencken's biographers, observed upon reprinting a 1910 "letter" by Mencken on socialism that the "essential" Mencken was anti-democratic and anti-humanitarian because he believed "man has no rights except those he can maintain by superior force or craft."[2] We need to look more closely at the period when the "essential" Mencken was formed in order to see that both style and attitudes were shaped by the muckrakers and their concerns. W. H. A. Williams, in *H. L. Mencken,* has surveyed the social criticism Mencken wrote before the war, noting that he discussed many progressive subjects, and concluding that "Mencken's attitudes during the progressive era seem so idiosyncratic, so lacking in either liberal or conservative consistency, that it is tempting to consider him a complete maverick."[3] But the consistency of his progressive views before 1915 is striking and significant, for Mencken supported many programs of exposure and reform. He was equally consistent in expressing outrage at what he took to be the lunatic fringe of fanatically dedicated vice crusaders, who sought by single and simple-minded means to uplift the moral standards of Americans: "All persons who devote themselves to forcing virtue on their fellow men deserve nothing better than kicks in the pants."[4] Often that condemnation has been taken erroneously to stand for his attitude toward *everyone* who sought progress through reform.

The concerns of the progressives had been very much an outgrowth of the genteel tradition, which was an important part of Mencken's heritage, with both public and private manifestations. Douglas Stenerson summarizes this aspect of Mencken's development clearly: "Mencken could not completely escape the genteel tradition any more than he could escape his middle-class assumptions. Although he did not accept the theology which, for many Americans, gave the Protestant virtues their final sanction, he retained a faith in the virtues themselves. He rejected puritanism and the glossing over of life's realities, but his basic conservatism and his conception of home and family had much in common with those of the upholders of genteel values."[5] One of the firmest, least shakable articles of genteel faith was a belief in progress. And Mencken, even in his later years when his popularity was waning and something like rancor infected his writings about American culture, reflected this faith: "There is, in fact, such a thing as progress," he wrote in 1934, and out of the moral systems man has produced, both sound and false, has flowed "a great richness, an immense enhancement of the human spirit."[6]

Mencken's sense of mission as an iconoclast and debunker was just as fervid as the evangelism of the most dedicated progressive and muckraker. He wrote in 1905: "The sham-smashing that is now going on, in all the fields of human inquiry, might be compared to the crusades that engrossed the world in the middle ages."[7] Sometimes he had written sympathetically about figures engaged in reform or progressive activities. For example, in the *Baltimore Morning Herald* on 8 July 1904, he described William Jennings Bryan in his decline as a heroic politician, forced at the Democratic National Convention to acquiesce to the majority of his party: "The smile upon his face as he acknowledged the cheers of friend and foe was not a pleasant smile to see. Behind it there lurked an infinite sadness and the glitter of his eyes seemed much like the glisten of tears." He admired Bryan's transparently genuine humanity. He called Bryan "gallant," an "eloquent Nebraskan," the progressive champion of reform who fought against the entrenched power of the affluent industrialists. He expressed sympathy for Bryan even in the "obituary"[8] written after Bryan's participation in the Scopes trial. While the Bryan of the obituary-essay is a ridiculous figure, a lisping fundamentalist and "the most sedulous flycatcher in American history" who spoke with "coo and bellow," he is a figure to be pitied. He was, Mencken wrote, a "poor mountebank" who had once been "a hero, a Galahad, in bright and shining armor." The rhetoric that ridicules him almost, but not quite, conceals a sense of pity for a heroic figure who could not adapt to the changes in his culture. The admiration Bryan deserved in 1904 had not been entirely canceled. Mencken ridiculed his provincial and puritanical background, but he admired his skill and success as a politician, just as earlier he had also been sympathetic toward the man and the causes he represented.

He expressed a similar respect for the skill with which Charles J. Bonaparte exposed graft and political dishonesty, calling him "a useful citizen," in *Frank Leslie's Popular Magazine* (1903). Later (1912) his attitude toward Bonaparte, as toward the progressive movement, had shifted, and he wrote about him as a man, like Bryan, who was obsessed by Puritan views. A similar shift occurred in his attitude toward Woodrow Wilson, with the war the central event in Mencken's growing disaffection. But in an article entitled "Dr. Wilson's Candidacy" (*Baltimore Evening Sun*, 1910), he had praised Wilson as president of Princeton and celebrated his entry into New Jersey politics: "He is practical as well as reflective, a man of action as well as a man of theory." Also in 1910, again in the *Evening Sun*, on 17 June, Mencken devoted a full page to Theodore Roosevelt, another key figure in the progressive era. Mencken applauded him as a trust buster: "The trusts, if not actually broken up, had, at least, been halted in their practices." In another essay he noted that "the muckraking magazine has blown up and is no more. . . . It came to grief, not because the public tired of muck-raking, but because the muckraking that it began with succeeded."[9] Mencken shared in the popular optimism of the time.

His editorials, articles, and columns in the *Sun* papers between 1905 and 1912 show a consistent awareness and support of the activities of practical, active reformers, while he ridiculed reformers whose concerns were aggressively and exclusively moral, such as the advocates of Prohibition. This was an incredibly prolific period for Mencken as a writer: often daily issues of the *Sun,* morning or evening or both, contained one or even two editorials, with one or even two columns opposite the editorial page, and sometimes an article or review elsewhere in the same issue. Of course, much of his writing was about subjects of a nonpolitical, noncontroversial, local nature, or commentary about timely state, national, and international events. There were obituaries, discussions of Baltimore food (usually oysters, crabs, and sauerkraut), Baltimore women, the weather, the happy condition of bachelorhood, the theater, and—an important recurring interest—the vitality of the American language. Many of these pieces were unsigned, but there is no question whatsoever as to the identity of the author, such is the distinction of Mencken's style even in the earliest of his writings. Running through these copious writings are the concerns typical of the progressive period. Mencken supported efforts to democratize voting processes; he favored and wrote at length about the direct election of senators; he was consistent and eloquent in his advocacy of women's suffrage. He favored efforts to limit the powers of the Standard Oil and sugar trusts. He supported and advocated reforms in public health programs.[10]

In 1905 there were editorials in the *Evening Herald* entitled "Oligarchy and Its Limits" (8 July) and "On Christian Endeavor" (8 July), as well as a series on graft (15 July, 21 August, and 24 August). The first was a celebration of the inevitable and proper defeat of the ring that ruled Philadelphia. The second was an affirmation of "the sublime idea of universal love" as manifest in such exemplary, practical, and active Christian organizations as the Y.M.C.A., the Society of Christian Endeavor, and the Epworth League. One of the series on graft was called "How Grafting Helps Us"; in it Mencken acknowledged the extraordinary effectiveness of muckrakers Ida Tarbell, Lincoln Steffens, and Thomas W. Lawson. Mencken echoed an assumption central to the muckraking point of view: "It is only when we shut our eyes to graft that graft will badly damage us," he asserted with unusual piety. In the last of the series, "The Art of Grafting," he ironically acknowledged that muckraking was important because it exposed the skill of the grafter, and did so skillfully.

There was no explicit conflict at this time between Mencken's acceptance of progressive morality and the amorality of his admiration for art or skill, although later that conflict became a subject of his writings. He wrote in an editorial ("Cardinal Gibbons on Agitators," 5 February 1906): "Those industrious gentlemen who have been entertaining us in the ten-cent magazines with exciting stories of graft . . . have dealt in overstatement; they have colored facts." And so it was with Mencken: he admired the artistry of the muckrakers, and he was learning something from them about a colorful and extravagant style. Typically Mencken's voice was that of the progressive editorial writer; he used the outraged cadences of the muckrakers, sometimes shading toward the Juvenalian in the contrivance of indignation. A *Sun* editorial in 1910, "Common Sense Reforms," praised the American Civic Association for its practical purposes and its refusal to purify "the habitable universe." Another *Sun* editorial (1911) was entitled "Murdering the Muckrakers"; in it he asked for a fair hearing on a bill before Congress that proposed an increase in the second-class postage rates. Mencken deplored one of the possible effects, which might have been to drive some of the muckraking magazines into trusts or out of business. In "The Muckrake in the Country" (*Sun* editorial, 1911), he drew attention to a news item about voting bribery in Ohio, then exhorted the muckrakers to turn away from "the shame of the cities," because, Mencken wrote, in the country "the worst foe of a free democracy is often that stupid and childlike mind in whose patriotism it is assumed to find its greatest security." A large proportion of the writings of Mencken's celebrity years (the 1920s) ridiculed aspects of American provincialism; therefore, it is especially significant to note that the earliest manifestations of his antiprovincial attitudes were those of a muckraker.

The pattern of his subjects and progressive attitudes during his journalistic apprenticeship is remarkably consistent. In 1911, from March 1 to 9, he wrote a seven-part series for the *Sun* on the Oregon Plan. These were articles in support of efforts for the direct election of representatives, and reforms such as the initiative, the referendum, and the recall. Mencken strongly favored the proposed amendment to the Constitution, and called the issue a "trial of democracy." Another trial for Mencken was capital punishment; he wrote about its "unspeakable savagery" and advocated its abolition in Maryland ("On Hanging," *Baltimore Sun*, 25 November 1910).

At about the same time there appeared in the *Sun* an article called "The Art of Lynching." Here Mencken developed a satiric technique that was to appear more and more frequently in his writing. He created a matter-of-fact, mock-rational voice like that of Swift's narrator in "A Modest Proposal" and wrote an ironic celebration of a Mississippi lynching as a "dignified and credible affair." This is the voice he assumed in the famous bathtub hoax essay—an extended, invented etymology of the word *bathtub*—where he parodied the authority of the journalist as historian, as the bringer of news, the creator of significance.[11] In this voice he also imitated the exaggerated earnestness of the muckrakers. Just as there were people who believed his hoax about the invention of the bathtub, there were those among his readers who may have believed that he advocated lynching—perhaps even Swift had readers who were willing to supply his cook with babies. In both Swift and Mencken the moral concern is fully operative; both parodied language that said the-thing-that-is-not. They were offended because people could be morally reprehensible and at the same time easily duped. Mencken's concern about the brutality of lynching remained consistent. In 1935 he went to Washington to testify before a Senate subcommittee at a hearing on the Costigan-Wagner Anti-Lynching Bill.[12]

Blacks were the usual victims of lynchings, and Mencken's efforts for the welfare of blacks were often vehement and outspoken. As reporter for the *Sun* he was concerned about the living conditions of Negroes as well as the abuse of their civil rights. Years later, as editor of the

*American Mercury,* he published many black authors and many articles about Negro life.[13] In the last column he wrote for the *Sun* (9 November 1948) he found "the spirit of the Georgia cracker surviving in the Maryland Free State, and under official auspices. . . . It is high time such relics of Ku Kluxery be wiped out in Maryland."[14] And his sense of racial injustice was frequently extended from blacks to Jews: "One of the things that makes a Negro unpleasant to white folk is the fact that he suffers from their injustice. He is thus a standing rebuke to them, and they try to put him out of their minds. The easiest way to do so is to insist that he keep his place. The Jew suffers from the same cause, but to a much less extent."[15] His defense of civil rights reached from racial minorities to all individuals; the humanistic basis for this attitude is obviously a basis for progressive morality, too. For example, in 1931 he wrote a letter to Hamilton Owens, editor for the *Sun,* asking him to send a reporter to Alabama to cover the Scottsboro case: "Obviously, the question whether the lady complainant lacked virtue before the alleged assault is irrelevant. A prostitute is just as much entitled to be protected against rape as any other woman."[16]

In 1912 there were *Sun* editorials in praise of the successes of the Civil Service reformers, and one called "Socialism as a Phase of Insurgency." In the latter he wrote about the success of the Socialist Party in elections around the country—as a sign that the "blind contentment" of the American people was being successfully challenged. In another context he had viewed socialism in ways we may at first glance associate with the libertarian Mencken of the 1920s. The occasion was a series of letters he exchanged with Robert Rives La Monte; these were gathered into a book entitled *Man Versus The Man: A Correspondence Between Robert Rives La Monte, Socialist, and H. L. Mencken, Individualist,* published in 1910. Mencken's posture was that of the debater, and he drew upon Darwin, Nietzsche, and Adam Smith to argue that the fittest properly survive, that there are a master class and a slave class, and that the measure of man's success is his superior skill and efficiency. Mencken's view of the world, he wrote, excluded "that sentimental reverence for the human being, *per se,* which credits him with a long catalogue of gratuitous and complex rights, all grounded upon the ancient theological notion that he is in some sense divine." The important qualifier here is the *per se,* for Mencken also wrote that his "view of the world . . . does not exclude those feelings of pity, charity, and good-will which grow out of habit and association, nor does it exclude that wise foresight which sometimes prompts the strong man to aid the weak man, that the latter, perchance, may shake off his weakness and become a helper instead of a pensioner."

The emphasis in his closing argument was upon the values of skill and efficiency. He celebrated what he called "unique service." His adjectives and adverbs describe the creative process; he spoke of craft, of invention, of better organization. Here, as was becoming more and more explicit in his writing, his ultimate value was art—which evokes an aesthetic, not a moral response. But he recognized the difficulties of his view, given the dominant humanitarian, progressive concerns of his culture at that time. The closing description of his letter is poignant, and reflects an anguish not usually associated with Mencken. He created the image of a workman laboring in the rain with pick and shovel:

> Contemplating the difference between his luck and mine, I cannot fail to wonder at the eternal meaninglessness of life. I wonder thus and pity his lot, and then, after awhile, perhaps, I begin to reflect that in many ways he is probably luckier than I.
> But I wouldn't change places with him.[17]

The generations upon whom Mencken had a profound influence—his own and the ones coming of age during World War I until about 1930—were also to emphasize, or to have Mencken emphasize for them, the "eternal meaninglessness of life," along with his antidote: the exercise of skill, the mediating, amoral, joyful effects of devotion to art.

Another antidote for Mencken, perhaps the most important to his equilibrium as artist, was simply the art of his life, directly acknowledged in his writing when he published his autobiographical books. The family home in Baltimore was the center of his comfortable, middle-class life, a home he inhabited until his death, with the exception of a five-year idyll with his wife in a household modeled after that of the Mencken family, and located a few minutes away. Mencken's many friendships and congenial professional associations were extensions of his domestic comfort. Other writers of his generation, notably Lardner, Lewis, and Marquis, sought the same balance between art and comfort, with Lewis conspicuously lacerated by the failures of his attempts at domestic relationship and friendship. But there was a tension between art and life for all of them, arising out of their inheritance of the romantic idea that great art seemed to emerge from suffering and loneliness. There was a rhetorical quality to their insistence that art mattered more than morality. There was also an unacknowledged irony, because comfortable, genteel, middle-class life was based upon strong moral perspectives with the wife and mother as delineators and judges of values. The humanitarian assumptions of the progressives and muckrakers had their parallels in the domestic values of Mencken's private life.

In March 1914, Mencken wrote (for the *Atlantic Monthly*) an article that assessed the power of muckraking journalism and that expressed what he had learned as an apprentice during the previous decade. The progressive journals, he said, had effectively conducted "emotional wars upon errant men," effective because they were "not intellectual wars upon erroneous principles." During this period of reform activity, he argued, journalists had properly and successfully manipulated the responses of ordinary readers, whose capacity for response was often naive, and who could only be persuaded by emotional rather than reflective means. But the result was "improvement in our whole governmental method," and the end, therefore, justified the means:

> Our most serious problems, it must be plain, have been solved orgiastically, and to the tune of deafening newspaper urging and clamor. Men have been washed into office on waves of emotion, and washed out again in the same manner. Measures and policies have been determined by indignation far more often than by cold reason. But is the net result evil? Is there even any permanent damage from those debauches of sentiment in which the newspapers have acted insincerely, unintelligently, with no thought save for the show itself? I doubt it.[18]

However, a few years later, Mencken's public attitude about reform journalism seemed to have changed, as he shifted from pragmatic approval to condemnation:

> The truth is that this crusading business is one of the worst curses of journalism, and perhaps the main enemy of that fairness and accuracy and intelligent purpose which should mark the self-respecting newspaper. It trades upon one of the sorriest weaknesses of man—the desire to see the other fellow jump. It is at the heart of that Puritanical frenzy, that obscene psychic sadism, which is our national vice. No newspaper, carrying on a crusade against a man, ever does it fairly and decently; not many of them even make the pretense. On the contrary, they always do it extravagantly and cruelly, pursuing him with dishonest innuendo, denying him his day in court, seeking to intimidate his friends.

The occasion was a review (in the *Smart Set,* July 1918) of *The Profession of Journalism,* a collection of essays that included Mencken's *Atlantic Monthly* essay of 1914 and a response (Mencken called it a "counterblast") by Ralph Pulitzer. Pulitzer had been offended by Mencken's extravagance, and he thought his pragmatic conclusion cynical and contradictory. Mencken took pleasure in revising his earlier position: in any argument he preferred to clarify the issues through the rhetorical creation of an opposing point of view. He said that in his 1914 essay he had made his "allegations . . . too mild": "All I can find in my discourse is a platitude—to wit, that the grand moral frenzy of newspapers is chiefly buncombe—that their true motive, nine times out of ten, is not to purge the republic of sin, but merely to give a hot show, stir up the animals, and so make circulation."[19] Pulitzer was right about the cynicism, although it had not been evident in 1914. Between 1914 and 1918 Mencken felt that the lunatic, vice-crusading mentality had taken charge of American political life, as evidenced for him in Woodrow Wilson's support of the Allies in the war and in anti-German sentiment. Part of the context, too, was his rhetorical assertion that puritanism was the root of evil in America. It was easy to condemn the puritanism of militant vice-crusaders, including Wilson, whose crusade was global in scope.

Nevertheless, his view of the power of journalism, which was almost religious in its intensity, and which had been lastingly influenced by the journalists of the progressive period, remained essentially unchanged. In April 1920 he wrote "On Journalism" for the *Smart Set,* and applied to the "yellow journals" the argument he had made in 1914 to defend the methods of the muckraking journals:

> I do not say that the yellow journals make any actual effort to be exact; on the contrary, they make a palpable effort to avoid a too literal exactness. But when they go on alleging, day after day, that every politician is a scoundrel and that every public service corporation is run by swindlers and that all the operations of Wall Street have the one aim of shaking down the plain people, they get near enough to the truth for any practical purpose.[20]

Those "truths" as he enumerated them were very like the "truths" explored and exploited by the muckrakers twenty years earlier. Mencken was consistent in his plea, however extravagant rhetorically, that journalism reach and affect people in compelling and progressive ways, and he argued that most moral appeals must be to the emotions. He had a practical sense of the growth of a mass audience in his time: he had begun to write when mass circulation was becoming a significant factor in journalism. In 1925 he reminisced about journalism at the turn of the century:

> The journalists of those days—or, at all events, those under the age of sixty—were unanimously convinced that they practiced a noble art, or, as they affected to call it, business, and that its public uses were lofty and indubitable. . . . The normal, right-thinking reporter of the time believed that journalism was fundamentally healthy and virtuous, and that every day in every way it was growing better and better.[21]

Mencken began his career as a commentator, very much in the dominant progressive style and tone of his time, on political and social events mainly from his perspective in the city of Baltimore. His interests in literature and culture were also important; they were in part expressed through his efforts to write poetry and fiction, through his drama articles for the *Baltimore Sun,* and through occasional reviews until 1908, when the opportunity to become the book reviewer for the *Smart Set* arose. This role stimulated his central interest, which was literature, and opened to him an audience beyond the city of Baltimore. The shift of his main concern from the political and social toward the cultural and literary was also the shifting pattern of intellectual commitment during these years. For Mencken, the shift occurred gradually, and the crucial period was from 1911 to 1915, the years of his daily "Free Lance" columns for the *Sun,* when he was also editor and book reviewer for the *Smart Set.* We can see in his writings of this period the development of his sense of function as a cultural muckraker, which had grown in part out of his disillusionment with the progressive movement and its attitudes, and in part out of the impact of the war. The Anglophilia that was the dominant tone of American life signified for Mencken the success of propaganda, of untruthful language, the triumph of bunk; this perception brought Mencken's interests into a sharper focus than heretofore. When the war became the subject of interest to his readers, Mencken was unable to write about it, except obliquely, because his own attitudes were so belligerently pro-German, and most of his readers' attitudes were not. He stopped writing "The Free Lance" in the fall of 1915.

The column carried Mencken's full signature, where prior to 1911 much of his newspaper work had been unsigned or initialed. Mencken's sense of auctorial identity, of having arrived as a journalist-artist, must have been enhanced. By midsummer of 1911 the tone of "The Free Lance" had been established. This tone ranged from the mock sermon (often the "brethren" were addressed, or he would begin by citing a text, in a parody of the structure of the sermon), to an enlightened rationality, to the indignation of the muckrakers. Such a tonal spectrum had appeared here and there in the earlier columns, editorials, and reviews, but now it was consistent. This consistency may have arisen in part because Mencken's audience had become more identifiable and more responsive to him: letters stimulated or provoked by "The Free Lance" were regularly printed next to the column.

Many of the subjects of the "Free Lance" columns were familiar ones to readers of the journalism of the progressive era: election fraud, administrative inefficiency, health and disease, women's suffrage. For example, Mencken wrote a chronology of the Standard Oil case (17 May 1911); he wrote about salaries of clerks and secretaries in City Hall, contrasted to the salaries of their overpaid superiors (17 June 1911). He wrote about adapting the public schools to the needs of the average child—a direct appeal to democratic principles. To Mencken such adaptation meant among other things the teaching of American rather than British grammar: an unusual call for freedom from the authoritarianism of linguistic purists and academically oriented teachers (14 September 1911). What he wrote for the column in defense of women's suffrage (as on 1, 3, and 6 February 1912) reflected the older progressive attitudes: his posture was humanistic and moral, to the extent that he deplored violation of individual human dignity. So, too, were the concerns of his essays against capital punishment, and his accounts of progress in controlling typhoid, cancer, and tuberculosis. The style of these columns was familiar to those brought up on muckraking journalism: extravagance was entertaining and also the outraged vehicle for truths which any morally sensitive reader was expected to accept without question.

The last column for 1911 (30 December) articulated Mencken's awareness of a shift of function: he called for a "permanent organization in Baltimore for warring upon stupidity, flapdoodle and buncombe." From this point on, with a few exceptions, his focus was the abuse of language, which he saw as the vehicle for fraud and evildoing. What was really wrong with life in Baltimore was what was said by the "boomers"—the politicians and some of the reformers. They produced, he wrote, "an endless saturnalia of bunk, of bluff, of stupidity, of insincerity, of false virtue, of nonsense, of pretence, of sophistry, of paralogy, of bamboozlement, of actorial posturing, of strident wind music, of empty words— even, at times, of downright fraud." What he wrote about Baltimore could as well apply to the nation, and his indignantly bemused attention turned more and more consistently to the fabrications of the "boomers" (Lewis called them "boosters")—the creators of bunk.

Significantly, Mencken's sense of the failure of muckraking to affect social and political life in America had developed slowly. The failure was articulated for him in 1913 by Walter Lippmann in a book important to the clarification of Mencken's attitudes, and also important as a statement of liberal ideas and ideals during this crucial prewar period of transition. This book was *A Preface to Politics;*[22] Mencken reviewed it in the *Smart Set* that same year, in a review-essay called "A Counterblast to Buncombe."[23] Lippmann's thesis that criticism in America needed to be directed not simply in muckraking fashion at the manifestations of evil in political and economic life, but at its sources in the human center of American culture reflected Mencken's attitude, too. The infected human center Mencken identified in the review was what he generalized as "a sort of revival of Puritanism," and he was to find the illness everywhere as he examined American life and letters in the years after 1913. The culminating moment was his 1917 essay, "Puritanism as Literary Force." The problem with reformers, Lippmann wrote, was their inflexibility and failure to respond to the reality of human needs. The failure was one of rigid moral insistence. Lippmann argued for new, inventive ways of thinking. He invoked some of Mencken's intellectual heroes—Nietzsche, Shaw, Wells—and added Freud, Bergson, William James. He wrote: "The enormous vitality that is regenerating other interests can be brought into the service of politics. Our primary care must be to keep the habits of the mind flexible and adapted to the movement of real life" (p. 29).

Lippmann noted that the significance of the feminist movement was greater than progressive concerns about the right to vote: "What women want is surely something a great deel deeper than the privilege of taking part in elections. They are looking for a readjustment of their relations to the home, to work, to children, to men, to the interests of civilized life" (p. 73). Similarly, a year earlier (in 1912) Mencken had written, with extravagant but unironic wit, that *his* feminine ideal was "a woman emancipated from convention and superstition, a free agent in human society, the full equal of her man." Lippmann went on to argue that both man and woman must be put at the center of politics, must be the measure of all things, because "without an unrelaxing effort to center the mind upon human uses, human purposes, and human results, it drops into idolatry and becomes hostile to creation" (p. 229). To combat this dropping into idolatry, iconoclasm was constantly necessary. Here Lippmann defined a role for Mencken and the debunkers of the 1920s, within a practical, philosophical context: "The best servants of the people, like the best valets, must whisper unpleasant truths in the master's ear. It is the court fool, not foolish courtier, whom the king can least afford to lose" (p. 149). He insisted upon "the importance of style, of propaganda, the popularization of ideas" (p. 179) in the interpretation of philosophical systems. Unlike Lippmann, Mencken was never a systematic thinker, but his style and attitudes had been influenced by the muckrakers; like them he was a propagandist, a popularizer of ideas who in the years after 1913 filled these roles brilliantly. Lippmann closed his remarkable book by observing that culture (the renderings of art) "enters into political life as a very powerful condition. It is a way of creating ourselves" (p. 235). Mencken accepted a role as remover of distracting idols and implicitly affirmed as a goal no less than the re-creation of American culture.

Mencken's disillusionment with the aims of the progressives and his more concentrated concern about those who fabricated or said the-thing-that-was-not were rendered in the April 1915 issue of the *Smart Set,* in an omnibus review ("The Grandstand Flirts with the Bleechers") that included comments on Lippmann's *Drift and Mastery.* Mencken approved of Lippmann's skepticism about Woodrow Wilson's New Freedom and "the multitudinous sovereign balms of the Hon. William Jennings Bryan." In previous years Mencken had written in praise both of Wilson and Bryan. Now he went on to criticize Wilson mainly for his abuse of language, for his use of "hollow and illusory words." Then he evaluated some of the major reforms brought about by the progressive movement: "What of the direct election of Senators? Has it improved the Senate? Far from it! . . . What of the initiative and referendum? The recall of judges? The direct primary? The vice crusade? Prohibition? Have these balsams cured the patient or even relieved him? Hardly. Has trust busting actually destroyed the Standard Oil Company? . . . Here, as everywhere else, the uplift has failed signally." This energetically indignant voice is the one we remember from the public image Mencken projected in the 1920s, but it is important to note that he, too, had written eloquently before 1915 in support of the "balsams" he ridiculed here. The war was an important controlling element in his disillusionment. The symbolic war of the muckrakers, in which Mencken had been a camp follower, had ended in defeat, as America began its commitment to a literal war. America had come of age, Mencken implied, and it was time for those with progressive concerns to turn to new subjects.

Mencken became more and more concerned about the quality of life in America; the creation of a better culture required an appropriate language and an appropriate style. Concern about style had always been expressed in his book reviews for the *Smart Set.* It was style he had in mind when he criticized Upton Sinclair for forgetting he was a novelist and becoming a "journeyman reformer." In a *Sun* article called "Literary False Alarms" (11 August 1908), he excoriated Sinclair's deliberate exploitation of his success at exposing the meatpacking industry in *The Jungle.* Sinclair, according to Mencken, had betrayed his proper artistic values as a novelist and had become afflicted by "the afflatus of a divine mission." He charged novelists Marie Corelli and Winston Churchill with similar betrayals. The distinction Mencken made was aesthetic; it was not that he condemned the values of the progressive sensibility, it was simply that in his lexicon of values a novel must provide realistic treatment of time, place, and character. In a later review of a Sinclair novel (*Love's Pilgrimage*) he responded favorably to the dramatization of conflict between art and morality. The hero of this novel is a writer, "afire with literary ambition," who discovers the practical realities of marriage and child-rearing. Mencken found the novel "an extraordinarily acute and interesting study of the conflict between the artistic impulse and the commonplace responsibilities of life." For once, he thought, Sinclair had managed to control his moral and socialist biases and had created a fiction about a complex reality.[24]

So, in his reviews, as his interests shifted, his values were more and more explicitly aesthetic, and his condemnation of the literature of what he called the Uplift became more pronounced. A review of Winston Churchill's *Far Country* (1915) led to a long and exuberantly extravagant polemic against the "whole rumble-bumble of the Uplift." Everywhere he saw the failure of progressive reformers and activists: "The ideal of service set up to conquer the old ideal of intelligent self-interest, has in a few short years been conquered and engulfed by it." Mencken compared the novel with Dreiser's *Titan*, for both dealt "with the conflict between the Uplift and the Invisible Government (The Money Power) in these States." But Dreiser rendered the conflict in its "elementals," and created a convincing central character (Cowperwood), where Churchill's was "puny" and "unconvincing," a "sentimentalist." Again, the failure was aesthetic: Churchill's "view of life and its wondrous mystery is the ethical, the Puritan view. He is too good an American to be an artist." The hero he had created had no sense of the quality of life, and Mencken asked a series of indignant questions: "What is his notion of beauty? What is his view of women, the sex war? Who are his heroes at forty-five?"[25] These were the important, the central questions for Mencken, questions that could be used to define civilized life in America, as well as to provide aesthetic measures for a novel.

Mencken shared Lippmann's view that art enlarges life, and behind this perspective was his deeply moral inheritance from the muckraking experience, with its democratic, humanistic values, including its concern about the status of women. Also behind this perspective was the influence of the muckraking style, with its sometimes deliberate and entertaining extravagance. Like the muckrakers, Mencken often attacked abuses of power. As he raked through the manifestations of American culture in the 1920s he found abuses of power everywhere, especially abuses produced by formulators of the myth of provincial American life and by glorifiers of the manners, history, and destiny of Americans. The excoriation of such abuses appeared again and again in the writings of his prime and most popular years. Underlying it was his staunch progressive idealism.

Louis D. Rubin, Jr., has described Mencken's sometimes concealed idealism in this way: "Mencken is no Rabelaisian chronicler of political buffoonery and no Puckian vivisectionist of knavery, but a vulnerable and bruised idealist who in order to function has evolved a formidably thick carapace of protective rhetoric. . . . The Mencken we most admire was continuously engaged in a game of exaggerated brag, whereby he said outrageous things and affected to be offhand and insouciant in so doing."[26] The celebrity Mencken of the 1920s spoke often in exaggerated brag, but there was a bruised, progressive idealist underneath. It is Mencken's fate, as well as his joy, sometimes to have had his progressive attitudes concealed by his deliberately outrageous extravagance.

Mencken, a muck-spattered cowboy (as Sherman had noted), rode the frontier of the spirit where ideas could be freely considered and transmitted. An idea could be raised to a higher power, could be transformed, by the language and form of its presentation. Similarly, the muckrakers had often stylistically moved beyond the limits of evidence. Mencken's efforts in prose exude a tremendous energy, when we hear a passionately and joyously committed dramatic voice, high in oath, convincing us by an exuberance beyond mere accuracy that language matters uniquely as the instrument of human progress.

# Chapter Five

## H. L. Mencken:
## Dancing with Arms and Legs

I am often wrong. My prejudices are innumerable,
and often idiotic. My aim is not to determine the facts,
but to function freely and pleasantly—as Nietzsche
used to say, to dance with arms and legs.

"Addendum on Aims," 1920

**H**ere, as an example of Mencken's mature style, are the opening
sentences of his essay on William Jennings Bryan, called "In
Memoriam: W.J.B.": "Has it been duly marked by historians
that William Jennings Bryan's last secular act on this globe of sin
was to catch flies? A curious detail, and not without its sardonic overtones. He was the most sedulous flycatcher in American history, and in
many ways the most successful. His quarry, of course, was not *Musca
domestica* but *Homo neandertalensis*. For forty years he tracked it with
coo and bellow, up and down the rustic backways of the Republic.
Wherever the flambeaux of Chautauqua smoked and guttered, and the
bilge of Idealism ran in the veins, and Baptist pastors dammed the
brooks with the sanctified, and men gathered who were weary and
heavy laden, and their wives who were full of Peruna and as fecund as
the shad (*Alosa sapidissima*)—there the indefatigable Jennings set up
his traps and spread his bait."[1]

These sentences appeal most obviously to the ear. We are very much
aware of alliteration of consonant and of vowel as a device for external
structural unity. Much of the unity and meaning of the sentences turns
on the repetition and slant rhymes in "act," "catch," "fly-catcher,"
"tracked," "backways," "Baptist pastors dammed," "shad," "indefati-

gable" and "traps." The main vehicle of meaning is the figurative language and the outrageous comparisons with which the main figure is developed. Bryan is compared to a big-game hunter whose quarry is an animal-insect called *Homo neandertalensis*. This animal-insect is never precisely identified, but one speaks to it with "coo and bellow" and its habits seem to be amphibian. The male of the species wallows "weary and heavy laden" in ponds whose muckiness is suggested by the "bilge" which these creatures have in their veins instead of blood—and the nature of their habitat is obliquely reinforced by the word "guttered." The female of the species is fishlike in its capacity to reproduce, and vaguely bovine in its eating habits, with the exception of "Peruna," a patent medicine popular especially during Prohibition and most noted for its high alcoholic content—although in the word there are echoes of Purina, a trade name for fodder fed to cows, pigs, dogs, and chickens. The irony, if not the exact nature, of these comparisons is clear, for we see Bryan as hunter pursuing an insect called man—Bryan whose last notable action was to insist that man descended from the angels and was in no way related either to animals or to insects.

Mencken has the ear of the versifier. While none of the unflattering cadences and comparisons in the Bryan essay and elsewhere is inherently poetic, one feels that in another era Mencken could have written the heroic couplet with brilliance and that he could easily have fit his metaphors into a variety of metrical forms. Finally, in his essay on Bryan, he projected a narrative voice which we hear in much of his best prose. His narrator asks "has it been duly marked by historians" and then goes on duly to mark in mock-historical rhetoric what Bryan's last secular acts were. One of Mencken's purposes is to debunk Bryan, and to do that he uses the satiric device of a narrator whose extravagance and outrageous comparisons are a calculated source of amusement for sophisticated readers. Mencken's narrator is a journalist-commentator who interprets a broad spectrum of contemporary experiences, a narrator who translates the circumstantial into the meaningful, fact into history, story into myth. An element of parody enters because of our awareness of the discrepancy between the earnestness of the voice and the outrageousness of the subject matter, or of the metaphoric and imagistic vehicles for the subject matter. But there is also a genuine seriousness behind Mencken's deft transformation of aspects of the Bryan legend into American mythology, for Mencken in his time and in his way was attempting to write what Edmund Wilson has called a "poetry of America."

In 1894, Mencken remembered in a reminiscence, he had been "torn between two aspirations: one to be a chemist and the other to be a poet."[2] He wrote verse, at least until 1903, when his first book, *Ventures into Verse,* was published. He also wrote short stories during these early years.[3] Literature was for him a form of release and escape from the mercantile world that his family assumed would be his by inheritance.

The "poems" in *Ventures into Verse* were about seafaring, adventuring, war, love, and such miscellany as Christmas, vaudeville, soup-eating, politics, and the city. A rather maudlin sentimentality pervaded many of them; others were modestly facetious or ironic in intent. He tried to leaven the sentimentality and seriousness by jesting on the opening pages. The book was subtitled: "Being Various BALLADS, BALLADES, RONDEAUX, TRIOLETS, SONGS, QUATRAINS, ODES and ROUNDELS—All rescued from the POTTERS' FIELD of Old Files and here Given DECENT BURIAL—(Peace to Their Ashes) . . . FIRST (and Last) EDITION . . . Preliminary rebuke[:] Don't shoot the pianist; he's doing his best." Two of the poems were dedicated to Rudyard Kipling. One, entitled "A War Song," ended like this:

> For 'tis ever the weak that must help the strong
>   Though they have no part in the triumph song,
>   And their glory is brief as their work is long—
>     (Sing ho! for the saints of war!)[4]

Many of Mencken's early verses and short stories were imitative of Kipling's style and subjects. His later prose cadences also had part of their source in the rolling and thumping verses of Kipling. He responded to Kipling's naturalism—that awareness and dramatization of internal and external forces which are seen as controlling the destinies and behavior of men and animals. In the quatrain quoted above this naturalism emerges as a simplification and misapprehension of a Darwinian idea: that the weak exist only to help the strong. No one would claim that Mencken had succeeded in giving this idea an effective transfiguration as poetry, or even as ballad. But he was struggling quite seriously with a process that, he hoped, would result in presentable verse. He had probably not yet discovered—and certainly had not yet interpreted—Nietzsche. It was not until after he read Nietzsche (he published his book on Nietzsche in 1908) that his ideology began to take less sentimental form, and at the same time he abandoned verse-making as an embarrassing, youthful affectation.

The struggle with sentimental commonplaces can be illustrated further in an eight-line poem called "Auroral," first published in 1900. Here we find Mencken again attempting to translate naturalistic perceptions into poetry. He used a particular circumstance of modern life (urban existence) as his material:

> Another day comes journeying with the sun;
> The east grows ghastly with the dawning's gleam,
> And e'er the dark has flown and the night is done
> The city's pavements with their many teem.
>
> Another day of toil and grief and pain;
> Life surely seems not sweet to such as these;
> Yet they live toiling that they may but gain
> The right to life and all life's miseries.[5]

Mencken in this poem (as he himself later on surely would have admitted) was heavy-handed, pompously solemn, and guilty of the kind of uplifting, moral perspective he was later to condemn. There is the promise of a rather startling, typically Menckenian effect in "the east grows ghastly," but that effect is quickly dissipated by the awkwardly "poetic" archaism of "e'er the dark has flown." There is an inept pathos underlying the naturalism of the notion that city dwellers toil only to "gain . . . all life's miseries." The verses do not survive the sentiment expressed in the line "Life surely seems not sweet to such as these," yet the idea with which we leave the last lines (if we have read that far), commonplace as it is, is one which has been transmuted into poetry by, for example, William Blake. In "London," life will endure even among the man-created horrors of the city. But Blake's rhetoric, unlike Mencken's, is effective because his diction is precise and his images vivid rather than abstract. At no point is the intensity of Blake's poem weakened by direct thematic statement.

Mencken's verse reflects his growing awareness of his failure as a poet. Awareness, not the failure, is the important factor: that Mencken turned away from verse-making and fiction does not mean that his imaginative impulses and ways of viewing reality atrophied or changed—only that he sought in journalism what for him were more suitable forms of rhetoric. This progression can be seen in a short poem published in 1905. It was called "On Passing the Island of San Salvador (the First Land Sighted by Columbus)."[6] In it Mencken's narrator had been moved to utterance because the sight of the island had inspired in Columbus "the deathless beauty of a dream come true." But this uplifting sentiment was offset by the rather startling metaphor which described the island as "forgotten offal of the land." Even as a maker of sentimental verses, which meant a special kind of full-blown posturing with "poetic" subjects, Mencken showed twinges of the iconoclasm, the satiric vision and the irony that later were formed into a muscular prose. The very title of his earlier verses, "Auroral," had expressed a simple irony which the rhetoric of those verses was too obvious in clarifying.

In much of his writing, Mencken's rhetoric was designed to startle and to provoke. He addressed his readers characteristically with an authoritarian, omniscient, hyperbolic, Juvenalian voice. Yet in his pronouncements on poetry, as in his own brief, early career as a versifier, much is revealed about the nature and development of his rhetoric as a satirist. In any essay called "The Poet and His Art" he wrote: "Poetry, then, is a capital medicine. First the sweet music lulls, and then its artful presentation of the beautifully improbable soothes and gives surcease. It is an escape from life, like religion, like enthusiasm, like glimpsing a pretty girl." He described the sickness which the medicine of poetry could cure as arising from the mood "of intellectual and spiritual fatigue, the mood of revolt against the insoluble riddle of existence, the mood of disgust and despair." He observed in the same essay that a "quality of untruthfulness pervades all poetry"; he cited Lincoln's Gettysburg Address as an example of poetry because of its "rippling and hypnotizing words."[7]

Nothing quite as clear as a poetics emerges from "The Poet and His Art," yet there is a pattern of ideas and attitudes (Mencken called them "prejudices") consistent with what he wrote about poetry elsewhere. In the essay he expressed the belief that poetry is nonintellectual in its appeal because it lulls the mind away from its normal or routine contemplation of reality; it also has the power to revive a mind weary with the "riddle of existence." Poetry is "artful"; that is, not accidental, and not simply a spontaneous overflow: the poet is fully aware of his techniques and functions. The rhetoric of poetry for Mencken was primary, for poetry could be "untruthful" as long as its language rippled and hypnotized. He made similar aesthetic judgments about prose style. For example, while he deplored Sinclair's tender-minded ideology, he praised him as a stylist: "He writes when his ideas do not harass him too much, with a fine feeling for the sough of words, the burble of phrases, the gaudy roll and hiss of sentences."[8] In citing the Gettysburg Address as an example of poetry he showed that he was not concerned with any simple, formal distinction between poetry and prose. He might, in fact, have been writing about his own prose style.

Mencken wrote in another essay[9] that prose was the language of truth and poetry the language of beautiful lies. Poetry "must soothe the ear while it debauches the mind." He explained that his own prose often had the effect of poetry, for he had eminently succeeded in debauching the minds of many of his readers. He was referring specifically to his bathtub-hoax essay of 1917, which he regarded as poetry because its rhetoric was misleading. His emphasis is significant: the essay was successful *because* "it was poetry, which is to say, a mellifluous and caressing statement of the certainly not true."[10]

In the bathtub hoax Mencken had written in mock-serious fashion about the invention of the bathtub in Cincinnati, Ohio, in the year 1842. His statistics were elaborate fabrications. For the purposes of the essay he assumed a particular dramatic pose; the narrator speaks with the authoritative voice of the journalist-commentator, one of the everyday, myth-and-legend-making voices of American culture. That some people accepted the voice as authentic was, of course, part of the joke.[11] In that acceptance there was an expression of a desire to see circumstances as history, to translate the trivial into the significant, fact into legend, reality into myth.

Those who saw the joke realized that the success of the essay depended upon an element of parody: Mencken had imitated the omniscient, myth-making voice with which the journalist-commentator addresses the reader from the editorial sections of newspapers and magazines. What was at issue for Mencken was the credibility of that voice, and there was a certain mad fiendishness behind the practical joke. It was 1917; Mencken, passionately pro-German, felt muzzled by the excesses of patriotism that dominated the attitudes of Americans. The "Free Lance" column had been a casualty, in 1915, of his unpopular views of the war. The war and all of its ramifications were excluded from his writing until after 1919; the central and most compelling subject for a journalist during these years was therefore closed to him. The bathtub hoax was in part an act of hostility directed at the audience upon which Mencken depended, and would again depend, for his livelihood and for approval. Looking back, in 1926 (when once more secure in his knowledge of the approval of his readers), he noted that the essay had been "thrown off as a relief from the patriotic libido of war time." About "the gaudy days of 1914–1918" he asked: "How much that was then devoured by the newspaper readers of the world was actually true?" The answer Mencken gave was "not one per cent."[12]

The bathtub hoax was Mencken's oblique way of working his own deceptive propaganda upon the gullible element in his audience; it was a hostile practical joke played upon the provincial one-hundred-percent American booboisie—the main object of his ridicule in the 1920s. He turned an aspect of the orderly, logic-loving, middle-class world upside down by ridiculing the faith of that world in the credibility of the journal as reliable interpreter of history in progress. The bathtub hoax especially illuminates aspects of Mencken's style because in it his rhetoric is almost typical: his narrator is authoritarian and omniscient; only the Juvenalian note (which, by destroying the element of parody, would have made the joke obvious) is missing. In other contexts this mock-serious voice became a supple and more subtle instrument of his style. The narrator of *In Defense of Women* praises women for their superior, practical intelligence. Some readers took that praise to be so exaggerated as to burlesque or ridicule what seemed to be affirmed. They took it as an elaborate hoax arising out of Mencken's misogyny. But Mencken, while his views of women were complex and rooted in the genteel values of his time, was not a misogynist, and he knew that a reader with a typical middle-class male orientation would find what he wrote so exaggerated as to seem to undercut itself. So he was ridiculing such a romantic, sentimental view of women by praising feminine superiority to the male in the practical world of commerce and events where the male liked to preserve the illusion of his own dominance. His posture was more complex than in the bathtub hoax because Mencken really meant what he seemed to mean. It is as if, when writing *In Defense of Women,* he extended his mockery to include among the credulous and unsophisticated those who thought he was not serious. We know that the "facts" about the invention of the bathtub were fabrications. But the evidence and attitudes he presents about women were not fabrications, when measured and evaluated against his observations and attitudes in other contexts.

The bathtub hoax essay obviously had fulfilled the requirements of Mencken's simplistic theory of poetry: it was untruthful, it was artful, it lulled the mind away from the routine contemplation of reality. When he wrote that he had succeeded through the bathtub hoax in debauching the minds of his readers, he was with an underlying seriousness calling attention to what he himself had defined as the poetic characteristics of his rhetoric. He was aware that poetry, whether satiric or lyric, in one of its aspects circles around the process by which reality becomes myth. Here, of course, the "reality" was false, fabricated, yet even so it entered the consciousness of some readers as if it were truth, and, as passed along by these readers, had all the power of myth. It was as surely created as a poetic metaphor for an aspect of reality. To Mencken's sophisticated audience it was an ultimate demonstration of the joy of dancing with arms and legs.

Edmund Wilson, in one of the earliest and one of the best appraisals of Mencken, compared Mencken's evocation of America with Walt

Whitman's.[13] Wilson wrote of the "comic portrait which Mencken has painted of himself," and saw behind that portrait a "critic, an evangelist and an artist." From what he called a Menckenian "prose poem" he quoted a series of descriptions on the topics "aspiration," "virtue," and "eminence." For example: "Aspiration": "College professors in one-building universities on the prairie, still hoping, at the age of sixty, to get their whimsical essays into the *Atlantic Monthly*. . . . Car-conductors on lonely suburban lines, trying desperately to save up $500 and start a Ford garage." "Virtue": "Farmers plowing sterile fields behind sad meditative horses. . . . Methodist preachers retired after forty years of service in the trenches of God, upon pensions of $800 a year. . . . Decayed and hopeless men writing editorials at midnight for leading papers in Mississippi, Arkansas and Alabama."[14] As if from an abbreviated Spoon-River anthology, many of the images evoked the small town, its loneliness and hopelessness, the small town of E. W. Howe, Sherwood Anderson, and Edgar Lee Masters, all midwestern realists whom Mencken admired. Wilson wrote further of Mencken's "gloomy catalogue" as the "poetry of America," comparable to Whitman's "enumeration of another set of visions"—many of Whitman's catalogues would serve for illustration.

The success of the bathtub-hoax essay as satire had depended on an element of parody—parody which arose out of Mencken's awareness of a myth-and-legend-making compulsion that sometimes affects both the newspaperman and his audience. Since the same kind of compulsion especially serves poets and versifiers, there is an affinity between Mencken's journalist-narrator who usually, but not always, mocks what he sees and Whitman's narrator who usually, but not always, celebrates what he sees; both narrators are expressions of the myth-and-legend-making impulses of their creators. Mencken as satirist usually dramatized the varied relations between his authoritarian, omniscient narrator and the setting and culture with which that narrator is in sustained conflict. Whitman as comic poet usually dramatized the affinity of his narrator to his setting and culture, a process in which conflict is diminished rather than sustained. But as satirist and comic poet, respectively, Mencken and Whitman had an artistic and dramatic device in common: the narrator in the characteristic works of each is authoritarian, omniscient, individualistic, and prone to hyperbole in expression.

Fecher shows, in an extended description of Mencken's style, that Mencken was a meticulous worker with his own prose. His detailed revisions demonstrate his care: "When it came to the use of words he had the keenest aesthetic sense. As much as any novelist or poet he sought precisely the right term."[15] Mencken had begun his career with serious aspirations to become a poet. These aspirations survived as he turned from verse to prose. Surely Wilson was right when he saw that Mencken in his time and in his way, like Whitman, was attempting to write a "poetry of America." Mencken's time and Mencken's way produced a writer of satiric prose, where Whitman's time and way had produced a comic poet. The Mencken who had once dreamed of being a poet was a figure the mature Mencken chose to have us forget—but something of that earlier Mencken survived in his rhetoric.

Some aspects of Mencken's rhetoric had their source in nineteenth-century traditions of American humor. He always tried for the fresh and startling image and in that respect his writing was related to the hyperbolic devices of earlier American humorists. One tradition in particular which pointed directly towards the tone of his rhetoric was the tradition of buncombe oratory. After 1820, when the phrase "talking from buncombe" became part of the language, the creation of buncombe oratory became part of the humorist's stock in trade. Often it was difficult to tell the buncombe from the real thing, so overblown, exaggerated, and windy was the oratory of the Jacksonian era, and so realistic were the burlesque imitations of that oratory.[16] There is in nearly all of Mencken's rhetoric the tone of burlesque; it is as if he were unconsciously parodying another Mencken who actually never existed. A fiery evangelist, this other Mencken might be imagined as having delivered windy diatribes from the pulpit calculated to separate the elect from the damned and brand the latter indelibly. Stylistically Mencken's work was affected in tone and cadence by this alter-ego, the arch-Puritan polemicist and preacher.

Forgue describes Mencken's humor as concealing his seriousness of purpose: his comic mask is a "caricature of his real traits." But he had many masks, and, therefore, many traits. Forgue characterizes Mencken's favorite pose as that of the "foreign observer"—like Tocqueville, Mrs. Trollope, or Dickens.[17] Mencken borrowed something of the aura of credibility as well as the tone of astonishment of these visitors to the strange and sometimes savage place that was America. But the comic dimension seems more American, deriving from buncombe oratory and from the wild individualism of frontier humor as it came to its fruition in Mark Twain and Bierce. Bierce's extravagant individualism was mirrored by William Cowper Brann, publisher, editor, and writer of *Brann's Iconoclast,* a monthly published at Waco, Texas, from 1895 to 1898. Brann was an irate journalist whose prejudices were more vehement than Mencken's, and whose style, although more florid, was often as startling and exaggerated. Brann's magazine had wide national and even international circulation. Mencken claimed in an autobiographical note that Brann had published an article by Mencken ridiculing "Methodist preachers of Baltimore."[18] Mencken responded both to the extravagance of Brann's publications and to his extreme libertarianism. Brann's and Bierce's were loud voices lamenting the passing of the frontier by sounding the wildly exuberant and belligerent cry of the gamecock of the wilderness one last time.

Mencken wanted to create a frontier of the spirit where ideas could be truly considered and transmitted. He had a closely related concern about the clarity of the language for consideration and transmission. Integrating both these concerns was his sense of the transcendent force of art. An idea could be raised to a higher power, could be transformed, by the language and form of its presentation. His efforts to write transformational language in verse form were stillborn. But often Mencken's efforts in prose exude a tremendous energy. We hear at these moments a passionately and joyously committed dramatic voice, convincing us by an exuberance beyond mere accuracy that language matters uniquely. There is in this energy the evocation of a stylistic commitment that has one immediate nineteenth-century American predecessor in Thoreau. Language like this can only come out of a tradition of expression that cares deeply about the human condition, a tradition like that of the progressives or Thoreau. Like Thoreau, Mencken wrote with the feeling that joyous and committed language was the ultimate weapon in the warfare against the murderous aspects of modern life, and that irony was not the negation or inversion of joy but its most profound evoker. For both, the highest value was an aesthetic animated by the mystique of craft: it is important to do, and love, well what must be left before long. Thoreau, in describing the aesthetic of his own writing, had expressed an American version of the Romantic sense of connection between reality and the power of language:

> I fear chiefly lest my expression may not be *extra-vagant* enough, may not wander far enough beyond the narrow limits of my daily experience, so as to be adequate to the truth of which I have been convinced. . . . I desire to speak somewhere *without* bounds; like a man in a waking moment, to men in their waking moments.[19]

Mencken, as thoroughly a Romantic in his aesthetic sensibility as Thoreau, celebrated the ironic potential of extravagance, too. To speak the convincing truth without bounds was for each the ultimate joy.

Mencken's special brand of polemic was an outgrowth of his style as a journalist. He was able to adapt journalism to his needs for self-expression. He had not been a success as a poet or writer of fiction; therefore, he chose journalism because as a journalist his talents had proved effective and he was almost immediately able to make his weight felt. He was not, of course, even as a journalist, always a debunker, that is, a purger of the nonsense in language. His interest in, and writings on, the American language were extensions of the techniques of his journalism; the journalist's clippings file, scissors, and pastepot were the heart and method of his lexicography. Words were endlessly fascinating to him and he handled them with the intuitive skill of a poet. Language was alive, colorful, absorbing, full of mystery, a kind of ritual central to the lives of all people. These were the attributes of the great religions, and the American language was a church that Mencken honored and helped construct. As he grew older his devotion became chauvinism: in 1948 he wrote: "General American is much clearer and more logical than any of the other dialects, either English or American. It shows a clear if somewhat metallic pronunciation, gives all necessary consonants their true values, keeps to simple and narrow speech tunes, and is vigorous and masculine."[20] As an expert on language he was able to make a devoted bid for respectable academic fame on his own terms. He liked to think of himself as a linguistic authority in the Johnsonian tradition.

Before the war he had shared many of the humanitarian concerns of the progressives, and he never changed his belief that art could enlarge the human center of life. It was Lippmann, not Mencken, who stated with great clarity the ideas about the role of art that had appeared from time to time in Mencken's writings prior to 1913. The occasion was *A Preface to Politics,* about which Mencken wrote an essay-review. Lippmann had observed: "art enlarges experience by admitting us to the inner life of others. . . . Literature in particular elaborates our insight into human life, and therefore, allows us to center our institutions more truly."[21]

Art renders the reality of experience, and that, after the removal of distracting idols, becomes the center of thought. Mencken took on as his role the removal of distracting idols, and underlying his conscious acceptance of that role was his concern about "insight into human life." He thought the individual self, both male and female, could be smothered by the genteel tradition with its Puritan ideology; he wanted to revitalize and conserve the values he thought had evolved when the self, male and female, was directly concerned with survival, as on the frontier: the values of courage, honor, pride.

Late nineteenth-century American culture had proved to be an affront to his sense of those values. He reacted through ridicule and frequently he was funny: people laughed, his hostility was accepted and approved often by the same public toward which hostility had originally been directed. This curious mixture of hostility and of need for acceptance and approval underlies all of Mencken's work, as indeed it does the work of Lewis, Lardner, Marquis, and other debunkers. That he usually tried to make people laugh at his outrageousness meant that he sought the most immediate and definite form of responsive complicity of which a reader or audience is capable. Therefore, he created an image of himself that his public could approve. It was the image of the lusty, noisy, Rabelaisian iconoclast, always omniscient, frequently Juvenalian, patronizing toward women, an irreverent heaver of dead cats, who lived by practical jokes and horse laughs. But that was not all of the real Mencken, any more than the "phunny phellow" was all of the real Mark Twain.

James K. Kilpatrick, who especially admired Mencken's journalism, observed that Mencken "was full of bluster, bravado, and bombast . . . with the discipline that marks every great entertainer. At bottom were the ideas—the original, outrageous, provocative, enchanting ideas that bubbled incessantly within him."[22] Those ideas were hardly original; they were the humanistic ones of his time and place, with a basis in the progressive idealism of the early twentieth century. Mencken accepted the duplicity inherent in satire and used a blustering, bombastic method to convey obliquely some of his deepest feelings about his culture. Those feelings were both masked by and expressed in the bravado of the civil libertarian: an aspect of his real self that he could not bear to have violated. But most important of all was a sense of himself as performing artist. He labored hard as a journalist, critic, and philologist, and above all at creating the exaggerated public posture. When he was at his best we are unaware of the labor. We respond to the sense of freedom and pleasure that radiates exuberantly from his writing.

# Chapter Six
## What Mencken Wrought:
## The Debunkers at Work

Lash the rascals through the world.

> Ambrose Bierce,
> "The Passing of Satire," 1909

Comfortable, complacent, middle-class citizens were targets for the satire and ridicule that the debunkers directed at them around 1910 and that reached a crescendo of loving contempt in the 1920s. They were laughed at for their provincialism, their puritanism, and their Americanism; their manners, their morals, and their politics were ridiculed. In matters of aesthetics they were called Philistines. At another extreme, their libertine brothers and sisters, or sons and daughters, were mockingly called aesthetes.

The process of deflation was in part a development out of the concerns of the muckrakers, those morally oriented members of the middle class whose revelations of sin in the cities had lost the capacity to shock and disturb by 1910. The debunkers turned with hostile joy against the staunch belief that in quiet country towns and hamlets one could always find kind, honest, morally impeccable, sensible Americans. No longer were provincial Americans to be allowed the comforting belief that they were guardians of the democratic virtues which, presumably, the mushrooming cities were so rapidly destroying.

Mencken's unique influence was exercised especially through his role as editor for the *Smart Set* and then the *American Mercury,* as well as through his copious writings for those publications, writings that made up the bulk of his *Book of Prefaces* (1917) and the six volumes of his *Prejudices* (1919–1927). The manifestations of that influence were extensive. His attitudes were reflected by Lewis, Marquis, Lardner, and hosts of other writers. Finally, the legacy of Mencken and the debunking point of view emerged in the *New Yorker* and in the writings of Nathanael West.

Mencken both helped create and added to the ridicule of the American provincial. Typically, in one essay he wrote that New York ought to be a free city, politically separate from the rest of the union. Although "every great wave of popular passion that rolls up on the prairies is dashed to spray when it strikes the hard rocks of Manhattan," nevertheless, as a free city, New York could "erect barriers and conditions around the privilege of citizenship, and so save itself from the double flood that now swamps it—first, of broken-down peasants from Europe, and secondly and more important, of fugitive rogues from all the land West and South of the Hudson."[1] New York represented civilization and sophistication, American commodities so rare that they needed to be carefully conserved. Much of Mencken's antiprovincial attitude was focused upon southern life and culture.[2] His classic essay identifying and ridiculing the cultural shortcomings of the South was "The Sahara of the Bozart" (1917).

The opposite of provincialism was the debunker's superior sophistication, and one measure for sophistication was appreciation of European culture. Again, Mencken, along with his friends George Jean Nathan and Willard Huntington Wright, established that superiority and exercised it. In 1912 they traveled in Europe together. A result of their trip was a series of articles published first in the *Smart Set* and then in 1914 as a book called *Europe after 8:15*. The book purported to be a guide to the real night life in Vienna, Munich, Berlin, London, and Paris—not the garish, Pigallic night life sought and often found by the American tourist. This typical tourist was caustically described in the preface and frequently ridiculed thereafter as the dollar-waving boob immune to the more sophisticated refinements of European travel. The preface, written by Mencken, and first published in 1913,[3] concentrated entirely on this now antique point of view. In each city the provincial American was depicted as the villain who had spoiled Europe for those whose cultural savvy was international. But not quite spoiled, for the bulk of the book laid before the discerning reader many romantic, intimate, private discoveries. Unfortunately, 1914 was not an auspicious year for a European travel book; it was 1919 before sensitive Americans began to go to Europe again for cultural or recreational reasons—or in order to expatriate themselves from American experience. In the 1920s the image of the American tourist abroad (usually from the Midwest), who was the victim of his own lack of sophistication, was to become a stock subject in debunking literature. Something like a reversal had occurred since the nineteenth century, when the middle-class American traveling in Europe was usually viewed as the innocent victim of European cultural pretensions and decadence.

In 1924, Donald Ogden Stewart (Ivy League educated and New York oriented) published a book that debunked a favorite middle-class symbol of success, the grand tour of Europe. It was called *Mr. and Mrs. Haddock Abroad* and facetiously chronicled the preparations and ocean voyage of a family from the city of "Legion, Midwest." The Haddocks are provincial, bumbling, and stupid; the book-length treatment of their inanities soon becomes as tedious as an encounter with real-life Haddocks would be. Their manners are meticulously and satirically recorded. Mrs. Haddock keeps a notebook, which is a middle-class guide as to things to see, do, and avoid. On Paris, she has: "Hotels not well heated. Cotton sheets. French not clean. Always rains in evening. Eiffel Tower unsafe. Morgue gone. Frenchmen unsafe. French immoral."[4] The American traveler's hopes and fears concerning his accustomed physical comfort are presented in monotonous detail. Trivial and farcical episodes are incongruously juxtaposed as the book moves into fantasy and nonsense; the Haddocks' status-groping trip degenerates into a ridiculous nightmare. The book was popular enough to be followed by a sequel in 1926: *Mr. and Mrs. Haddock in Paris, France.* Their comic plight must have furnished amusement and a sense of superiority for those numerous enlightened Americans who escaped the provincialism of their own country during the 1920s in European travel or expatriation.

Ernest Hemingway, in *The Sun Also Rises,* used expatriation as the condition through which his characters both illustrated and refuted Gertrude Stein's observation that they were all members of a lost generation. Hemingway made complex and profound fictional use of the antiprovincial attitude. His characters had, in part, sought expatriation in order to escape from the provincialism of life in America. Occasionally in the novel they refer to life back home in a satiric, bantering, debunking manner very like the manner of Stewart in the *Haddock* books. Some of the conversations between Jake Barnes, hero of *The Sun Also Rises,* and his close friend, Bill Gorton (for whom Stewart may have been a real-life model), are very like the dialogues in Woodward's novels. There is no extraliterary evidence that Hemingway was influenced by a reading of Woodward's *Bunk* or by any of his other novels, although on chronological evidence alone he could have read *Bunk* (1923) before writing *The Sun Also Rises* (1926) and *The Torrents of Spring* (1926). Certainly both writers had noticed similar elements in the conversations of their contemporaries. *The Sun Also Rises* reflects more convincingly than any other work the speaking rhythms and the attitudes of the disillusioned expatriates of Hemingway's time.

On their fishing trip in Spain Jake and Bill amuse themselves with repartee that includes satiric commentary on expatriation, the Civil War, Bryan, Mencken, and businessmen as dreamers:

> "You're an expatriate. You've lost touch with the soil. You get precious. Fake European standards have ruined you. You drink yourself to death. You become obsessed by sex. You spend all your time talking, not working. You are an expatriate, see? You hang around cafes."

> "Abraham Lincoln was a faggot. He was in love with General Grant. So was Jefferson Davis. Lincoln just freed the slaves on a bet. The Dred Scott case was framed by the Anti-Saloon League. Sex explains it all. The Colonel's Lady and Judy O'Grady are Lesbians under their skin."

> "Gentlemen," he said, and unwrapped a drumstick from a piece of newspaper. "I reverse the order. For Bryan's sake. As a tribute to the Great Commoner. First the chicken; then the egg."

> "Let us not doubt, brother. Let us not pry into the holy mysteries of the hen-coop with simian fingers. Let us accept on faith and simply say—I want you to join with me in saying—What shall we say, brother?" He pointed the drumstick at me and went on. "Let me tell you. We will say, and I for one am proud to say—I want you to say with me, on your knees, brother. Let no man be ashamed to kneel here in the great out-of-doors. Remember the woods were God's first temples. Let us kneel and say: 'Don't eat that Lady—that's Mencken.' "

> "I loved Bryan," said Bill. "We were like brothers."
> "Where did you know him?"
> "He and Mencken and I all went to Holy Cross together."

> "You ought to dream," Bill said. "All our biggest business men have been dreamers. Look at President Coolidge. Look at Rockefeller. Look at Jo Davidson."[5]

Here the cynical attitudes and the disaffection dramatize Jake's and Bill's position as expatriates. Their conversations reflect the vernacular of Hemingway's generation, and are symbolic of an aspect of the novel's meaning, for in them hostility is directed not only against provincial, puritanical America but also against assessors of that America, such as Mencken and the new historians. These conversations show that Jake and Bill are acting out a ritual of close friendship, through a facetious display of their shared sense of sophistication. There is an anguish underlying these flippant exchanges: in ridiculing Mencken they are recognizing the superficiality of the disaffected attitudes they had learned from him. The close companionship they affirm through their kidding and debunking is the masculine companionship of the fishing-hunting idyll away from civilization and away from women. The desperation and seriousness underlying their wit is emphasized by the setting: their idyll takes place near Roncevalles, in Spain, where Roland and his friends fell together on a point of honor. In this scene Hemingway uses the vernacular of debunking so as to dramatize the tragic emptiness of these lives. As he saw so profoundly, the rejection of provincial, traditional American experience meant also the loss of deeply rooted values and carried with it a sense of disorientation. Wit and cynicism were superficial ways of concealing nostalgia for a way of life that would never return, if it had in fact ever existed.

The most graphic as well as the most satiric chronicles of provincial midwestern manners during this period of cultural introspection were also fictional, and were set out in the novels of Sinclair Lewis. Lewis's best novels (*Main Street,* 1920, and *Babbitt,* 1922) contained satire of midwestern, middle-class provincialism, but in these novels Lewis the satirist was secondary to Lewis the realist and novelist of manners. Carol Kennicott and George Babbitt are partly victims of midwestern provincialism and they are viewed sympathetically; however, they are also victims of their own pretensions. Much of the popularity of *Main Street* and *Babbitt* rested on the jubilant reception of Lewis's relentlessly realistic descriptions, which had the effect of debunking small-town values and manners. In *The Man Who Knew Coolidge* (1928) he responded to the public acclaim for his talents as a debunker by writing deliberately as a satirist. Lowell Schmaltz, businessman and friend of Babbitt from Zenith, delivers a windy monologue in which his tediousness, his crude conformism, and his belligerent Americanism are bluntly portrayed. Lowell Schmaltz, unlike Babbitt, is totally ridiculed; he has none of Babbitt's idealism or sense of a life missed and unfulfilled.

*Main Street* and *Babbitt* were the best of many books in the 1920s whose authors had constructed as dramatic background a provincially mannered, morally repressed, narrowly patriotic, and culturally sterile midwestern world. The hero of Floyd Dell's *Moon-Calf* (1920), Felix Fay, seeks to escape from the worst of a similar world, and the hero of Ben Hecht's *Erik Dorn* (1921) does escape, but into an equally meaningless cynicism. In Homer Croy's *West of the Water Tower* (1923), the hero, Guy Plummer, son of a minister, rejects his father's puritanism, but he is also incapable of his father's directness and honesty; he ends, like Babbitt, by accepting the stagnant, materialistic values of Junction City, Missouri. In *An Unmarried Father* (1927) Dell created a respectable, practical, provincial Illinois environment from which his hero, an indecisive, romantic idealist, tries unsuccessfully to escape. In all these novels there is satire of midwestern manners and attitudes, but the satire is incidental and secondary. The midwestern setting in each is represented with as much affection as disaffection. Novelistically, as background, the provincial life is affirmed as a crucible for the formation of virtues which the heroes of the novels usually are incapable of assuming. Instead of their fathers' moral solidity they have only a vague romantic idealism. The heroines, not the heroes, of these novels are the ones who carry over into the modern world the best of the old virtues. In none of them is there satire of the unremittingly savage kind that Lewis created in his portrait of Lowell Schmaltz. Nevertheless, these writers all borrowed from and reflected the attitudes of Mencken and Lewis.

Mencken was the most influential and widely read debunker. He identified America's Puritan traditions as the source of repression and of what he called the benign booziness. Late nineteenth- and early twentieth-century Protestantism, he contended, was simply puritanism in a degenerate, proselytized form. Puritanism was the source of the moral attitudes characteristic of the middle class, attitudes predominant in American life. Mencken never defined, described, or established puritanism as a historical phenomenon; it was, for him, an easily derived cultural abstraction, hypothesis, and point of departure (like the frontier, or the economic interpretation of the Constitution) for multiple diatribes and critiques of contemporary America. The Puritan, he thought, was one who believed that he not only had the right but also the duty to watch over and correct the morals of others: "The objection to Puritans is not that they try to make us think as they do, but that they try to make us do as they think." Thus Prohibition, censorship, the Mann Act, reform, the cherry-tree myth, and American democracy appeared in the world, all of them products of the same evangelical ethic. All were manifestations of a deeply rooted hostility which Mencken defined in this way: "At the bottom of Puritanism one finds envy of the fellow who is having a better time in the world, and hence hatred of him. At the bottom of democracy one finds the same thing. This is why all Puritans are democrats and all democrats are Puritans."[6]

The American provincial, with his unsophisticated, bucolic, middle-class soul, was, according to Mencken, the inevitable product of the

Puritan spirit. This provincial was responsible for, and especially susceptible to, such American institutions and phenomena as fundamentalism and Prohibition. Such plots for "making men good by force" as Prohibition and legislation against birth control were invariably more successful in the country than in the city, because "the yokel is trained from infancy to suffer espionage."[7]

Mencken's most ecstatic orgy of gleeful hostility against an extreme and to him typical form of the benign booziness fostered by puritanism occurred in his reporting of the Scopes trial at Dayton, Tennessee, in 1925. He had a national audience, through his articles in the *Baltimore Evening Sun* (which were syndicated in newspapers all over the country), and through the *American Mercury*. He was completely in his element: Dayton was typical of the backward, rural America, populated by boobs and yokels, that he had been satirizing for years; the fundamentalists cooperated by being thoroughly, even belligerently, fundamental. There was not much need for exaggeration; straight reporting and the roll and thump of his most restrained rhetoric produced the satiric effects he wanted. Even the *New York Times*'s coverage of the trial (10–27 July) reflected reportorial sarcasm, irony, or simple comic astonishment. But underneath what Mencken wrote of fundamentalists and especially in his portraits of the aging, weakening Bryan, there was sympathy, particularly for the demagogue who had known better days. Fundamentalists were but rural manifestations of the greater middle-class, Anglo-Saxon, Puritan affliction that he called the "benign booziness."

This aspect of the humanitarian surfeit in the 1920s was manifest according to Mencken in reform and the reform attitude. The reformer, Mencken wrote, believes in "all the revolutionary inventions for lifting up humanity." He is the "forward-looker" who is "chronically full of hope"; he is "tender-minded," and "pathologically sensitive to the sorrows of the world."[8] He is, in short, the muckraker; Sinclair was Mencken's prime example and prototype, although a few years earlier Mencken had spoken appreciatively of Sinclair's skill as a novelist. Reformers in the 1920s, Mencken thought, gravitated toward Washington, where they became securely established in government jobs. The new reformer

is the fellow who enforces the Volstead Act, the Mann Act, all the endless laws for putting down sin. He . . . tours the country teaching Mothers how to have babies, spreading the latest inventions in pedagogy, road-making, the export trade, hog-raising and vegetable-canning, waging an eternal war upon illiteracy, hookworm, the white slave trade, patent medicines, the foot and mouth disease, cholera infantum, adultery, rum. . . . He represents the new governmental tyranny; he is Vision, vice the spoils system, retired.[9]

This essay was written in the early 1920s when Mencken's attitudes about the progressive movement had shifted, at least ostensibly. At this time in his career Mencken was confirming and enhancing his hard-won popularity as an iconoclast.

Dorothy Parker wrote "Reformers: A Hymn of Hate" which was an echo in verse of the Menckenian point of view: "I hate Reformers; / They raise my blood pressure." Her verse was one of the contributions in a book called *Nonsenseorship,* which was published in 1922. A collection of essays, verses, and drawings, the book debunked censorship in America. Censorship was viewed as one of the institutionalized, repressive effects of neopuritanism. Throughout the book the methods and attitudes of Mencken are evident. The cartoons by Ralph Barton invariably depict the censor in Pilgrim garb. One of the contributors, Frederick O'Brien, called the missionary-censor the "wowzer," one who wants to do unto others as he has done unto himself: "Wowzerism dies hard. . . . The Anglo-Saxon American has it in his blood as an inheritance from the rise of Puritanism four hundred years ago, while in many ways it is an idiosyncrasy to be explained by the glands regulating personality. . . . We must attack and extirpate the wowzerary gland."[10]

The lead article in *Nonsenseorship* concentrated on the most spectacular affront of all to the sophisticate in the early 1920s: national Prohibition. Heywood Broun, who wrote the article, occasionally rose to Menckenian scorn: "This will be a nation composed entirely of men who wear rubbers, put money in the bank, and go to bed at ten."[11] Mencken, too, was a vehement and influential anti-Prohibitionist. He wrote in 1918 that "teetotalism does not make for human happiness; it makes for the dull, idiotic happiness of the barnyard."[12] Prohibition was one of the waves of popular passion that had swept up from the prairies, and was, Mencken thought, directed against the intelligent city-dweller by puritanical provincials. In an essay called "The New Galahad" he praised one admirable result of Prohibition, the bootlegger: "An ideal hero. . . . The true heir, not only of the old-time Indian fighters and train robbers, but also of the tough and barnacled deep-water sailors."[13] In short, the bootlegger, like the debunker, was the individualistic defier of society.

Ben Hecht's contribution to *Nonsenseorship* was an essay on literary censorship. In it he acknowledged Mencken's influence and effect as a champion for literary realism, and wrote with a hint of Mencken's extravagance. He thought that the crusade for realism in literature had lost its vitality. He deplored what he considered to be a lack of significant, inspiring dialectic in American letters between the iconoclasts and the censors. Literary iconoclasm had come to be tolerated "in a land alive with caterwaulings of virtue." The censors, he wrote, were too ignorant to appreciate the machinations of the iconoclastic intellect: "Our books were over their heads. Our broadsides aimed for their vitals whizzed by their ears and lulled them into slumber. A hideous victory is in our hands."[14]

Literary censorship was a manifestation of the reform attitude that Mencken especially resented. His most famous battle occurred in 1926 when the *American Mercury* was banned in Boston; Mencken defied the ban, was arrested, tried, and acquitted. His motives were not entirely libertarian or altruistic. He was concerned about freedom of expression and freedom of the press, but he also was motivated by a shrewd businessman's concerns: the two-year-old *American Mercury* would benefit from the national publicity.[15] The specific issue was alleged explicitness about sex as a subject in the *Mercury,* and about this issue Mencken's attitude was ambivalent. He had as a reviewer been outspoken in his praise of Dreiser, especially in the context of the suppression of *Sister Carrie.* However, he felt that by the 1920s the American writer was quite as free to write about sex as he or she needed to be. The fight for realism in the earlier years of the century had been successful enough; at one point in the 1920s Mencken wrote: "The most virtuous lady novelists write things that would have made a bartender blush to death two decades ago."[16] As an editor he was never especially radical in his selection for publication of manuscripts that were graphically realistic in their treatment of sex; he had too shrewd a sense of how much his audience would tolerate. His own attitude toward sex was strictly genteel. He liked to pose as a lusty Rabelaisian, but was actually a perfect Victorian gentleman.

Like Mencken, most of the debunkers were curiously and characteristically fastidious in their attitudes toward sex. Militant woman's suffrage and emancipation, but not sexual freedom, were sources of comic material. Their own latent puritanism remained a conditioning factor. Marquis created Hermione, a flighty, newly emancipated, middle-class young lady who lived in Greenwich Village during the prewar years and who was a prefiguration of the flapper. But in spate of her advanced ideas, Hermione remains quite chaste. Marquis's Mehitabel was another comic creation through whom he both debunked and admired the hardy individualism of the flapper. Free love is a necessary aspect of Mehitabel's way of life, but she is frequently penalized with kittens, which she promptly, and somewhat guiltily, deserts. Lardner's sense of propriety became overt in his crusade against the off-color allusions that were commonplaces of radio fare. The flapper, as conceived by the cartoonist John Held, was depicted with a satirist's fastidious hostility. But his caricatures were accepted and celebrated as symbols of female emancipation, not as symbols of sexual liberation. One feminine opinion of the flapper was a little apologetic; Helen Bullitt Lowry, writing on "The Uninhibited Flapper" in *Nonsenseorship,* offered the widely held view that the flapper would never have flapped if puritanism had not driven her to it.

Sex was more often than not treated as a serious subject before and after the war. A rare exception was the book called *Is Sex Necessary?* by James Thurber and E. B. White, published in 1929; it was a mock-cultural history of sex in America. It is the half-humorous conceit of the book that the male is bested by the female in the relationship between sexes. He is the victim of feminine knowingness and aggression. In America, the authors began, "the biological aspects of love . . . are distorted and transcended by emphasis upon its sacredness." The female, in order to defend herself from masculine strength and impetuosity, surrounds herself "with a nimbus of ineffability." One aspect of her defense is the "Diversion Subterfuge," of which historically, the "first manifestation was fudge-making." Another manifestation was the parlor game, which developed when the man tried to foil the fudge-making subterfuge by bringing a box of candy. Frustration entered the picture when diversion was sought in long rides on tandem bicycles. Then (around 1907) the epoch of the den in America began and men withdrew completely, thereby bringing about "the first general separation of the physical and the psychic in this country." The Sexual Revolution occurred when women "concluded that sex was recreational rather than procreational." New York became the capital of the revolution and drew "young ladies from the South and from the Middle West whose minds were not quite made up about sexual freedom."[17] They usually lived in Greenwich Village. The book went on in this mock-historical, pseudo-sociological way as woman's descent from her nineteenth-century pedestal and her emancipation from the Puritan tradition were traced. Perhaps Thurber and White were in part parodying a 1929 symposium called *Sex in Civilization,* edited by V. F. Calverton and S. D. Schmalhausen. They mocked the startling historical inclusiveness and solemn scientific aplomb of the sociologist's method and style. Part of their humorous effect was achieved through parody of popularized writings which were designed to make modestly affluent and moderately intelligent readers nodding acquaintances with virtually everything. There were not, until the late 1920s, very many authoritative treatments of changes in sexual behavior (Havelock Ellis was available only to specialists until the Random House edition in 1936; Freud was translated in 1908 and thereafter, but usually reached the public in simplified or sensational form). Sex was a serious subject; even Thurber and White's comic approach retained a residue of Victorian reserve.

Mencken never tired of ferreting out other manifestations of puritanism in American life. He expended more energy and covered more paper in this particular crusade than did anyone else in his time, or any other time. Another example of his dogged pursuit of the benign and uplifting booziness was what he wrote of birth-control advocates. He thought that some of the proselytizing energy which in earlier periods might have been absorbed by abolition, philanthropy, or muckraking was caught up by the newer scientific faith in the human capacity to influence the environment. Birth control was one of the impassioned crusades of the 1920s for those who sought to apply their faith in science. Mencken called them the "birth control fanatics" and recognized them only so long as their rights of expression were opposed "by an evil combination of theologians and politicians." But his attitude toward birth control was expressed through a Juvenalian pose: "I believe that the ignorant should be permitted to spawn *ad libitum*, that there may be a steady supply of slaves, and that those of us who are more prudent and sanitary may be relieved of unpleasant work."[18]

His bombastic extravagance seemed designed to conceal his distaste for the subject, which touched upon matters he in his gentility thought should remain private and personal. Other debunkers of his generation shared that distaste. The tone of parody is also an element here: what may seem offensive because of its antihumanitarian windiness and conservative insensitivity is in part satire of just such windiness and insensitivity. In spite of Mencken's comic scorn and anger, the damned spot of puritanism at which he scrubbed so persistently and which he doused so generously with the antiseptic of his rhetoric proved to be ineradicable, especially in himself. In their similar obsessions, other debunkers only partially concealed their own puritanism-in-reverse.

Puritanism, usually compounded and hardened by provincialism, was manifested in the political life as Americanism, according to the formula most of the debunkers applied. Few of them went as far as Mencken in extravagantly asserting that puritanism and democracy were equally offensive, but the tendency was there. In *Erik Dorn* (1921), Hecht expressed the characteristic attitude of the debunker toward puritanism-Americanism when he described a character (George Hazlitt) in this way: "His puritanism had put an end to his brain. Like his fellows for whose respect and admiration he worked, he had bartered his intelligence for a thing he proudly called Americanism, and thought for him had become a placid agitation of platitudes."[19]

In the preface to *The American Credo* (1920) the kinds of platitudes which the debunker found especially offensive were defined by Mencken and Nathan as "rhetorical gasbombs upon the subject of American ideals and the American character, so copious, so cocksure and withal so ill-informed and inconclusive." They set out in their ironic and blunt way to put "into plain propositions some of the notions that lie at the heart of those ideals and enter into the very substance of that character." They collected in *The American Credo* many of the "rhetorical gasbombs" which the one-hundred-per-cent American accepted as self-evident truths. They had been publishing samples in their regular column of commentary, "Répétition Générale," in the *Smart Set,* since 1919. Their main purpose, further stated in the preface to *The American Credo,* was to explode the American's notion of himself as "the chief exponent of liberty in the whole world," since in point of fact "his political liberty is fast succumbing," as evidenced by such things as his silence before the tyrannies of the Espionage Act and his approval of Prohibition.

Mencken and Nathan further consolidated their ridicule of Americanism in a section of the *Smart Set* called "Americana." Begun in 1923 and carried over to the *American Mercury* the next year, "Americana" were unedited clippings from American newspapers and journals illustrating the banality, chauvinism, and narrow bigotry of aspects of American life, usually provincial life. Something of the success of "Americana" was dramatized when the *Saturday Evening Post,* a popular and genteel family magazine, responded with its own selections of "Americana," designed to celebrate cheerful, comic, patriotic, and poignant elements in the lives of Americans.

Mencken and Nathan became editors of the *Smart Set* in 1914 (although Mencken had been writing the book reviews since 1908) and, after the relatively quiet war years, from 1919 to 1923 filled the magazine with satiric writing. Two series called "The Nietzschean Follies" and "The Higher Learning in America," like other nonfiction in the *Smart Set,* frequently ridiculed American culture and life. Fiction ranged from sophisticated romance to stories reflecting the debunkers' subjects, especially their antiprovincialism. Among those published were Lewis, Parker, and Stewart. The *Smart Set* also gave the first significant national exposure to Eugene O'Neill and to F. Scott Fitzgerald. It continued to publish some of Fitzgerald's best early fiction, and surely some of the ironic perspective of Fitzgerald's most accomplished writing developed out of what he learned Mencken would accept. One of the stories Mencken printed (in 1921) was "The Diamond as Big as the Ritz," a major achievement in the Fitzgerald canon, which took as its underlying tension the corrupting power of great wealth. This sense of corruption had its sources in *The Gilded Age,* in the writings of the muckrakers, and in Thorstein Veblen's *Theory of the Leisure Class.* Mencken recognized the maturation of Fitzgerald's talent in a review of *The Beautiful and the Damned* (April 1922). Earlier (August 1920) he had called *This Side of Paradise* "the best American novel I have seen of late." Although a few years later he dismissed *The Great Gatsby* as "a glorified anecdote," his support of Fitzgerald as an emerging writer was significant.[20]

The style of the *Smart Set* as much as its substance had been responsible for its success among readers who valued it as "a magazine of cleverness" and as "lively entertainment for minds that are not primitive." But its modest circulation, combined with the dissatisfaction of the publisher and of advertisers at the editors' irreverence, led to the departure of Mencken and Nathan in 1923 for the greener covers and greater success of the *American Mercury.* Although Nathan's interest was drama, he participated fully in editing all aspects of both the *Smart Set* and the *American Mercury* during its first year. His purpose as a critic was to attack "the stupidity of the native professional stage" (November 1916) and his style complemented Mencken's as they ridiculed other stupidities of American life. Sometimes, because of the forest of pseudonyms each enjoyed using, it is difficult to see what is Mencken and what is Nathan. Their shift to the *Mercury* brought them a publisher, Alfred A. Knopf, who supported them more substantially both in finances and in editorial freedom. In appearance and format the *Mercury,* with its dignified green cover and good paper, looked classier than had the pulpy, slick *Smart Set.* There was less fiction and poetry in the *Mercury,* in fact less emphasis on literature and fine arts: those were Nathan's interests. Nathan's departure as editor after a year left the magazine to Mencken and the cultural muckraking that especially engaged him. Much of the debunking style and many of the objects of that muckraking had already been established in the *Smart Set.*[21] The *Mercury* built quickly to a circulation peak of 84,000 in 1928, as compared to a peak of 50,000 for the *Smart Set* in 1920.

As journalists, then, to a great extent through the pages of the *Smart Set* and the *Mercury,* Mencken and Nathan were influential in affirming and sometimes even directing assessments of many aspects of American life, not only by debunkers but often by more methodical, scholarly critics and historians. Arthur Schlesinger observed in *New Viewpoints in American History* (1922) that the public had been in the main unaware of a revolution in historical method. For a number of years, he wrote, new viewpoints brought about by the scientific study of economics, sociology, and politics had been applied to the American past. Much of this work was still "buried in the files of historical society journals," but there was a growing demand for popularizations of the new history.[22] The deflation of contemporary heroes, heroines, politicians, and demagogues had its analogue in reappraisals, and frequently satire of the American past and of America's earlier heroes and leaders whose exploits had been exaggerated beyond credibility. The popular biographies of George Washington written by Hughes and Woodward in 1926 were aspects of this reappraisal of the past.

In 1928 Woodward published another biography, *Meet General Grant*. Reviews by Mencken and Brooks pointed to the brilliance of Woodward's estimate of Grant as a man,[23] but some of the professional historians were less sure of the thoroughness and accuracy of Woodward's methods. His popularity continued to depend on his reputation as a debunker, although he tried to live down the appellation. In his autobiography he wrote: "I am an admirer of George Washington and there is not a debunking paragraph in the whole book." When his *Tom Paine: America's Godfather* was published (1945), he noticed with disgust that the *New York Herald Tribune* had headlined the review: "Woodward Debunks the Debunkers of Tom Paine."[24] Frequently the popular histories and biographies presented the findings of researchers who had carefully and thoroughly examined their sources. Many of these presentations inevitably resembled irreverent exposures, and most popular historians, brought up on the style of the muckrakers, had an eye for the sensational. Thus Woodward's 1923 coinage, for all that it stuck with him in later life, was not an inappropriate description of what the popular historians were doing.

Mencken's influence on the popularization of American history and biography was (as in so many other areas involving criticism of American culture) direct and extensive. In 1918 he attacked the glorified image of George Washington: "He was not pious. He drank whisky. . . . He knew far more profanity than Scripture. . . . He had no belief in the infallible wisdom of the common people, but regarded them as inflammatory dolts, and tried to save the republic from them." Mencken closed this evaluation, which was first published in the *Smart Set*, with the suggestion that, had there been a Mann Act in the eighteenth century, Washington could have been arrested for violation of it.[25] Mencken was debunking not Washington but the false image that had been created of him; creating a new and strictly accurate image was not so important to Mencken as the deflation of the old one. However, he was aware of the need for new histories and biographies, and as an editor and reviewer he was in a position to encourage researchers who were more thorough than himself, but who shared with him the debunking attitude that rejected the use of inflated rhetoric for celebrating the past. In 1920 he wrote: "Where is the first-rate biography of Washington—sound, fair, penetrating, honest. . . . How long must we wait for adequate treatises upon Jefferson, Hamilton, Sam Adams, Aaron Burr, Henry Clay, Calhoun, Webster, Sumner, Grant, Sherman, Lee?"[26]

The answer was to be, Not long. Hughes and Woodward brought out their biographies of Washington in 1926, and a flood of biographies and histories on the American past followed. As an editor Mencken was able to select articles about the tendency to reexamine the American past. For example, to the first issue of the *American Mercury* Harry E. Barnes contributed "The Drool Method in History."[27] He wrote in indignant and bumptious Menckenese that "the drool method" had provided certain American shibboleths which were never violated. According to the method, Americans were primarily of Anglo-Saxon stock; religious and political liberties were the goals of the colonists; such men as George Washington, Ulysses S. Grant, and John Brown were always virtuous, godlike heroes.

Biographies such as the ones by Woodward and Hughes (especially Hughes) did not lack documentation or authenticity; they served the purpose of debunking the false image of Washington, not Washington himself. But sometimes the new images of past heroes were exaggerated; sometimes hostility toward the old images and eagerness to ridicule them led to further distortion. Even Mencken, keeping his initial perspective, or perhaps resenting inept intrusion upon his turf, objected to some of the things that were being written. In March 1926 he reviewed biographies of Jefferson, Hamilton, and John Adams; he wrote that they had lived in a heroic age, that "they were men of complete integrity." Then he objected: "I fear that the gallant iconoclasts who revise our history books sometimes forget all this. Engaged upon the destruction of legends, all of them maudlin and many of them downright insane, they also, at times, do damage to facts."[28] Mencken's own sense of fact as it related to history was highly selective, since it usually led him unerringly and protectively to aristocrats and individualists. "Maudlin" and "insane" legends, he thought, could invariably be traced to and blamed on the influence of the Puritan tradition.

Critiques of patriotism after World War I, Merle Curti reported in his study *The Roots of American Loyalty,* were "part and parcel of the disillusionment that affected many intellectuals and a considerable part of the sophisticated or would-be sophisticated post-war generation."[29] There was often good reason for ridicule and mockery. One of the main sources of gaseous rhetoric was the Committee on Public Information, which was established in April 1917. Under its director, George Creel, the committee issued propaganda in an effort to marshal public opinion for the all-out war effort. Pamphlets were published by the millions; thousands of public speakers promoted the sale of war bonds and stimulated patriotism; foreign language newspapers were censored and many other newspapers were persuaded to exercise self-censorship. Although well-intentioned and perhaps necessary for promoting effective war mobilization, the committee fostered attitudes that resulted in intolerance and needless suppression of individual liberties. By the time of the national elections in 1918 large segments of the public were beginning to resent the absolute control the government had demanded; a Republican majority changed the political balance in Congress. Protests against the regimentation of the war, against the suppression of free speech and against the excesses of the Espionage and Sedition acts were heard more often.

Americanism inevitably produced demagogues to perpetrate it, heroes who exemplified it, and rogues who profited by it. The demagogue was to Mencken the man who had risen to crow at the top of the dung heap in the provinces, whether the Midwest or the South. A typical aspect of the democratic delusion, of the triumph of provincial simplicity, was the demagogic ascendance of Warren Gamaliel Harding, an Ohio politician, to the presidency in 1921. One irreverent commentator was Clinton W. Gilbert, who anonymously published *The Mirrors of Washington* during the first year of Harding's administration. His book was made up of caricatures of prominent political figures. In the chapter on Harding he wrote with the debunker's bellicose authority. He described Harding as plain and provincial; as president, Harding represented the triumph of these qualities in American life:

> We have the perfectly typical American, Warren Gamaliel Harding of the modern type, the Square Head, typical of that America whose artistic taste is the movies, who reads and finds mental satisfaction in the vague insanities of the small town newspaper, who has faith in America . . . with a quantity production mind, cautious, uniformly hating divergence from uniformity.

Provincialism of mind was to blame for the reverent Americanism which had pushed Harding to the top: "The 'why' of Harding is the democratic passion for equality. We are standardized, turned out like Fords by the hundred million, and we cannot endure for long anyone who is not standardized."[30]

Harding was an indefatigable source of platitudes which glorified America. Harding did not really need a debunker, for his writings and speeches sound like self-parodies. He began his campaign book of 1921 with the observation that "America is at the threshold of an era of good will." He proposed to keep govermental hands off business: "Let us put an end to holding success to be a crime." In addressing the American laborer he was evasive: "Work is the supreme engagement, the sublime luxury of life." He cautioned immigrants to "think of 'America First.' " He encouraged Americans to cultivate active recreations in order to work out "the poisons in good sweat." He ended by glorifying the American small town as the home of the democratic virtues: "There is more happiness in the American village than any other place on the face of the earth."[31] Harding and his administration seem incredible; even matter-of-fact accounts of his era sound exaggerated. The remnants of his presidential dignity were shattered in 1927 with the publication of *The President's Daughter.* Presumably written by his mistress, Nan Britton, the book told of her seduction by Harding, which resulted in the birth of a child, Elizabeth Ann. Many readers must have been more amused than shocked by the book, which was written with prurient coyness, and reads like a debunker's hoax.

Harding's less loquacious but more articulate successor, Calvin Coolidge, was elected on the basis of the same narrow Americanism. In his inaugural address, 4 March 1925, he piously insisted: "We believe that we can best serve our own country and most successfully discharge our obligations to humanity by continuing to be openly and candidly, intensely and scrupulously, American."[32] Harding and Coolidge were agile bunk-makers; it is not surprising that their era spawned debunkers. Coolidge in his demagogic simplicity was the arch-Puritan provincial to the debunkers. Gilbert, again, in a campaign book of 1924 called *You Takes Your Choice,* applied the "singed-cat" metaphor to Coolidge: "Like the singed cat, he is better than he looks." Gilbert's debunking irony was direct and irreverent; he did not publish anonymously, as he had in *The Mirrors of Washington.* He wrote that Coolidge's singed-cat nature had grown out of his Puritan background: "He 'walks humbly' because some of his Pilgrim ancestors found that it paid, here and hereafter."[33] Coolidge jokes were common conversational currency during the era of what was judged to be his phlegmatic inaction. One journal in particular, the *New Yorker,* established its sophistication by means of numerous Coolidge jibes.

Other aspects of Americanism which were treated in deflationary fashion were the exploits of explorer heroes and heroines, American adventurers on land, sea, and in the air, whose accomplishments were magnified and sometimes created by extravagant public-relations schemes. Corey Ford, who appeared frequently as parodist and humorist in *Vanity Fair,* parodied autobiographies and tales of adventure written by female explorers in *Salt Water Taffy: The Almost Incredible Autobiography of Capt. Ezra Triplett's Seafaring Daughter* (1929), and in its sequel *Coconut Oil: Jane Triplett's Amazing Book out of Darkest Africa* (1931). These books were illustrated with composographs for which Ford's friends obligingly posed. In 1926, the year Richard Evelyn Byrd flew to the North Pole in a monoplane, Ford also wrote a burlesque for the *New Yorker* called "The Pole at Last." It describes an expedition to the North Pole by Mr. Eustace Tilley, the bemonocled, top-hatted dandy who adorns the cover of the *New Yorker*'s anniversary issues.[34]

Wolcott Gibbs, staff writer for the *New Yorker,* was also reacting to Byrd's extravagantly publicized exploits when he wrote *Bird Life at the Pole* (1931). The publicity about American heroes and their exploits was and is often absurdly breathless and solemn. There were elements of the ridiculous and the pompous in what Byrd accomplished, and certainly coverage by the various media was in many instances excessively ecstatic and extreme in its chauvinism. Byrd unquestionably had a sense of the extravagantly dramatic; his character as well as his expeditions offered many opportunities for debunkers. His 1928 expedition to Antarctica was heavily sponsored; he imported a mountain of supplies and a small army of personnel; he managed to keep in constant radio communication with the outside world; he named mountain ranges for Rockefeller and Edsel Ford. In 1929 after flying over the South Pole he was greeted as a conquering hero and promoted to rear admiral by special act of Congress. He lectured and wrote books on his exploits for several years. There was as much of the ridiculous as of the sublime in his life and adventures; Ford and Gibbs did not miss the opportunity to parody accounts of what Byrd did.

Mencken and Nathan drew many of the "rhetorical gasbombs" through which they ridiculed Americanism from the pages of journals and newspapers. The development of the large syndicates, which standardized and actually made news through a process of selection, emphasis, and exaggeration, was a twentieth-century phenomenon. One journalist, Silas Bent, was concerned in *Ballyhoo: The Voice of the Press* (1927) with the changes that had come over American newspapers since the beginning of the century. He wrote that the Spanish-American War and the World War had spawned "gargoyle journalism," through which the public appetite for sensation was fed. Sports, crime, advertising, and illustrations were being emphasized and given two to three times as much space as before, while editorials, letters to the editor, and society news had shrunk to insignificance. Bent's style echoed the indignant tone of the muckrakers, with some infusions of humorous Menckenian hyperbole.

One expression of Americanism which received both debunking and muckraking treatment was American sport. Lardner expressed more and more his disillusionment with sports and athletes as heroes after the World Series fix of 1919. John R. Tunis, who wrote sports columns for the *New Yorker*, both muckraked and debunked sport in his 1928 book, *$port$: Heroics and Hysterics*. He objected to sport as big business. He exposed the "Great Sports Myth" as an aspect of Americanism, for, according to the myth, sports are competitive, and competition makes for nobility of character." The reality, he pointed out, is that "many, if not all, of our sporting gods are muscle-bound between the ears."[35]

Another latter-day muckraker was Stuart Chase, who in *Tragedy of Waste* (1925) criticized the excesses of capitalism, the heart and soul of Americanism. Chase did not attack capitalism itself. He criticized loss of manpower through the production of nonessentials and through faulty methods of production and distribution. He also cautioned against the waste of natural resources. In 1927 he teamed with F. J. Schlinck to write *Your Money's Worth: A Study in the Waste of the Consumer's Dollar*. As an exposure of advertising fraud it was, again, a muckraking book, but there was also mockery of consumers for their gullibility, mockery expressed with the debunker's authoritarian and joyful bellicosity. The American's anxiety about skillful consumption, which dates from the 1920s, was certainly extended and perhaps even created by the muckraking and debunking points of view.

The debunkers did not stop with ridicule of middle-class manners, morals, and patriotic attitudes. Another part of their gleeful scorn was directed at attitudes toward the arts. They identified and mocked the Philistinism of those who distrusted and disliked the arts, and who believed that literature was primarily a vehicle for information. They also reflected their own Philistinism in their hostile deflation of the manic artistic pretensions of middle-class aesthetes. The pattern for the satire of Philistinism had been set in the 1890s by Gelett Burgess of the *Lark* and Vance Thompson of *M'lle New York*, both editors of little magazines for small audiences who knew that they disliked the tastes in the arts of affluent Americans. The debunkers had little to add that was new in subject matter, attitude, or method, except their scorn for Bohemianism, even while they often enjoyed some of the advantages of the Bohemian life. Comic hostility was turned against what Mencken called the divine afflatus:[36] the urge to create, the call of art, which produced flourishing Bohemias in New York and Chicago after 1910.

Middle-class culture, whether manifested as Philistine rejection of the arts or as the pretensions of would-be aesthetes, was bad enough, but some of the debunkers discovered something they took to be much worse: mass culture, especially as conceived and perpetuated by Hollywood and the radio. They viewed aspects of mass culture in America with something of the squeamish censoriousness which they had ridiculed as the basis for middle-class morality. Thus they revealed once again something of their own backgrounds, traditions, and allegiances.

Mencken, as usual, was leader of the band. He saw American puritanism as the source of cultural Philistinism. More than once he attacked that aspect of New England culture, which, he thought, had set the dominant tone for American letters. He objected to the application of ethical notions of right and wrong to aesthetic problems. He concentrated his attack on the humanistic critics, the most sophisticated of Philistines, who supported the "decaying caste of literary Brahmins." "You will spend a long while going through the works of such typical professors as More, Phelps, Boynton, Burton, Perry, Brownell and Babbitt before ever you encounter a purely aesthetic judgment upon an aesthetic question."[37] Mencken identified a new group of writers in America who formed what he called "an undercurrent of revolt. . . . Skepticism shows itself: in the iconoclastic political realism of Harold Stearns, Waldo Frank and Company, in the groping questions of Dreiser, Cabell and Anderson, in the operatic rebellions of the Village." Mencken himself did more than anyone else in his time to direct and affirm the iconoclastic undercurrent of revolt. He immediately recognized the importance of Brooks's *America's Coming of Age* (1915); he noticed that Brooks had rewritten " 'The American Scholar' in terms borrowed almost bodily from 'Democratic Vistas'—that is to say, he prophesies with Emerson and exults with Whitman."[38]

Mencken's own most profound and enduring manifesto directed against those who knew rigidly what they liked in literature was the equally rigid essay, published in 1917, "Puritanism as a Literary Force." One of the results of the influence of puritanism on American life in the nineteenth century, Mencken wrote, was that men of "ability and ambition turned to political activity for self-expression." Literature and the other arts were left "to women and admittedly second-rate men." The result was a feminized literature "almost completely disassociated from life as men were then living it," and a consequence was that important writers (realists and naturalists) had few readers and little cultural effect. Another consequence, Mencken noted, was that most American humorists capitulated to the dominant Puritan-Philistine culture of their time. Even his favorite American writer, Mark Twain, was "the victim of his nationality," for, with the exception of only a few writings, Mark Twain was unable to "throw off his native Philistinism."[39]

Mencken identified himself with those who were in revolt against the sentimental literature of the nineteenth and early twentieth centuries. However, he ridiculed middle-class cultural aspirations that sought fulfillment in Bohemian life, with its exclusion of everything except art. To Mencken, the Bohemian rebellion was "sterile of direct results," although it had some redeeming aspects: "The poet hugging his Sonia in a Washington Square beanery and so giving notice to all his world that he is a devil of a fellow, is at least a better man than the emasculated stripling in a Y.M.C.A. gospel-mill, pumped dry of all his natural appetites."[40] Distrust and scorn for Bohemia were expressed by other debunkers, too. Marquis was the most persistent anti-Bohemian, but the attitude was shared by Woodward, Lardner, and Hemingway, and was inherited by West.

In his autobiography Hecht explained the meaning of art for his generation from, roughly, 1915 to 1925: "If you did not believe in God, in the importance of marriage, in the United States Government, in the sanity of politicians, in the necessity of education or in the wisdom of your elders, you automatically believed in art."[41] As editor of the *Chicago Literary Times* in 1923 and 1924, with the help of Maxwell Bodenheim, Hecht had debunked the cultural, political, and moral shortcomings of the middle class. The paper was especially a declaration of artistic independence. Hecht and Bodenheim aimed both playful and angry polemic at anyone who stood in the way of the antitraditional, modern movement in the arts. It was characteristic of most of the debunkers, however, that they ridiculed both traditionalists and antitraditionalists in cultural matters. Their attitude of dissent was provoked by any extremist position or point of view, whether avant garde or conservative. It was one of Mencken's comic affectations to consider the creative act itself as a way of relieving a condition of flatulence. Marquis made Archy, his *vers libre* bard, a cockroach, while his flighty Hermione associated with "Hobohemians" and tried always to feel the "Cosmic Urge." Hemingway, in *The Torrents of Spring,* made his comic declaration of artistic independence through ridicule of what had for him become the affectations of his immediate mentors.

The first issue of Mencken's *American Mercury* contained an attack by Ernest Boyd entitled "The Aesthete, Model 1924."[42] In it Boyd ridiculed the aesthetes of the 1920s as pale imitations of the aesthetes of the 1890s. Born with the century, Boyd wrote, usually Harvard-educated, the aesthete began as a conformist and a Babbitt. Then a subtle change occurred, and he began to read *The Masses* and the *Little Review*. He went to war, where he avoided combat and edited the *"Doughboys' Dreadnought."* He became disillusioned and stayed on in Paris after the war. Eventually repatriated, he lived in Greenwich Village. His poems and a war novel were published. These creative efforts were "remarkable chiefly for typographical and syntactical eccentricities, and a high pressure of unidiomatic, misprinted French to the square inch," and for a "breathless phallic symbolism." His literary career took a new direction, Boyd continued, when he became a literary critic. His criticism consisted of a series of obscure *obiter dicta* upon works of art, and in this nonmethod he was very like the unknowing Philistines for whom he professed hatred. The aesthete was "the literary counterpart of the traditional American tourist in Paris." Gradually "an aesthetic of Philistinism" emerged. Typical of this aesthetic was the aesthete's discovery of the American "lively arts," and his application of obscure criticism "to matters within the experience and comprehension of the plain people." Eventually, Boyd predicted, the aesthete's aestheticism would disappear as his ingrained Philistinism reasserted itself; he would return "to the cosy hearth of the American family."

Boyd's hostile and satiric treatment was one of a series of portraits he wrote in 1924 for Mencken's *American Mercury*. Another of them was called "A Midwestern Portrait"[43] and was also an oblique attack on aestheticism. In it he wrote that midwestern intellectuals had been migrating to the East. Either as aesthetes or satirists these intellectuals became "boosters" for literature and culture by attacking Philistinism. Therefore, the midwestern aesthete was just a Philistine in new guise. The result of this homesteading on the sophisticated frontier of the East was simply "brighter and better Babbitts."

Boyd's 1924 *American Mercury* essays were collected in book form. He added to the "imaginary" portraits a note in which he described the reaction to them, especially the one called "Aesthete: Model 1924." He was bombarded, he wrote, with telephone calls, telegrams, and letters from "aesthetes," some of whom offered personal abuse or injury.[44] The principal retort was in the form of a one-issue magazine called *Aesthete, 1925*. It was published in February and included contributions from Allen Tate, Slater Brown, Kenneth Burke, Malcolm Cowley, John Wheelwright, Hart Crane, Matthew Josephson, and William Carlos Williams. Allen Tate relates that the magazine was written one Saturday night (and Sunday morning) in January 1925 at a New York hotel.[45] The magazine's exuberant satire was directed against Ernest Boyd, and Mencken and Nathan as the editors of the *American Mercury*. It also dealt in general with those critics who in their criticism concentrated not on the work of art itself but on matters peripheral to the work. Thus Brooks was ridiculed as a literary sociologist, Santayana was mocked for his philosophical bias, Paul Elmer More for his insistence that a work of art have moral content. Mencken was viewed as a nationalist in literary matters; he was called "an American Eagle." Boyd's portrait of the aesthete was criticized by Matthew Josephson with the stricture that he had offered no "reasoned opinions as to the direction of taste, for discovery, or constructive proposals. . . . Mr. Ernest Boyd is a fundamentalist!" Slater Brown was more exuberant than angry, for his attack on Boyd took the form of a parable. He ridiculed Boyd's method as a series of unrelated accidents and coincidences, and likened Boyd's creative impetus to a sparrow's (a "boid's") excrement. The back cover of the magazine was an advertisement for the "Mencken Promotion Society." The pitch was "Get Self Respect Like Taking a Pill—Menckenise!"

In the Boyd-aesthete controversy debunkers and counter-debunkers attacked each other with sometimes extraordinary extravagance and hostility. In 1925 a segment of the intelligent reading public was disenchanted with Mencken and the new *American Mercury*. Mencken had been the dominant critical voice in America for over five years. Some readers were tired of his prejudices; he was being left behind by the cultural movement of the 1920s. To those who were seeking a genuine aesthetic he was coming to seem boorish and reactionary.

In *The Torrents of Spring* (1926), Hemingway ridiculed both Mencken and aestheticism. The book was dedicated to "H. L. Mencken and S. Stanwood Mencken [*sic*] in Admiration." Linking these two names together was an insult to each, for S. Stanwood Menken was a vice-crusader whose antipathy for H.L. was as violent as H.L.'s for him.[46] The book is an extended debunking orgy. There are irreverent references to well-known literary figures; in addition to Mencken, Henry James and Willa Cather are among the writers ridiculed. Sherwood Anderson and Gertrude Stein are parodied, especially the Anderson of *Dark Laughter* (1925), and the Stein of *The Making of Americans* (1925). Hemingway was probably thinking of Henry Fielding's *Shamela,* a parody of Richardson's *Pamela,* when he decided to write *The Torrents of Spring;* there are quotations from

Fielding at several points, and also notes addressed to the reader, in
the manner of Fielding. Hemingway spoofed Anderson's elaborate
method of flashbacks, and commented upon the nonsensical method of
the narrative in the author's notes to the reader. Parody of Anderson's
style was more direct:

> Why shouldn't he work with his hands? Rodin had done it. Cezanne had been
> a butcher. Renoir a carpenter. Picasso had worked in a cigarette-factory in his
> boyhood. Gilbert Stuart, who painted those famous portraits of Washington
> that are reproduced all over this America of ours and hang in every school-
> room—had been a hod-carrier. James Russell Lowell had been, he had
> heard, a telegraph operator in his youth.

The parody here also echoes the tonal facetiousness with which members of a sophisticated generation addressed each other. We can hear
the same quality of voice in fiction by Marquis and Woodward. Lewis,
who could mimic anything, is reported sometimes to have talked like
this. In the characterization of Shrike, the newspaper editor in *Miss
Lonelyhearts*, West provides a coda for the tone in which many debunkers ironically assessed their world.

Part Four of *The Torrents of Spring* concentrates on parody of Gertrude Stein; it is called "The Passing of a Great Race and the Making
and Marring of Americans." Hemingway wrote: "Ah, there was a
woman! Where were her experiments in words leading her? What was at
the bottom of it?" And in a spoof of her style: "He had a new feeling. A
feeling he thought had been lost forever. Lost for always. Lost. Gone
permanently. What a botch he might have made of life. Killing himself.
Let Spring come now. Let it come. It couldn't come fast enough. Let
Spring come."[47]

Some of the writers attacked by parodists were considered to be
panderers to the needs of Philistine audiences for simplified information
about a rapidly changing and complex culture. Other writers who became subjects for parody were those whose rejection of traditional,
moral, and usually sentimental nineteenth-century literature had led to
an aesthetic glorification of the work of art for its own sake. Stewart was
one of the best parodists. In *A Parody Outline of History* Stewart deflated the styles of Cabell, Lewis, Fitzgerald, Lardner, Burgess, Wharton, and O'Neill. Other parodists who appeared frequently in *Vanity
Fair* or the *New Yorker* were Ford (alias "John Riddell") and H. W.
Hanemann. Ford's parodies were collected in *Meaning No Offense*
(1928), Hanemann's in *The Facts of Life* (1930).

At the heart of the debunking attitude was a sense of the offensiveness and even destructiveness of over-inflated language. Therefore, chauvinistic interest in the past and popularizations of history were often subject to parody. In *A Parody Outline of History* (1921) Stewart took the debunker's stance when he contended that H. G. Wells's *Outline of History* (1920) had not dealt with *all* the important events in American history. Hendrick Willem Van Loon was another popularizer of vast subjects whom Stewart must have had in mind (*A Short History of Discovery*, 1918; *Ancient Man*, 1920; *The Story of Mankind*, 1921). In the process of parodying this state of historical overinclusiveness, he debunked puritanism, Prohibition, expatriation, and the extravagant ideology created to justify the war that was to make the world safe for democracy.

In 1923 Stewart assumed the bedtime-story manner of Thornton W. Burgess to write *Aunt Polly's Story of Mankind*. Subtitled *From Jelly-Fish to Uncle Frederick, or; The Ascent of Man*, the book ridiculed the staunch Americanism of the Anglo-Saxon, Protestant middle class. The book was a parody of what Barnes had called the "drool method." Uncle Frederick is a successful businessman who believes in Christian principles and the teachings of Benjamin Franklin; Aunt Polly is a prim defender of the values and virtues that go with their station in life. The book tells the story of what happens as Aunt Polly indoctrinates her nieces, nephew, and son in the evolution of mankind to its present perfect embodiment in the middle-class American. It is Aunt Polly's belief that "the great need for the younger generation is a return to the safe and sane standards of before the war." The book ends with a description of the Armistice Day pageant of the progress of mankind, as directed by Aunt Polly. The parts in the pageant are to be played by a group of youths known as the Christian Scouts and by the members of a rival marching group: " 'Mankind,' aided by 'Peace' and 'Big Business' and 'Finance' and 'Christianity' was to take up the torch and hold it high and 'History' was to smile happily and step to the front of the stage and ask all the audience to join in singing the 'Star Spangled Banner.' "[48]

A more general mockery of the Philistine's desire to have all human knowledge displayed neatly on library shelves was a burlesque called *The Outline of Everything*. Published in 1923, it bore the name "Hector B. Toogood" on the title page, but its sophisticated facetiousness and unrelieved irony are very like Stewart's. The *Outline of Everything* was also a parody of H. G. Wells's *Outline of History*. Both Wells's massive inclusiveness and his pompous simplicity were ridiculed; one section in the *Outline of History* begins "Biologists, that is to say, students of life."[49] It is the facetious aim of *The Outline of Everything* to provide "the sum total of Human Knowledge in *one* volume." To this end "a system of classification by terminations" was adopted. The "Ologies," such as Biology, Psychology, Theology, are taken up first, followed by the "Tures" (Literature, Agriculture), then the "Utions," the "Ics," the "Ographies," the "Osophies," the "Isms," and the "Onomies." This system provides material for other debunking subjects; for example, the section on the "Ographies" subdivides the world "into countries that are *dry* and countries that are *wet.*" The section on philosophy provides a novel pedagogy: "Every night before I go to bed, I myself visualize at least one branch of human knowledge." Toward the end of the *Outline* there is a chapter entitled "How to Prepare an Outline at Home in Your Spare Evenings." And finally, there is included "A Bedtime Story of Mankind" in which the underlying hostility of the book toward an emasculated cultural condition is more directly expressed: "we have seen how the Mid-dle Ages was the age of the School-men. It fol-lows log-ic-al-ly that the pres-ent day is the age of the school-marm."[50]

"John Riddell" (Corey Ford) laughed at Van Loon's exasperating metaphor-making in a 1927 parody, published in *Vanity Fair.* Van Loon is "reported" to have said:

> History is a suspender-button. It ties up the past with the future. Its right to exist depends entirely upon this ability to hold up the past to the present. As long as it covers the facts we are content.
>
> But as civilization gradually grows a little older, yea, and stouter, and fuller, the strain upon history becomes greater. And finally, one fine day, pop! goes our suspender-button, and down comes the past and for a moment we see the facts of existence.[51]

Parody satirizes the creators of verbal excess whether they be politicians, Philistines, aesthetes, or writers for whom in another place and time the parodist may have felt genuine respect. The debunker operating as parodist was expressing oblique concern about the affliction of distorted, deceptive language upon the sensibilities of those who love words and their power above all else—who feel intensely that at the very least the word should be cousin to the deed. The abuse of language was, in the ears of the debunkers, the major offense committed by provincials, Puritans, patriots, Philistines, and aesthetes. What the Babbitts and Coolidges and, sometimes, Gertrude Steins said and wrote was more horrifying than what they did, for they sometimes said or wrote the-thing-that-was-not.

Another effect of the excited flatulence that produced art in America was identified by the debunkers as mass culture, which they conceived as the expression of both middle-class Philistinism and aestheticism. Mass culture, after the enthusiasm for the lively arts that ran rampant in the 1920s, became in the eyes of some sociologists and critics the ogre of American life. The tabloids, the pulp magazines, radio, and Hollywood were blamed for this neo-Philistine, American travesty of sophistication. Mass culture meant sensation rather than feeling, sentiment rather than sensibility, platitude rather than idea. Some of the debunkers in the late 1920s were among the first to express their concern over aspects of mass culture. For example, in *Off the Arm* (1930) Marquis identified Hollywood as a major source of cultural banality. At about the same time Lardner satirized another source in a series of columns on radio. Underlying their satire was a sense of horror; residual Puritan instincts shared by all the debunkers shaped their responses. However, mass culture metastasized with deadly vigor. One manifestation of the disease appeared ironically at the height of Mencken's reputation as prober in the cultural muck of America. The *Smart Set,* shortly after Mencken left it, became in 1924 an organ for everything that Mencken disdained and ridiculed in American life, a travesty of its former self. It was acquired by a Hearst-owned subsidiary, and the first editorial under the new management asserted: "We believe in the American people. We believe in Main Street. We believe in the farmer, the laborer, and the mechanic. To *Smart Set* we comprise one people, indivisible, with our eyes set on a goal."[52] Mencken's reaction to this direct challenge to all he stood for has not been recorded, but we can imagine that his delight must have been as great as his pain.

What Mencken wrought was a change in attitude toward American culture. Most of the materials and subjects for his craft were already at hand. His was not an inventive skill, but the craft he fashioned was a powerful force that was rooted in earlier American experience and style. We see his influence everywhere in the 1920s. Both influence and parallels in career and attitudes are reflected in others of his generation, notably in Lewis, Marquis, and Lardner.

# Chapter Seven
## The Mimic as Artist: Sinclair Lewis

Institutions . . . insinuate their tyranny under
a hundred guises and pompous names, such as
Polite Society, the Family, the Church, Sound Business,
the Party, the Country, the Superior White Race;
and the only defense against them, Carol beheld,
is unembittered laughter.

*Main Street,* 1920

A n early story about Lewis, told by a contemporary, illustrates his
eager mimetic ability, a lifelong characteristic. Lewis's new stepmother had taken him to call on the DuBois family in Sauk
Centre, Minnesota; it was 1892 and Lewis was seven years old.
Ben DuBois, who was slightly younger than Lewis, recalled that Lewis
"raced about on the lawn on his hands and knees, his face on the
ground, crying, 'I eat grass like cows!'—and ate it."[1] Probably it was a
good imitation, if we can judge by Lewis's extraordinary mimetic skills
throughout his life, but obviously the most striking thing about it in the
memory of Ben DuBois was its weirdness as a social gesture.

As every child learns sooner than later, imitation can be used for
satiric effect—that is, it can become parody. The situation into which
the parody is introduced can be as important as the imitation itself; the
weirdness of Lewis's cow-imitation suggests that in some mixed, probably partly conscious way, it was designed both to please and to offend.
This double impulse lies behind Lewis's lifelong mimetic compulsions
and is also a motivation for an aspect of his writing. Again and again
Mark Schorer, in his biography of Lewis, describes the astonishing and
diverse mimetic performances with which Lewis regaled and often overwhelmed or bored those whose attention he captured in his desperate

need for applause and appreciation. For example, Schorer quotes Vincent Sheean's description of one Lewis performance at a party in Berlin when he imitated the styles of Vachel Lindsay, Longfellow, Swinburne, and Tennyson: "The rhymes and meters were perfect, the parodies so keen that even the Germans did not need to be told what they were. . . . I have never heard anything like those improvisations" (p. 492). And of the same occasion, Dorothy Thompson, Lewis's second wife, said: "We all sat with our jaws dropped. No one had ever witnessed such a tour de force, or likely ever will again. Lewis threw away, on his friends or casual companions, enough talent to have made another writer" (p. 492).

Mimetic skills demand a certain quality of detachment, an ability to listen, to observe, to analyze with an ear finely tuned to both the spoken and the written word. Lewis's researches for his novels had a kind of sociological thoroughness, a capacity for the accumulation of copious details about the surfaces of reality. Part of this capacity is like that of the muckraking journalists, whose attitudes and styles dominated the media during his college years; Sinclair praised *Main Street* as "a lovely job of muckraking" (p. 300). His ability to reflect the reality of particular American types, then to exaggerate it, or make it grotesque, had its basis in his mimetic skill. His novels, like Lardner's short stories, are full of the energy and rhythms of American speech. Among his best mimetic characterizations are George Babbitt, Elmer Gantry, and Lowell Schmaltz (especially of *The Man Who Knew Coolidge*). Indeed, Schmaltz and Gantry move beyond the illusion of reality to become grotesque composites of what Mencken called the American boob and the preposterous Puritan demagogue.

With the publication of *Main Street* in 1920, Lewis became a success as a writer and a central literary interpreter of American culture. His influence extended through the 1920s and culminated in 1930 with international recognition for *Main Street, Babbitt,* and *Arrowsmith,* which brought him the Nobel Prize. This award was in a sense an affirmative action decision on the part of the Nobel Committee, which had first determined that an American writer would be the winner (Theodore Dreiser was the runner-up). In the words of Anders Osterling, a member of the committee, they wished "to recognize a vigorous trend in modern literature—high class American humor, the best traditions of which had been continued with such marked success by Sinclair Lewis" (p. 547). That "high-class American humor" is the satirical humor of the group headed by Mencken and exemplified by Lewis, Marquis, and Lardner. Lewis was the best known in Europe of these writers, and he was perceived to be in a tradition that evolved most immediately from

Mark Twain. He also, as Schorer writes, "shared in another tradition, the tradition of provincial manners as depicted by Midwestern and Western humorists—George Ade, Artemus Ward, Josh Billings, Finley Peter Dunne" (p. 289). Part of Lewis's mimetic skill lay in his imitation of their success at rendering the patterns of American speech.

But Lewis's gift was unique and his extraordinary ear for words spoken and written went beyond the imitation of the American stereotypes that many European (and, for that matter, American) readers found in his fiction. There was something more to his writing than the revelation and ridicule of the crass, materialistic, superficial lives of Americans in the Midwest. Lewis's satire becomes at its best an ironic vision: two of his characters, Carol Kennicott and George Babbitt, discover and endure the imprisonment of modern life in ways that touch upon modern experience whether it be American or European. For each, conflict leads to the imagination of rebellion. The imagery of warfare, which Lewis uses to objectify conflict, is implicit in Babbitt's flirtation with rebellion, and is an explicit pattern in *Main Street* for delineating Carol Kennicott's disaffection with the values of her midwestern life and world. In writing a novel with a woman as its protagonist Lewis was deliberately following in a genre that includes (to name only two American heroines) Edith Wharton's Lily Bart and Dreiser's Carrie Meeber. *Elmer Gantry,* another book Lewis wrote before he received the Nobel award, derived from a novel of the late 1890s by Harold Frederic—*The Damnation of Theron Ware.* The similarities are remarkable. Lewis does not imitate or plagiarize Frederic; he transmutes Frederic's acerbic irony into his own devastating satire. This is mimetic activity of a very sophisticated sort: like any major writer Lewis made extensive and brilliant use of the literary tradition available to him. The grass he eats in this kind of mimetic rumination is very green indeed.

In choosing to write a novel about a woman Lewis was responding to a current issue in American life. Like Mencken and some of the other writers of his generation, Lewis recognized the tension created by the shifting attitudes of women during a period of political emancipation and social change. Like Mencken, Lewis sympathized with the needs of women to create lives for themselves free of the ordinary domestic values of traditional middle-class American life. Carol Kennicott is a woman who, subject to these changes, struggles for self-definition. George Babbitt also experiences a struggle for a new sense of self, and at least imagines a condition of freedom from many of the same values that confine Carol Kennicott.

The dilemma of women in assessing and in breaking out of the conditions of middle-class life was also the dilemma of the middle-class novelist, and Lewis sensed the similarity. The dilemma both for women and Lewis was that of loving and depending emotionally upon what must be changed or left behind in seeking new conditions of self-fulfillment and achievement. Like Carol Kennicott and George Babbitt, Lewis had early in his life questioned the values of the comfortable, provincial world in which he was brought up. And, sometimes without knowing it, he found himself in conflict with that world's genteel expectations that one pursue a useful mercantile or professional career. Lewis lived the ordeal of the artist in a world indifferent or hostile to literature.

The first person in his life to tolerate his queerness was his stepmother. She played a very traditional role for him as a domestic authority essential to his sense of equilibrium, and part of the character and situation of Carol Kennicott must have derived from her.

His stepmother had married his father, the village doctor, when Lewis was seven. She became more than a stepmother to him—she was "psychically my own mother" (p. 18), and perhaps his cow-antics were an attempt to gain her attention and approval. In a correspondence that began in 1903, when he went off to the academy of Oberlin College, and lasted until her death in 1922, he expressed his feelings and aspirations to her more than to any other person. As in so many middle-class homes she was the emotional center of the family, because the role of arbitrating feelings had been relegated or abdicated to her. She was the first audience for many of his earliest "literary" efforts.

Upon her death, Lewis wrote a letter to his father, using the rhetoric of formal grief; his letters to his father were always formal, dutiful, even when insisting on his own special vocation as writer-artist. Through the formality there are moments that reflect his sense of her special significance to his emotional life. While he describes her as "an eternal fact" and an "incessant influence," he thinks that "her life was a triumph," largely, the letter implies, because of her presence as the responsive center for his feelings. He does not describe her significance to his father directly—such statement of emotion would violate the puritanical restraints of the formal father-son relationship. But at the end of the letter there is a projection of his grief into the character he hopes really exists beneath the father's emotional reserve. He was living in England, and several letters he had written his mother did not reach their destination until after her death; he wrote to his father, "I hope, terribly, that it will not hurt you to have them coming for her." This imaginative, in effect literary projection is as close as we ever come to Lewis's real feelings. But his father, in response to a cable inviting him to assuage his grief by coming to England, maintained his distance: "The Roberts have moved into our house and are taking fine care of me and it leaves me with my old room all the furniture and things going on just as they have for years" (pp. 313–14). This distance was a function of the traditional patriarchal relationship. In fact, the father whom Lewis created imaginatively in what must have been an agony of longing seemed only to exist in his verbal projection.

Lewis was like his father in that his feelings remained private; and we can only guess what the emotion within must have been, or infer it from the sensitivity of his best characters. Schorer describes a life in Lewis's childhood and adolescent years lacerated by loneliness, by unfulfillable longings for human relationship and contact. Ugly and awkward, he was saved only by the mimetic skill which allowed him to achieve a sense of artistic grace and respite from the grief of being so different. So it seems natural and inevitable that he had begun to think of himself as a poet as early as 1901, when at sixteen he began to send verses to magazines such as *Harper's* (they were rejected). In 1902 he began the lifelong practice of keeping an account of his journeys, not as recollected in tranquility but as they occurred. The aesthetic value behind this practice was the value of immediacy, perhaps influenced by his readings of the sensational and seemingly successful muckraking reporters, whose exposures were above all timely. His devotion to literature had all the intensity of religion; he wrote in his diary in 1902: "To read books, to gaze at pictures, to wander through green fields and stately woods and by sapphire water, ever thinking and progressing ever, though slowly or swiftly, to the divine purity!" (p. 41). The passionate intensity of his self-consciousness is like that of the young Stephen Dedalus in Joyce's *Portrait of the Artist as a Young Man.*

In addition to his devotional passion for literature and his exploratory attempts to define himself as an artist, there were more traditional evangelical expressions. About a Y.M.C.A. meeting he wrote: "It impressed me very highly as an indication of positive earnest muscular Christianity" (pp. 97–98). His missionary zeal began very soon to center on his longings to be a poet or the writer of pretty poetic prose. He never seemed fully to discover that his true medium as a writer was to be in the immediacy of a reportorial prose. Nor is there any apparent source for the disaffection with organized religion that appeared rather suddenly in his diaries around 1903 and that became characteristic of his later writings. A similar disaffection with the middle-class world that had nurtured as well as hurt him as a child emerged during his sophomore year at Yale (1904–1905).

Perhaps this disaffection was a reaction that set in after the wild evangelical enthusiasms of his adolescence. Or perhaps it was because he could not "make it" in the genteel, clubby world of Yale College. Perhaps both of these reactions were operative, as well as a more general influence coming to him in the journals of the time. It had become popular to expose what seemed defective in some of the institutions of American life, to rake through the muck in order to salvage and cleanse what was of enduring value. His first published piece of writing, *The Critic* (1904), was an act of literary muckraking: he showed how a currently popular novel had been plagiarized from an older one (pp. 97–98).

By his sophomore year at Yale, he was acting as if he had discovered his vocation. He was sending out his stories, poems, songs, and articles to commercial publications before submitting them to the Yale *Lit,* which rejected many more than it accepted. If his true sense of vocation led him to seek the larger audience, he also had to find an audience, and seek recognition, outside of his immediate environment. Because he failed to be appreciated by his peers in the usual collegiate ways, he sought to create a sense of satisfaction as an artist and as a human being by studying and emulating the successes of other published writers.

From the time of his departure to Oberlin in 1903 until his death in Italy in 1951, he seemed constantly to be on the move, traveling across the country, across the oceans, making attempts (they always failed) to create "homes" in such places as Long Island, Connecticut, Vermont, Minnesota, England, Italy. Always he searched for a world elsewhere: geographically, in his human relationships, and in his imagination, lacerated always by his need for approval and affection. His stepmother had initially provided the support he needed, and again and again in a series of failed relationships with women he sought the emotional security that could only be generated by approval. His second marriage, to Dorothy Thompson, was the most spectacular of these failures—she was too intelligent and successful a woman to give the uncritical adoration that he craved and demanded. She was, at least in sensibility, the Carol Kennicott of his real life. The tragedy is that he could only apprehend and celebrate feminine integrity such as hers in his fiction.

Perhaps only late in his life—he was fifty-four—did he find the kind of female relationship that seemed to fill some of his needs. Marcella Powers was eighteen; she seemed to adore, even worship him, but also in obvious ways she was May to his January. He dominated her, or tried to, attempting to play the traditional male role of both lover and father.

There is a curious closing image for the centrality of the mother, and therefore of the woman, to Lewis's buried emotional life, and this is the figure of Mrs. Powers, the mother of Marcella Powers and the companion of his last years. Hemingway had met Lewis and Mrs. Powers in Venice. It was he who described her aptly (in *Across the River and into the Trees*) as "the elderly wholesome looking woman who was with him. She looks like anybody's mother in an illustration in 'The Ladies' Home Journal.' "[2] Lewis's relationship with her seems to have been quite formal and impersonal. If he could not have the daughter—she had developed other, younger interests—he could have her mother by buying her companionship in an odd and sometimes grotesque reconstruction of an older stepmother-son relationship: odd because she was a silent foil to his endless, often drunken verbosity, and grotesque because he treated her not as a human being but as a metaphor for a mother, a role she seemed to relish, prostituting herself, as it were, to his regressive emotional needs. He created her as a character and placed her in his life as deliberately as he created and placed characters in his fiction. She was an imitation, a mimetic, mother.

It is a sad irony that some of that mimetic skill so necessary to his best fiction spilled over into his life, where we find a pattern of ludicrous and sometimes tragic efforts to apply such skills to life itself, ranging from the weirdness of eating grass like a cow to the creation of a synthetic mother in a time of emotional need.

*Main Street* was in part a mimetic work because Lewis was responding to what his age demanded. It was an enormously popular novel, in large measure because Lewis recognized a state of mind and an irate posture that had begun to find satiric expression around 1910. Mencken was the central figure in the creation of this state of mind and posture. Lewis sought Mencken's approval in the writing of *Babbitt,* which is in a sense a sequel to *Main Street,* and he credited Mencken with helping him focus on the idea for *Babbitt:*

> A year ago in a criticism of *Main Street* you said that what ought to be taken up now is the American city—not NY or Chicago but the cities of 200,000 to 500,000—the Baltimores and Omahas and Buffaloes and Birminghams, etc. I was startled to read it, because that was precisely what I was then planning, and am now doing.[3]

In major book reviews Mencken enthusiastically reacted to all of Lewis's writings of the 1920s. He established and in some ways created Lewis's reputation as the most successful and most read American novelist of the decade. Lewis's sense of his role as a satirist derived from Mencken, and he was quickly labeled "Mencken's Minion." He imitated—or shared—Mencken's attitudes and ideas; it is difficult to draw a line between what was inspired by Mencken and what was original.

While he relished the popularity and success that came to him as Mencken's minion, he was at his best as a novelist when he was able to transcend his somewhat limiting reputation as a satirist. In his best work (*Main Street* and *Babbitt*) the satiric point of view is but one element of an ironic perspective that has signficant novelistic effects. Mencken too recognized his achievement as a novelist. What Lewis imitated especially in Mencken issued in the novels *Elmer Gantry* and *The Man Who Knew Coolidge,* novels in which the heroes became grotesques and in which satire overwhelms novelistic form and effect. Of these, *Elmer Gantry* (1927) is significant as a response to Mencken's cultural criticism because it reflects typical Menckenian attitudes; it also reflects Lewis's attitudes as an artist working in the tradition of the novel, while at the same time exploiting his reputation as a debunker.

Mencken, in his reaction to the failures of the progressive movement, had concerned himself more frequently and more indignantly than anyone else with what he took to be the source of moral repression in America: Protestantism, the predominant faith of the American middle class. "Faith," Mencken wrote in 1916, is "a mellow and caressing ecstacy, a benign and uplifting booziness."[4] According to Charles Angoff, his assistant editor on the *American Mercury,* Mencken carefully read Protestant publications, looking for items to run in the "Americana" section of the magazine. He kept up a custom of gleefully mocking the earnest ineptitudes of Methodists and Baptists well into the 1930s, even after many readers had expressed their boredom.[5] Lewis certainly was one of his faithful readers.

Protestantism, Mencken thought, had gathered to itself all the "imbecilities" that had accumulated in the church over the centuries and had cloaked them "with religious sanctions."[6] Due, apparently, to this accretion, the Protestant was caught between two tendencies in his church: one toward an emulation of Catholic orthodoxy and ritual, the other toward evangelism. In one essay on Protestantism, Mencken wrote that certain remedies had been concocted by the Protestant hierarchy in order to combat destructive tendencies. One involved consolidation and reorganization; another involved making the church a center for many extrareligious activities: this was "the scheme of putting bowling alleys and courting cubicles into church cellars, and of giving over the rest of every sacred edifice to debate on the Single Tax, boxing matches, baby shows, mental hygiene clinics, lectures by converted actors, movie shows, raffles, non-voluptuous dances, and evening classes in salesmanship, automobile repairing, birth control, interior decoration, and the art and mystery of the realtor."[7] Mencken's report on the increasing social function of the Protestant church was developed with both satirical and novelistic thoroughness in *Elmer Gantry*.

Lewis had accepted his public's and Mencken's estimation of him as a satirist when he wrote *Elmer Gantry*. He also had been influenced by Mencken's Baptist baiting, for his novel was dedicated to him "with profound admiration." In his "Essay in Pedagogy" (1926), Mencken had chastised novelists for not making use of "the most salient and arresting of American types." Among the types he listed was the evangelist: "the malignant moralist, the Christian turned cannibal, the snouting and preposterous Puritan."[8] Lewis responded with the characterization of the Reverend Elmer Gantry, which was an unrestrained attack on a segment of the Protestant clergy and on the public imagination that boosted such bigots and demagogues as Gantry to positions of influence.

Lewis's research for writing the novel proceeded with the care and sociological thoroughness that went into most of his books. To advise him, he gathered what he called his "Sunday School Class," a group of fifteen clergymen with whom he met in Kansas City once a week during 1926. At these sessions Lewis assumed the role of teacher and preacher rather than the one taught. As in so many other areas of his life and fiction, the distinctions between mimicry and real feeling became blurred—if indeed there ever was such a distinction for him. Schorer quotes one of the fifteen clergymen, who reported:

> Soul-shaking moments come when Lewis speaks with the passion of an Old Testament prophet, demanding, "What sacrifices do you make? What risks will you take to end these paralyzing influences which you tell me are creeping over your church? Who will give up his wife and children, house and bank account? Who will literally follow Jesus into loneliness, ridicule, and death?" Lewis had been reading the New Testament and its iron and flame have gotten into his blood. "Why do you men stay in pulpits and use terms that mean nothing to you, and repeat creeds you have denied to me?" (p. 449)

In the passion that we hear transmitted by Lewis there may have been a basis for implicit moral condemnation of Elmer Gantry, although rhetoric like this never occurs in the novel. But Lewis was clearly acting out a preacher-teacher role and thereby dramatizing a concept of the hero as a combination of preacher, teacher, and artist—a man of dedicated, lonely, Christ-like intensity who is capable of sacrifices for romantic ideals and values. He must also have been aware of his artistry as a mimic, and of the relation of that ability to his skill as a novelist. One ideal of the artist (the man of skill) as hero had already been dramatized by him in the character of Martin Arrowsmith (1926).

None of this ideal is expressed in the characterization of Elmer Gantry, for the book presents, as Schorer writes, a "nightmare image of a world that, totally empty of human value, monstrously, and without relief, parodies the reality" (p. 478). Lewis may have assumed that a moral measure for the satire of the book need only be implicit, or he may have assumed that his readers had come to *Elmer Gantry* via *Main Street, Babbitt,* and *Arrowsmith,* where moral perspectives and a concept of the hero are clearer. Mencken, at any rate, assumed the moral dimension; in writing about both Lewis and Lardner, he observed: "It is difficult, even for an American, to contemplate the American without yielding to something hard to distinguish from moral indignation."[9] Parody of reality is the central element in *Elmer Gantry* and in Lewis's next book, *The Man Who Knew Coolidge.* Parody carries its own measure of success; it is amoral and succeeds insofar as it creates an illusion of the reality of what it ridicules. The measure is aesthetic, not moral. For Lewis, the ultimate hero is the artist, that lonely novel-writing self who mimics and manipulates reality.

Gantry is a product of provincial Kansas. Educated in Baptist Terwillinger College and Mizpah Theological Seminary, he is thoroughly the product of an arid, narrowminded, bigoted midwestern culture; he is like the earlier George Babbitt in his Rotarian bumptiousness and avid Americanism, but he has neither Babbitt's saving grace of self-doubt nor Babbitt's vague sense of the shortcomings of his way of life. A large, handsome man, Gantry has a commanding physical presence: magnetic sexuality charged by a resonant, impressive voice. Temporarily fired from the ministry when apprehended on one of his drunken sprees, he falls in love with, and goes to work for, a woman evangelist. Together they are tremendously successful, and Gantry finds his true métier as a soul-saver and rabble-rouser; remembering his days as a football hero at Terwillinger College, he invents the "Hallelujah Yell": "Hallelujah, praise God, hal, hal, hal! / Hallelujah . . . !"

Sharon Falconer, the evangelist of "intense brooding femininity," is Gantry's female counterpart. She thinks of herself as "the reincarnation of Joan of Arc, of Catherine of Sienna [*sic*]"; some of Lewis's readers must have thought of Aimee Semple McPherson. Her sense of mission reaches a formidable intensity: she believes that "the next Messiah might be a woman, and that woman might now be on earth, just realizing her divinity."[10] An ex-stenographer from Utica, New York, she has gathered to herself the trappings of gentility: a new name, a southern mansion, the clothes, mannerisms, and artistic interests of what both she and Gantry believe is a higher, more sophisticated way of life. The scene in which she takes Gantry as a lover is both comic and grotesque. The mutual seduction occurs at the altar of a specially constructed chapel, the inner sanctum of her southern mansion. In this chapel not only is Christ represented in effigy, but also a profusion of pagan deities.

This setting and situation derive from a scene in Frederic's *The Damnation of Theron Ware* (1896), an earlier satire on an aspect of American puritanism, specifically, that of Methodists in upstate New York. (It is not a coincidence that Sharon Falconer comes from Utica, Frederic's birthplace.) Lewis drew substantially upon the most immediate and relevant novelistic model available to him; his mimetic impulse extended to another novel within a respectable tradition with which he wished to identify himself. He also indirectly established for his novel an aura of historical connection: writers of the 1890s had similarly located division and conflict in American culture.

Theron Ware is a preacher who is lured away from the austerity of the Methodist church by his vague, romantic apprehension of an orgiastic future. This future is embodied for him in a woman appropriately named Celia Madden. To Theron Ware she represents art and culture, and the dream of leisure, romance, and love—a sophistication similar to that which Sharon Falconer personifies for Elmer Gantry. Celia Madden too maintains an inner sanctum in her Greek revival home; Lewis was probably thinking of it when he described Sharon Falconer's chapel. The Celia Madden sanctuary is decorated with Christian paintings and Greek statuary; a piano, which looks at first like an altar, is in a central position. The scenes in the two books are similar in that in each the minister is seduced by his own romantic apprehension of the sophisticated paganism of his surroundings. Both Frederic and Lewis are unmistakable in their satiric intentions, and the surroundings they describe in realistic detail are grotesque. There is, moreover, a similarity in the structure of both books: in each a stifling, provincial, repressive, Protestant environment forms a common naturalistic background. There is a common irony in that although both Theron Ware and Elmer Gantry move toward more complete damnation, nothing is made of the original innocence of each. Neither is allowed the dignity of becoming aware of what he ought to be. The satiric aspect is savage; if there is a moral dimension against which to evaluate either, it is in each novel implied rather than stated or dramatized.

Elmer Gantry's damnation proceeds relentlessly. He saves himself in a cowardly way when the Waters of Jordan Tabernacle burns down. He works as a New Thought "psychologist" for a while, then takes a step up

in social prestige by deserting the Baptist faith in which he was educated; he becomes a minister of a Methodist church in Zenith, home of
George Babbitt and Lowell Schmaltz. Gantry begins his ascent as a
demagogue when he preaches for Prohibition and conducts a campaign
against vice. He rises further on the thesis that liberalism of any kind
leads to atheism. His respectability is crowned with an honorary degree
(Doctor of Divinity), acquired through a fund-raising deal he makes
with the university. He takes to radio broadcasting, and continues to use
race-hatred, vice-crusading prurience, and narrow-minded Americanism as the tools of his self-centered demagoguery. His grand scheme is
to combine all the reform and anti-vice organizations in the country
(and eventually in the world) into one association with Gantry as its
head and dictator. His uncontrollable sexuality delays him briefly when
he is blackmailed, but he outblackmails the blackmailers. At the end of
the book he is called to a large church in New York and at the same time
becomes executive secretary of the National Association for the Purification of Art and the Press. He moves confidently toward greater demagoguery on the slogan "We shall yet make these United States a moral
nation!"[11]

 Behind Lewis's tone of omniscient superiority we are persistently
made aware of a background of sinister forces and passions. We are
allowed no sympathy for Gantry, no sense of a violated humanity in
him. If we read Lewis sympathetically—if we share his implicit attitude
of disgust—then we also accept his method of partially relieving that
disgust through ridicule, mimicry, and laughter. Part of a culture is
ridiculed in *Elmer Gantry* for its provincialism, its hypocritical puritanism, its brutal, mechanical conformity. The same kind of cultural indictment formed the background of much of Lardner's writing; it was an
ingredient of Marquis's fastidious horror, partly relieved by humor; and
Mencken was its expository source. All of them condemned what they
took to be the moral hypocrisy of puritanism in American life. But so,
too, had Frederic. The evocation of Frederic's novel in *Elmer Gantry*
was deliberate. Lewis must have thought of himself as writing *Elmer
Gantry* within a tradition, however recent and however brief; this identification would, to his mind, lend a kind of mythological power and
authority to his novel, and help make it at least artistically respectable.

The popularity of *Elmer Gantry* was guaranteed when it was banned
in Boston and other places. Harcourt, Brace (Lewis's publishers) antici-
pated its success with a first printing of 140,000 copies, at that time "the
largest first printing of any book in history." Its initial sale was over
600,000, but eventually, Schorer reports, it was to be exceeded by total

sales of the earlier novels *Babbitt, Main Street,* and *Arrowsmith* (pp. 468, 473).

Artistic respectabilty is all he could have hoped for from *The Man Who Knew Coolidge,* which is a parodic tour de force, the extension to boring length of one of his cocktail-party imitations. It is an entirely programmed book. Its narrator, Lowell Schmaltz, is a minor character in *Babbitt,* a booster personified, with none of Babbitt's sensitivity or humanity. Lewis's delight in the book was that of the skillful parodist turning out yet another caricature in response to what he took to be public demand. It was a facile performance, spun out in a few weeks. For a Lewis book, it sold poorly.

Lewis's greatest achievement is in *Main Street* and *Babbitt.* In them satire and novelistic sensibility exist in a fruitful and generally controlled reciprocation, whereas in *Elmer Gantry* and expecially in *The Man Who Knew Coolidge* the impulse toward satire had proved dominant. This reciprocation becomes reflected in the metaphorical structures of *Main Street* and *Babbitt,* structures in which Lewis depicts a kind of warfare between a confining social mechanism and the romantic longings of the characters Carol Kennicott and George Babbitt for lives and worlds elsewhere.

Sometimes in the literature of the early twentieth century we find the metaphors of warfare, imprisonment, and escape, as aspiring writers like Lewis sought to define themselves in relation to the conflicts of American life. In an important book, Paul Fussell has shown the centrality of the metaphor of warfare in the modern imagination, and its sources both in the First World War and in some of the literature immediately preceding it. While his focus is on British writers, he suggests that his thesis may apply to American writers as well, and I believe it does.[12]

Of course, conflicts and antitheses had existed in American life from its beginnings, as had the experience of war. What was especially characteristic of the early twentieth century was a consciousness of the resultant tensions. A sense of conflict between East and West, culture and vigor, the Apollonian and the Dionysian, sophisticated and provincial, affected both Lewis's life and his writing. Schorer describes the result this way: "He stood in Main Street, midway between the 'East' and the frontier, only a little closer to the second than to the first, pulled toward both and free to choose neither" (p. 166).

The heroine of *Main Street* and the hero of *Babbitt* are powerless before the forces of provinciality, puritanism, and belligerent bad taste. The battle on the prairies was just as much a war as that in the trenches, and in both conflicts the participants experienced powerlessness. The consciousness of powerlessness is a characteristic of the literature of the 1920s; for that generation, war was more than an event, it was metaphor as well. The debunkers sought literary ways to deal with its effects. Intuitions of powerlessness are part of the orientation of many characters in early twentieth-century American literature; some examples are Carrie Meeber, Lily Bart, Martin Eden, McTeague. But these intuitions have extensive nineteenth-century sources as well, and both sources and analogues in European literature. The important twentieth-century distinction is the *consciousness* of loss or failure of power, with war as an expressive metaphor. Both the soldier and the artist have in common their attempts—sometimes their mad, deranged attempts—to find or create senses of coherence through the invention of connections and relationships.

*Main Street* dramatizes and illustrates the major concerns both of Lewis's fiction and of his life. His age recognized the conflict between provincial, rural values and urban, sophisticated values; the typical means of expression was satire. Lewis accepted the satiric mode, and yet there was something more, because he was so profoundly a provincial himself. In *Main Street,* and somewhat less in *Babbitt,* the provincial Midwest is represented in oxymorons: again and again images of ridicule are set beside images of affection, hate beside love, revulsion beside attraction, death beside life. As a child of the middle class, the inheritor of its idealism and materialistic aspirations, Lewis was agonized by a conflicting sense of the murderousness and repression of humanity that could at times be the results of those hopes and aspirations.

In much of *Main Street* the conflict between attraction for and revulsion against Main Street life is deliberately, although unevenly, constructed. Lewis's own ineffable longing for identification with his heroine is expressed initially with sentimental uncertainty in the opening lines: on seeing Carol "the heart of a chance watcher on the lower road tightened to wistfulness over her quality of suspended freedom." But also on that first page he sketches part of a controlling mythological framework for the novel—he introduces a sense of the frontier's recent passing, as Carol's "quality of suspended freedom" becomes focused by the adjective "rebellious" and her sensibility implied by the adjective "bewildered": "The days of pioneering, of lassies in sunbonnets, and bears killed with axes in piney clearings, are deader now than Camelot; and a rebellious girl is the spirit of that bewildered empire called the American Middlewest."[13] Sentimental language becomes modified by ironic detachment as the narrator's voice takes on tonal assurance, and a structure for irony is created, as it were, before our eyes.

What Lewis does better in *Main Street* than anywhere else is to see his heroine and her midwestern environment satirically yet sympathetically. He develops his mythological framework carefully. Carol is given a vision of the "northern Middlewest" as "the newest empire of the world": "a land of dairy herds and exquisite lakes, of new automobiles and tar-paper shanties and silos like red towers, of clumsy speech and a hope that is boundless" (p. 24). This vision is Lewis's vision, too, and while it comes to be deflated it is never canceled out. Lewis is careful to sketch in one of its sources: Carol comes from a town in Minnesota which "in its garden-sheltered streets and aisles of elms is white and green New England reborn" (p. 6). She has her roots in an old-world America and her vision of paradise derives from the old Puritan one of the garden. That haunting sense of an ideal landscape is always with her, as it was for Lewis, too.

Carol's vision is abruptly and devastatingly altered by her first view of Gopher Prairie: "Oozing out from every drab wall, she felt a forbidding spirit which she could never conquer" (p. 34). But Lewis immediately juxtaposes her view to that of Bea Sorenson, a farm girl, who sees bigness and firmness and loveliness everywhere. Neither view is meant to prevail, both are satirized, Carol's for its affectations and Bea's for its oafish simplicity. Somewhere in between there is a mediating ironic perspective; here Lewis is at his best, and his book succeeds best as a novel when this perspective is sustained and controlled.

But there are many places, especially in the second half of the novel, where the author's voice intrudes, often in Mencken's mock-indignant tones, to ridicule aspects of small-town behavior and mentality. Again and again Lewis insists with evangelical fervor that Gopher Prairie and Carol Kennicott have thousands of look-alike counterparts throughout the country; Gopher Prairie is but one manifestation of an epidemic. The tendency toward generalized polemic destroys the finer irony of which the book is often capable, while long set speeches mimicking the extravagances and stupidness of Gopher Prairie boosters satirize provincial complacency. This aspect of Carol's repressive environment is presented with numbing thoroughness. Perhaps Lewis had been too successful as a cocktail-party satirist, and could not bear to delete any of these practiced caricatures. He knew he had a theme—the exposure of American provincial mediocrity—that was popular and current, because Mencken had made it so. At times even Carol's sensitivity is forgotten and she sounds as deliberately and raucously irreverent as Mencken at his most boisterous.

But sometimes he achieves for her a larger significance. She becomes a twentieth-century heroine, even while her passion has a comic intensity, because she articulates the feelings of women. Lewis has Carol say about "the darkness of women":

> We're all in it, ten million women, young married women with good prosperous husbands, and business women in linen collars, and grandmothers that gad out to teas, and wives of underpaid miners, and farmwives who really like to make butter and go to church. What is it we want—and need? Will Kennicott there would say that we need lots of children and hard work. But it isn't that. There's the same discontent in women with eight children and one more coming—always one more coming! And you find it in stenographers and wives who scrub, just as much as in girl college-graduates who wonder how they can escape their kind parents. What do we want? . . . I believe all of us want the same things—we're all together, the industrial workers and the women and the farmers and the negro race and the Asiatic colonies, and even a few of the Respectables. It's all the same revolt, in all the classes that have waited and taken advice. I think perhaps we want a more conscious life.
> (p. 201)

This polemic is given an ironic context when a few pages later Carol's sensitivity is rendered trivial: Lewis objectifies her loneliness and discontent by having her wistfully overhear a flirtation between the servant girl, Bea, and Miles Bjornstam, an amiable local radical. Through her romantic yearning, Lewis dramatizes the insidious limitations her culture imposes upon her capacity to imagine. In other scenes he represents traditionally "feminine" fantasies in Carol: she longs to escape to exotic places, sometimes with a lover; she attempts, with "religious fervor, a surge of half-formed thought about the creation of beauty" (p. 217), to transform the cultural life of Main Street. We see her powerlessness before romantic fantasies that are characteristic of the culture she wishes to escape.

Sometimes Lewis treats the women's suffrage theme with heavy male-chauvinist ridicule. Carol talks with a "generalissima of suffrage" who says: "You have one thing. You have a baby to hug. That's my temptation. I dream of babies—of a baby—and I sneak around parks to see them playing" (p. 441). While his view of the dilemma of women is sympathetic, here the compulsion to undercut the more strident tones of the feminist movement prevails. This double perspective was Mencken's, too.

There are other places where clumsy satirical intrusion violates the finer novelistic context. For example, the narrator describes what Carol really finds attractive in the younger, artistic Erik Valborg: "It was not Erik to whom she must escape, but universal and joyous youth, in classrooms, in studios, in offices, in meetings to protest against Things in General" (p. 361). This voice is that of a novelist explaining; there is no implicit ironic judgment of her matronly romantic urges. And sometimes the narrator's interpretations are so heavily sarcastic as to be ludicrous. For example, there is this moment in the genteel flirtation between Carol and Erik, when he visits her house in the absence of her husband: "It is women who are the calm realists once they discard the fetishes of the premarital hunt" (p. 368).

So the ironic tone is not consistent in *Main Street*. Many of the violations seem designed to please diverse elements among Lewis's readers, as if in his plan to write something novel he had deliberately introduced attitudes and subjects he knew were current and contemporary. However, there is also in *Main Street* a more detached, Joycean irony, through which Lewis shows how Carol longs for liberation from Main Street life. One dimension of her longing is perceived by Lewis as the rebellion of a woman against the male-dominated values of that life, and her vision is both personal and political.

Carol has the urges of the pioneer to escape the pressures of time and place and seek a world elsewhere. She tries to satisfy these urges by actual travel—to a neighboring town, to California, to New England, New York, Washington—or by fantasy. But at the end she returns in time to a specific place, to Gopher Prairie, and to a commitment to accept and transform that place. Lewis makes this return powerful by showing us the extent to which her feelings have been conditioned by the myth of the frontier, by its romantic associations of limitless expectation and opportunity. The myth is preserved with the potential for transformation, but about that transformation Lewis is finally ambiguous, and the mediating tone through which he represents the ambiguity is ironic. Lewis's control is at its most impressive when he shows us how Carol's feelings are released or generated by visions of landscape or of the natural world. For example, immediately following her meditation about the Middlewest, Carol's feelings are objectified for us in a striking development of pastoral imagery:

> The grass beside the railroad had been burnt over; it was a smudge prickly with charred stalks of weeds. Beyond the undeviating barbed-wire fences were clumps of golden rod. Only this thin hedge shut them off from the plains—shorn wheat-lands of autumn, a hundred acres to a field, prickly and gray near-by but in the blurred distance like tawny velvet stretched over dipping hillocks. The long rows of wheat-shocks marched like soldiers in worn yellow tabards. The newly plowed fields were black banners fallen on the distant slope. It was a martial immensity, vigorous, a little harsh, unsoftened by kindly gardens. (p. 25)

Carol is approaching Gopher Prairie for the first time, and clearly it is as if she is entering a battlefield, with its charred devastation, barbed wire, and stubble as if from the effects of bombardment. We are told that her view of the prairie is objective, but she is not conscious of its significance, although she feels it. What she *is* conscious of is that "all this working land was turned into exuberance by the light. The sunshine was dizzy on open stubble; shadows from immense cumulus clouds were forever sliding across low mounds; and the sky was wider and loftier and more resolutely blue than the sky of cities" (p. 25). These images objectify the ambiguity that lies at the heart of *Main Street:* Gopher Prairie exists in an environment that is both a natural paradise and a land wasted as if by warfare. There is a pattern of descriptions like this one embedded in the structure of *Main Street.*

At the end of the novel Lewis closes with a scene that includes a final version of pastoral imagery, and the ironic effect is remarkable. Carol is returning from duck hunting, where she has just learned to shoot a gun; she now feels like a veteran on the symbolic battlefield:

> She looked across the silent fields to the west. She was conscious of an unbroken sweep of land to the Rockies, to Alaska; a dominion which will rise to unexampled greatness when other empires have grown senile. Before that time, she knew, a hundred generations of Carols will aspire and go down in tragedy devoid of palls and solemn chanting, the humdrum inevitable tragedy of struggle against inertia. (p. 450)

It is a moment of tragic resignation, given its power by Carol's image of a receding, endless frontier—as poignant an image as that of the receding green light in *The Great Gatsby.* Then Lewis deliberately interrupts this eloquent rumination with the sound of a human voice: " 'Let's all go to the movies tomorrow night. Awfully exciting film,' said Ethel Clark." Lewis, sure here, at the end of his novel, about the necessity for perspective, closes by mimicking the most banal of midwestern voices. The effect is ironic, the contrast of loving hatred, of ugly beauty is completed.

At the beginning and at the end, and in many places especially in the first half, Lewis wrote with the assurance of a novelist whose satire is both necessary and informing. His heroine and his landscapes prepare the way for Fitzgerald's *The Great Gatsby.* More than that: they may have made *Gatsby* possible.

One other side of Lewis's development needs to be explored in order to place his role and reputation as debunker in perspective. Like Mencken, Marquis, and Lardner, Lewis wanted to succeed as an artist, not as a satirist or humorist, and the novel was his medium. Again, mimesis is the essential element, and this time the pattern of influence can be found most immediately in Edith Wharton. Probably her central work for him was *The House of Mirth* (1905).

*Babbitt* (1922) illustrates Lewis's consciousness of the function of the satiric perspective in the construction of the novel; in *Babbitt* he worked more explicitly with elements that in *Main Street* were instinctive or implicit; he was fully conscious of himself as a craftsman-novelist. Part of this consciousness was expressed by his dedication of *Babbitt* to Wharton. *The House of Mirth* reflected her sense of a culture whose values in the early twentieth century were shifting ominously and irrevocably. At the center of those changes, both symptomatic and symbolic of them, was her perception of the changing role of women. This subject was a central one for Mencken, too, and Lewis had addressed it directly in his characterization of Carol Kennicott.

"I never had any choice," says Lily Bart, heroine of *The House of Mirth*. She is trying to assess what it would mean to be free from the complex social obligations demanded by the pursuit of money and material things. Her sense of entrapment by forces she cannot control or resist is like the entrapment that Lewis creates for Babbitt—although Babbitt never comes to realize as fully as she the futility of his position, nor is there for Babbitt a tragic termination in death. Nothing tragic nor even dramatic can ever happen to Babbitt.

Lewis was expressing more than admiration for Wharton's writing when he dedicated *Babbitt* to her; he was identifying a source for the ironic tone of his book. He was locating it among the American novels of manners, to be placed, he must have hoped, on a nearly empty shelf beside Wharton's novels and many of Henry James's. He was interested in the dominant, repressive effects of the social and cultural environment created by what he took to be the ruling class in America: the middle class of the Middlewest. Edith Wharton was interested in the effects of a similar dominance and repression, except that her turf was walked by New York society. *The House of Mirth,* which Lewis probably first read in 1905, when he was in college, illustrates the extent of his admiration.

While Babbitt is a character to be laughed at (primarily) and Lily one to be admired (primarily), they are most alike in their ambivalent feelings—shared by their creators—toward the classes that defined and circumscribed their existences. Neither these characters nor their creators could escape from worlds that are depicted with harsh irony, yet within which they find redemptive potential. New York society is as stupid and narrow as that of Babbitt's Zenith; the "Four Hundred" of the metropolis are as indifferent and hostile to genuine human sensibility as are the Boosters of Babbitt's little city. Both Lily and Babbitt are given depth by their unfocused and unfulfilled longing for freedom from the worlds of which they are so much parts. In each novel, landscape provides the imagery through which the longing for freedom is expressed; conversely, the metaphor through which the destruction or attenuation of freedom is described is that of the machine. The scene in which Lily Bart comes to the self-realization that she "never had any choice" is enacted in a lovely, quiet, natural setting: "The landscape outspread below her seemed an enlargement of her present mood, and she found something of herself in its calmness, its breadth, its long, free reaches." Suddenly this moment of clairvoyance and discovery—it is like reaching a "forbidden height" as if on climbing a mountain—is destroyed by the intrusion of a motor car, and this machine is the sign that brings her, powerless, back into the social mechanism that controls her. Her final awareness, shortly before her death, is expressed also in the figure of the machine, bringing to the surface a nexus of images that is the metaphorical structure of the novel: "I have tried hard—but life is difficult, and I am a very useless person. I can hardly be said to have an independent existence. I was just a screw or a cog in the great machine called life, and when I dropped out of it I found I was of no use anywhere else."[14]

Lewis found in Wharton's writing, and precisely, I believe, in *The House of Mirth*, figurative patterns for expressing the powerlessness of the individual caught up in a social and cultural mechanism. Babbitt's awareness of the power and pervasiveness of that mechanism can be just as explicit as Lily Bart's:

> He beheld his way of life as incredibly mechanical. Mechanical business—a brisk selling of badly built houses. Mechanical religion—a dry, hard church, shut off from the real life of the streets, inhumanly respectable as a top-hat. Mechanical golf and dinner-parties and bridge and conversation. Save with Paul Riesling, mechanical friendships—back-slapping and jocular, never daring to essay the test of quietness.[15]

Babbitt is given a sensibility and longing for self-definition that are meant to make his final acquiescence to his world all the more pathetic and ironic. Often this sensibility seems ludicrous, yet it is the only measure of Babbitt's depth as a character. It is clear that, in creating Babbitt, Lewis is mimicking—both loving and hating—an American type. Sometimes the strokes of love seem sentimental, and the ironic vision of the narrator-observer is lost. The novel begins in April, the cruelest month, with Babbitt dreaming fantasies of escape into a pastoral setting with a sexy fairy child. This is ludicrous, but it is also pathetic and touching. The setting for his dream is the cot on the sleeping porch of his house, where he sleeps winter and summer, expressive both of his conformity (every Floral Heights home has a sleeping porch) and of his vague yearnings to escape his life so as to enter a simpler world elsewhere, not dominated by the accumulation of things. As part of his rebellion, which is seen as a comic disaffection, he goes off with his one sensitive friend to an idyll in the wilderness, and Lewis invests the description of the landscape with heavy significance: "Over everything was a holy peace" (p. 148). Then Babbitt and his friend speak: "He patted Paul's shoulder. 'How does it strike you, old snoozer?' 'Oh it's darn good, Georgie. There's something sort of eternal about it' " (p. 149). The human voices in this garden are mimicked by Lewis in cadences that deliberately destroy the scene's sentimentality, but the idyllic power of the natural setting remains intact.

Babbitt's doubts about his standardized, mechanized life are redeeming doubts, and, vague as they are, it is out of those doubts that he shapes a brief rebellion from wife, home, business, club life, and the demands made on him for cheerfully conforming behavior. He is capable of a playful whimsy, as when we see him, plump and pink, squatting in his bathtub to shave. It is as if he wants to escape even the confinements of his own masculinity, for in a frivolous, slightly erotic, stereotypically "feminine" gesture, he shaves one of his legs. He is bored at his own dinner party. His need for freedom is powerful, even if it is just freedom from domestic life. Confronted by the risks of freedom he is as terrified and as much at a loss as was Lily Bart fifteen years before him.

Once he has doubted his world, it comes to seem absurd, but that is a perspective he cannot sustain. So he acquiesces and conforms, bound by the force of the city of Zenith, which, even before Babbitt's rebellion is completed, Lewis describes in this way: "More than mountains or the shore-devouring sea, a city retains its character, imperturbable, cynical, holding behind apparent changes its essential purpose" (p. 308). So the force of the city is stronger than the force of nature; it is part of Lewis's ironic purpose to create this pastoral conflict and to resolve it in this way. Babbitt's attempts at escape into a less standardized, more natural way of life are defeated. He is absorbed back into the complacency of urban middle-class culture. There is no escape for him, no hint even of such a redemptive, if melodramatic death as comes to Lily Bart. But

Babbitt's situation as well as the figure of the repressive social mechanism had been derived by Lewis from *The House of Mirth*. Wharton admired *Babbitt*—although not without criticism of its endless caricatures of midwestern manners—and recognized that Lewis's real achievement grew out of his response to the quality of her irony: a novelist's recognition of influence and mimetic activity of a high order.

When Lewis went to New York in 1910 (like Lardner, Marquis, and many other aspiring midwesterners) it was with the clear conviction that he was "born a writer," as he wrote to his father (Schorer, p. 173). He kept to this goal with a lifelong religious dedication. He was bitterly resentful of critics who praised him for the accuracy of his pen, for his sociological amplitude, but never talked of his skill as an artist (p. 320). He was not closely identified with the resurgence in cultural life that animated New York during these years, but he did share the great respect for Wells and Shaw current at the time. He lived in Greenwich Village, consciously an artist, but remained skeptical about the Bohemia that flourished there: he called it "Hobohemia" perhaps because he was not accepted by its society.

He worked hard at being an artist, and this work often meant to him the writing of poetry. These poems are terrible, as was much American poetry during the first decade of the twentieth century. Shortly before he died he was still trying to write poems, often in rhyming couplets, as if at least the form of a long tradition of English satiric poetry were on his mind. Some of these poems were intensely personal and introspective. Two of them close in images of the monastery and of the monastic life, as if his long religious dedication to art were figured forth in final metaphors of withdrawal and penitence (p. 802).

Dorothy Thompson identified the character of his devotional commitment to the art of writing: "You aren't a husband or a lover or a father but a person of expression, a man of words, who positively presses words into and out of anyone who feels you closely" (p. 622). The sexual metaphor she uses to describe the urgency of his need expresses the erotic quality of his violent devotion to language. Her metaphor also shows the terrible limitations of his emotional nature: the expression of passion was only possible for him through his art. He had none of the capacity for tenderness that a husband-lover-father needs for even ordinary human relationships. Something of the same lack—at times under the guise of simple emotional reserve—appears in other men of his generation, as does a similar ambivalence toward women.

So it was his religion of art that sustained him through a lifelong series of failed human relationships. The novel *Work of Art* (1934) illustrates his commitment to art clearly. It also affirms the midwestern, middle-class values that his works of the early 1920s had in some aspects de-bunked. In *Work of Art* there are two brothers, counterparts, one an affected literary type, the other a solid and true hotel manager. The literary brother is very like Lewis as he had been when a boy; he is one of Lewis's caricatures, this time of himself, in what seems to be a ritual of purification through artistic confession. The hotel-manager brother is depicted as the real artist; his work of art will be the transformation and management of a tourist court in Kansas. We are a long way from Carol Kennicott, whose disaffected sensibility is more credibly that of the artist. It is also a long way from Arrowsmith, another artist-hero in the Lewis canon. Arrowsmith's art is that of the doctor, and Arrowsmith is an idealistic, rebellious, optimistic hero, a Babbitt transformed.

The satire in his best novels was the vehicle for effects that accurately delineated conflicts within the American character, both female and male, at a time when so many elements of American life were shifting irrevocably. The popularity of *Main Street* and *Babbitt* goes beyond their appeal as narratives (Lewis's structures are typically episodic rather than narrative), beyond their currency as books debunking provincialism, puritanism, and Americanism, to their clarity of characterization. Carol Kennicott and George Babbitt are American types because they are reflective of the aspirations and frustrations of middle-class Americans caught up in a complex social and cultural mechanism they seem power-less to control. They are manifestations of twentieth-century heroines and heroes for whom there are no dramatic solutions—only violated sensibilities and existences made meaningful (in Carol's case) by the love of art or (in Babbitt's case) by immersion in the amicable social interac-tions of friends and neighbors. Lewis was serious about his own love of art, and yet he could, in the 1920s at least, ridicule such seriousness as affectation. He was serious in his own need for amiable social interac-tions, and yet he could mimic the need and the process.

Lewis's audience was enormous in the 1920s. Both *Main Street* and *Babbitt* penetrated deeply into the American consciousness, not just because they ridiculed provincial life and manners but also because they portrayed through imitation and mimicry aspects of the twentieth-century American's perception of self—the self with a sense of con-strained choices, with longings for freedom through the seeking of new landscape, new experience, in a world that seemed sometimes like a ponderous mechanism beyond human control.

All his life Lewis sought to become an artist with an appreciative audience: again and again he ate grass like a cow, hoping to please someone—anyone—with the quality of the imitation. But Lewis was not only skillful as imitator: he was responsive to the essential formulations about American culture in the literature immediately preceding and surrounding him. Mimetic skills were central to his fiction: his success as a satirist depended upon his ability to imitate the manners, attitudes, and voices of Americans in his time; his skill as a novelist turned upon a sophisticated mimetic capacity to derive imagery and structures from the tradition of the modern novel. Although its motivation may have been political, the Nobel Committee of the Swedish Academy showed considerable insight when it recognized in Lewis's work "a vigorous trend in modern literature." As an American writer Lewis transmitted to us a legacy from our past—a kind of ironic detachment that is to be found in our best literature and that informs some of our most vivid views of ourselves. Satire became in the best parts of his best works the vehicle for a vision of American life. Rourke has described Lewis's importance this way:

> Lewis turns his abundant fables into critiques and challenges, but the transcendent effect is the traditional effect: the American portrait, a comic portrait once more, has been drawn in amplitude. Babbitt takes a place beside the archetypal Yankee; and for the first time an archetypal native scene is drawn in Main Street.[16]

Compulsiveness about art, about what Mencken variously ridiculed and celebrated as the divine afflatus and as beautiful letters, was an animating force in the life of another midwesterner and contemporary, Don Marquis. Marquis, like Lewis, sought to transcend his reputation as a debunker and make his way as a poet, essayist, and writer of "serious" novels and plays. Like Lewis, he could never fully appreciate that his most enduring and complex achievement as an artist was in his satiric work of the period from 1915 into the early 1920s.

# Chapter Eight

## A Puritan's Satanic Flight:
## Don Marquis, His Archy, and Anarchy

Things fall apart; the centre cannot hold;
Mere anarchy is loosed upon the world.

> Yeats, "The Second Coming," 1921

**A**rchy, the *vers-libre* bard and cockroach, observes that great men succeed not "by sudden flight but they / while their companions slept / were falling upwards / through the night."[1] Like his maker, Archy is an extravagant romantic who with nighttime inspiration challenges, defies, and sometimes overcomes gravity. To fall upwards through the night is to escape the sucking earth and to enter the landscape of the imagination. In that landscape Archy is immortal and godlike because he is able to create a condition that allows his soul to transmigrate freely from the form of one cockroach to another. As an imaginative extension of his creator, he retraces Satan's fabulous voyage and seeks to discover and repossess a lost paradise. That he is doomed to failure, and that he is, finally, only a cockroach, is Marquis's expression both of an ironic sense of himself and of the romanticism of his time.

In Archy, Marquis created a mock-heroic image for the years from roughly 1910 to the mid-thirties. Although he died in 1937, his verse still appears in anthologies, two Archy books are in print, and a Marquis legend lingers in the minds of those who knew him or knew about him. A romantic whose closest archetype was probably Byron, he wanted, sometimes desperately, to succeed as a writer of heroic and lyric verse and prose. But he wrote most successfully when the ironic, satiric, or satanic mood was upon him. Like many satirists he could be both congenial and uncongenial, both smiling and savage. Like all satirists he had discovered the grave absurdity of his world, and he wrote about it in such a way that a concerned hostility could be expressed rather than repressed. His talent and his era combined to make him a memorable satirist, even while he sought compulsively to transcend such a role.

Marquis was very much a member of the generation that included Lardner and Lewis. All three followed the example of Mencken in reflecting and ridiculing the sense of renewal and resurgence that characterized American culture during this period. They all debunked the provincialism and puritanism that they found as bases for the values, manners, and morals of the middle class. Like the others, Marquis ridiculed Americanism, and especially the demagogues and politicians who were indefatigable sources of windy platitudes about America, its heritage and its destiny. He mocked the Philistinism of the middle class. Yet at the same time he scoffed at an affected aestheticism and Bohemianism.

Marquis and Mencken were strikingly alike in several respects. Both were born of middle-class families, Marquis in 1878, Mencken in 1880. Both rejected the provincialism of late nineteenth-century life, yet both looked back on that life with a sense of loss and nostalgia. Marquis, coming as he did from rural Illinois, was in this respect more truly a provincial than Mencken, who commuted between Baltimore and New York. Still, Mencken, in a reminiscence fifty years later, recalled the "rural delights" in the 1880s of what is now suburban Baltimore: "Here was everything from wide and smiling fields to deep, dense woods of ancient trees, and from the turbulent and exciting life of the barnyard to the hidden peace of woodland brooks."[2] Such nostalgic recall was part of the mythology of their generation, leading even a cosmopolitan like Mencken to evoke (or imagine) a quieter pastoral world, a paradise lost.

Like the young Mencken, Marquis wanted first to be a poet; unlike Mencken, he did not reject poetic yearnings as the folly of youth, but continued all his life to write and publish serious as well as satiric verse. Both were journalists; Marquis in fact made his reputation almost entirely as a newspaper columnist.

They were alike too in their curious mixture of sanguine liberality and Puritan fastidiousness. Marquis may never have read or been directly influenced by Nietzsche, but he was in his Nietzschean individualism like Mencken, who had interpreted and often misinterpreted Nietzsche for his countrymen. Both Mencken and Marquis hated the hypocrisy and repression of individuality that they found in militantly humanitarian movements, and especially in organized religions. They shared, too, an admiration for Mark Twain. Mencken's admiration was directly expressed in his criticism and reminiscences; Marquis reflected his debt especially in his imitative early writings. Mencken projected the image of the iconoclast, the joyful heaver of dead cats into the parlors of the genteel, who nevertheless openly asked Mark Twain's bitter question: "What is Man?" Marquis followed Mark Twain's lead as a lecturer-humorist, thereby joining the ranks of such others as Major Jack Downing, Artemus Ward, Petroleum V. Nasby, Josh Billings, and Orpheus C. Kerr. It was a devious tradition, because satire was hidden behind the mask of congenial humor. Two of Marquis's most notable characters in this tradition were the Prohibition-inspired character called the Old Soak and Hermione, who epitomized the modern, emancipated, middle-class young woman of the prewar era.

But it was when Marquis took one step further into fantasy with the creation of Archy the cockroach and Mehitabel the alley cat that he discovered the proper medium for both his satiric and romantic impulses. In the preface to *Archy and Mehitabel* E. B. White wrote that "at bottom Don Marquis was a poet" (p. xxiii). All his life he longed to break free of the drudgery of journalism and to make a place for himself as a writer of what he considered to be serious poetry and prose. His published writings, in addition to anthologies of his work as a journalist, include plays, several novels, and books of verse. His sense of a creative life unfulfilled was expressed in a letter he wrote in 1928 to Christopher Morley:

> I have never told anybody, how deep and abiding my professional disappointments are. I have had for fifteen years the consciousness of rather unusual powers—I can say this to you and have no risk of it being misunderstood as mere egoism. . . . But you cannot understand, nor won't until you get to be 47 or 48, the continual internal gasping hurrying sense that they are not started yet, the big things.[3]

Marquis may have been frustrated by the knowledge that younger men such as Hemingway and Fitzgerald had already conspicuously achieved by 1928 what he still hoped to achieve. Yet he had accomplished what he himself could never fully appreciate: the creation in Archy the cockroach of an enduring, ambivalent image of the poet as both myth-maker and myth-destroyer, as revealer of the absurdities of his time, as a figure of the lightweight who defies gravity and precariously survives in a dark, urban world overrun by predators. While a cosmopolitan Archy shares Mencken's attitude of horror and mock-hostility toward provincial life, there is also the oblique expression in his ridicule of a nostalgia for an insect-Eden where snakes and birds don't eat bugs, a pastoral world where the penalty of Adam, and of Satan, is not felt.

Donald Robert Perry Marquis was born the son of a physician in the town of Walnut, Illinois. In an autobiographical novel called *Sons of the Puritans* (which remained unfinished at his death in 1937) he left some vivid impressions of late nineteenth-century life in a small midwestern town, which for the purposes of fiction he called Hazelton, Illinois. Hazelton, like the real Walnut, is located in flat country where corn is grown and where hogs and cattle are raised. Like Lewis's Gopher Prairie, Anderson's Winesburg, Masters's Spoon River and Robinson's Tilbury Town, Hazelton's insularity and Puritan conformism combine in the novel to produce among its citizenry certain repressed and unfulfilled characters. The majority of its citizens, Marquis wrote, "were rather prosperous on the whole; they were satisfied; they were smug and complacent; they resisted change. The only living thing, in reality, was the church; and this church (whatever its denomination) they distorted to their own image." They are fiercely puritanical and devote themselves to waging war on drink, free thought, and prostitution: "Puritanism has always been unable to exist without an Adversary, an Enemy—the Church of Rome, the Church of England, Apollyon, witches, Negro slavery (in the North), Negro equality (in the South), the barroom, the bootlegger. . . . It carries in its bowels a kind of fire which demands combat."

The novel tells the story of a boy, Jack Stevens, into whose character Marquis projected much of himself. Jack talks like Huck Finn and has Huck's honest perceptiveness. As he grows up, he becomes disaffected with the values and attitudes of his Protestant environment, but he does not rebel against it until he has begun college. Religious revelation arouses powerful emotions in him. He tends to confuse these emotions with the revelations that come to him when reading and writing poetry, a confusion that is compounded when he meets and makes love to a pretty evangelist. He finds that the ecstasies of sexual abandon are similar both to the ecstasies aroused by his religious sensibilities and to the creative joys of the artist when what Mencken called the divine afflatus strikes. Jack is enough of a Puritan, in his view of himself, to feel guilty about his discovery, and enough of a romantic to begin to move away from the religion and values of his midwestern world. Marquis comments: "Youth is never sure where he is going. He starts out to walk toward God, and the song upon his lips is a chant in praise of God, and lo! the song subtly changes, and suddenly it is not God after all toward whom he is walking, but a woman."[4]

Marquis showed fully the ambivalence of other debunkers toward the changing status of women. His first wife, Reina, was a writer who had begun a career as a successful novelist, and Marquis was sympathetic to her need to "justify her existence by doing something well," as she wrote about a character in her first novel. At the same time she accepted and fulfilled all the domestic responsibilities of a woman with two children in a household with limited financial resources. After her early, tragic death due in part to exhaustion at trying to sustain both of these roles without help, Marquis married Marjorie Vonnegut, an actress, who similarly accepted a double life as a professional and a mother. The pattern, ending with her death at forty-four, was repeated. Such conflicting allegiances between the professional and the domestic reflected the changing status of women in Marquis's time. The attrition that in each case led to early death resulted in part because neither woman was physically able to meet the demands of both worlds, and also because it was assumed that the husband need not take on any significant domestic role. Marquis understood their professional ambitions. But at the same time he relished, and in his emotional life expected, the comforts of the traditional, middle-class domestic environment they struggled to provide. Sympathy, and perhaps a similar ambivalence about it, existed in his earliest memories of his mother, too. In an unpublished autobiographical fragment, he wrote, "It was terrible that she had to spend so much of her life in a commonplace little village such as Walnut, Illinois."[5]

Like his prototype Stephen Dedalus, Jack Stevens discovers new sources of revelation in art and poetry (although Hazelton is no Dublin, and Marquis is not a Joyce). Here *Sons of the Puritans* breaks off, incomplete. Marquis left some notes which indicate that Jack was to go to New York, where between 1910 and 1917 he was to forge a career and to enjoy liberation among the literary salons of that city. Like the hero of his novel, Marquis came to New York in 1909. There he joined the staff of the *Evening Sun,* and on 7 April 1913 began the "Sun Dial" column for which he became famous. In 1922 he switched to the *Tribune,* where his column was called "The Lantern."[6] He quickly became both a humorous commentator who celebrated aspects of American life and a satirist who debunked other aspects of that life. Some of his humor in the early New York years was in the gentler, smiling vein of the nineteenth-century local colorists, but he soon developed a more characteristic mode of expression as a debunker-satirist. This pattern appears in two early works of fiction in which Marquis seemed to be searching for a medium that would express his sense of the destructive contrasts in American culture. He also was seeking an audience, and his uncertainty as to the interests of that audience is frequently apparent.

His first published novel appeared in 1912 and was entitled *Danny's Own Story*. It displays Marquis's affection for and indebtedness to Mark Twain. A frank and superficial imitation of *Huckleberry Finn*, it has few of the accomplishments of that book. Danny, the hero, is more a Tom Sawyer than a Huck Finn, and it is as if Marquis felt his audience could not tolerate the subversion of its values that a true re-creation of Huck would demand. The book is frankly and unashamedly sentimental. In his first bid for literary fame Marquis responded to Mark Twain the funnyman—to that smiling, genteel Mark Twain, the popular author whom everyone knew and understood was really Samuel Clemens. The early fiction of Lewis followed this same pattern, in its exploitation of sentimentality and romantic adventure, but Marquis was quicker than Lewis to discover that what his age wanted was satire.

The crucial period of transition for Marquis, as it had been for Mencken, was in the several years following 1912. The mood of the local colorist and spinner of genteel romances changed: in 1916 he published a farcical romance called *The Cruise of the Jasper B*. Here he debunked the romantic excesses of the adventure-detective story. Along the way there were jibes at such contemporary American phenomena as women's suffrage, anarchy, free verse, expatriation, and easy success on Wall Street. The hero of the novel is Clement J. Cleggett, a copyeditor on a New York newspaper who inherits money and promptly quits his job. Cleggett is a Quixotic figure (he is an expert swordsman whose favorite author is Dumas) with many of the whimsical desires and urges of James Branch Cabell's Jurgen (1919) and of James Thurber's Walter Mitty (1937). Cleggett becomes the champion, protector, and lover of the beautiful Lady Agatha, an English suffragist ("I was one of the first militant suffragettes to break a window"). Her admiration for Cleggett is summarized when she tells him: "A great suffragist leader was lost when fate made you a man." Like Candide, Cleggett collects an odd assortment of derelicts. One of them, his chaplain, the Reverend Simeon Calthrop, wants to go on a pilgrimage because he has kissed a married woman. This moral defection is the result of holding a tango class in the basement of his church every Thursday evening. At the end Cleggett takes a tip from a barber and makes a fortune on the stock market. He explains that he is "a little mad; but I would rather be mad with a Don Quixote than sane with an Andrew Carnegie and pile up platitudes and dollars."[7]

*The Cruise of the Jasper B*. is a very lightweight book indeed, but it is laced with satire, fantasy, and farce. It is as if Marquis by slipping from topical satire into farce that borders on the nonsensical was seeking to provide for himself and for his reader escape, release, and relaxation from a contemporary world that seemed at once amusing and appalling. The tone of *The Cruise of the Jasper B.* was present a few years later in such books as Cabell's *Jurgen* (1919), Woodward's three novels, *Bunk* (1923), *Lottery* (1924), *Bread and Circuses* (1925), and Hemingway's *The Torrents of Spring* (1926). Hemingway's book is an act of liberation by a major writer from his immediate literary heritage and must be assessed in the context of what he parodied. Parody provided a frame for Hemingway, while one problem with the others, and especially with Marquis's novel, is that fantasy, farce, and nonsense do not serve as vehicles for the expression of anything in particular. We do not know what is being parodied. In their very incoherence these techniques reflect what we are asked to view as the confusions of the culture for which they are mirrors. The issues do not seem very significant to us; there is a faint tone of hysteria, suggesting that their authors did not find them very significant, either. And Marquis had not yet caught the rhythms of the language of his time, as had Hemingway. Nor had he yet created a character who could effectively serve the purposes of irony and satire.

Then, in his newspaper column, there appeared Hermione. She was a young lady of the prewar era, a prefiguration of the more liberated, worldly Mehitabel, whose exploits Archy was soon to celebrate. Hermione became the heroine of a collection of anecdotes and verses entitled *Hermione and Her Little Group of Serious Thinkers,* published in 1916. *Hermione* ridicules the affectations of middle-class Bohemians in New York just before and during the first years of the war. The book consists of Hermione's monologues, with the author's ironic verse and prose comments interspersed. Hermione is the daughter of a wealthy Philistine ("Papa has very little sympathy for advanced ideas") and of a genteel, "mid-Victorian" mother.[8] Hermione conducts a "salon weird where congregate / Freak, Nut and Bug and Psychic Bum" (p. 1). These were the years in New York of Mabel Dodge's famous evenings; perhaps Marquis had her in mind, or one of her less-noted imitators. At Hermione's sessions, "thought, within, / Roared through the rooms as red and hot as Sin" (p. 104). Hermione tries to keep up to date on all the new intellectual fads. Her discussion group has, she says, "taken up Bergson, socialism, psychology, Rabindranath Tagore, the meaning of welfare work, culinary science, the new movements in art—and ever so many more things I can't remember now" (p. 90). (Evolution, science, Nietzsche, the Superman, the Superwoman, symbolism, astrology, trial marriage, the house beautiful, heredity, environment, hedonism, and cosmic consciousness are other subjects that send shivers of delight through this culturally manic female.) At night, before going to bed, she holds what she calls her "psychic inquisitions." She questions herself concerning the new person she is trying to become:

> "Have I vibrated in tune with the Infinite today, or have I failed?" "Have I been independent today? Or have I *failed?*" "Have I shown the sacrificial spirit . . . ?" "Have I been sympathetic . . . ?" "Concentration! Concentration! That is the key to it all! Nearly every night when I am alone with my own Ego I go into the Silences for a little period of Spiritual Self-Examination and I always ask myself: 'Have I Concentrated today? Really Concentrated? Or have I failed?' " (pp. 15, 31, 58)

Hermione's principal affectation is that "one's subliminal consciousness must ever vibrate in harmony with the Cosmic All" (p. 161).

One of her faithful attendants is the poet Fothergil Finch; he is "radical and advanced and virile" (p. 24). For Fothy "life is one long, grim, desperate struggle against Conventionality, and Social Injustice, and Smugness, and the Established Order, and Complacence. He is forever being a martyr to the New and True in Art and Life" (pp. 24–25). Another admirer of Hermione's is Voke Easeley, who paints sound portraits with his larynx: "He has gone right back to the dog, the wolf, the cave man, the tiger, the bear, the wind, the rockslide, the thunder and the earthquake for his language" (p. 87). Hermione thinks "the primitive is just simply too fascinating" (p. 159). She longs to be alone under the stars with her cave man. But she retains her sense of propriety, in spite of her intellectual freedom; when she finds out that plants have sex, she says: "Isn't it frightful to think that this agitation has spread to the vegetable kingdom?" (p. 169). Finally, Hermione summarizes her comic ambivalence between the Victorian and the modern when she says: "Stimulation! Stimulation! That is the secret of Modern Life!" (p. 179).

Marquis created Hermione in order to ridicule what seemed fraudulent and precious in the cultural resurgence that became, around 1910, a conscious, even self-conscious, movement in American life. The posturings of would-be intellectuals and artists continued to offend him all his life. Perhaps his hostility drew intensity from his own frustrated efforts to become known as a writer of plays, poems, and novels. In 1919, probably inspired by Mencken's *Book of Prefaces* (1917), he published a book that he called *Prefaces*. Some of these prefaces were parodies, some were serious essays; his most frequent subjects were varieties of literary pretension.

One of the parodies was called "Preface to a Book of Literary Reminiscences." We are told that the "Eheu Fugaces Chop House" has been torn down to be replaced by a publishing house. Marquis's narrator is a somewhat senile, name-dropping belletrist: "I remember Lincoln regarding little Billy-Cul Bryant quizzically as Billy sat in the Upper part of the icebox, unconsciously crushing a consignment of ripe tomatoes, writing 'Thanatopsis.' 'Read it aloud, Billy-Cul,' said Abie. And when Billy-Cul had done so Abie remarked humorously: 'It's got some awful good words in it Billy-Cul, but what's it all about?' " Another preface ("Preface to the Prospectus of a Club") had in it a defense of the Bohemian life in Brooklyn:

> Walt Whitman used to live over there. . . . Once an old Long Island skipper sunk a harpoon into Walt's haunch when he came up to blow, and the poet, snorting and bellowing and spouting verse, towed the whaler and his vessel clear out to Montauk before he shook the iron loose. Is there a bard in Greenwich Village who could do that? Not even Jack Reed who writes like Byron and swims like Leander, could do that.

And there was the inevitable spoof of the "New Art," this time on the efforts of a Greenwich Village couple to discover a new source of artistic material and inspiration, using recently popularized Freudian concepts. They successfully harness their Uncle Peleg to a sound instrument which amplifies his snores: "When man sleeps his subconscious mind is in control and his ego ranges back through all the past life of the race. . . . In Uncle Peleg's snores we hear the cave man fighting with the boar, in Uncle Peleg's snores is the orchestral expression of the evolution of the human being."

Although the wit in these representative examples is about as compelling as that in college humor magazines, apparent in them are the tone, manner, and elements of parody that Frank Sullivan was beginning to make the hallmarks of his style. Marquis's influence was probably direct, for the younger Sullivan also wrote for a New York newspaper (the *World*). The feature pages of the *World* and the *Evening Sun* served as schools for humorists and as sounding boards for satirists.

Marquis did not confine his satire to the harmless excesses of newly-liberated, middle-class aesthetes. While he was sometimes funny in his writings on aspiring artists, we inevitably sense his own irate Philistinism. Certainly there was a good market in conservative, genteel, American homes for writings flattering to the middle-class sense that artists were eccentric and need not to be taken seriously. But Marquis did not pander to middle-class convictions in other respects. Also in his book of *Prefaces* he wrote in Menckenian tones: "We live in an age so remarkably pure, because it is so frequently reformed whether it likes it or not, that our apprehension of the iniquity in the minds of others has become almost abnormally acute" (although Mencken would not have written "almost"); and, "Censors are necessary, increasingly necessary, if America is to avoid having a vital literature."[9] These were hardly radical ironies in the year 1919, but they did serve to identify Marquis with sentiments that Mencken had expounded earlier.

With the coming of Prohibition Marquis introduced a character whom he called the Old Soak. The Old Soak appeared in the *Evening Sun* columns, and the pieces were gathered into two books: *The Old Soak and Hail and Farewell* (1921) and *The Old Soak's History of the World* (1924). The early Old Soak pieces, in a gentle, comic way, did little more than flatter the indignation of those who opposed Prohibition— and nearly everybody around New York, at least, considered Prohibition both a drastic affront and a source of comic inspiration. Gradually, however, the Old Soak became more than a flat, comic figure. An element of ugly savagery was injected by Marquis into this placid, laughable character. Here was a hint, a prefiguring and reflection of that dangerous, primitive world of violence and sudden death inhabited by Archy and Mehitabel, their friends and enemies. The Old Soak's belligerent American individualism is struck through with a terrible bigotry and provincial narrowness. On the subject of modern witch hunting and persecution the Old Soak says: "Well now and then they burn a colored man in this country, but this is a repubblikin form of government and a man gets burned in a repubblikin form of government can say to his self he is getting burned for something different than in the old witch burning days and it orter be a great comfort to him to realize he is getting burned in a free country." At another point the Old Soak, provoked by talk about evolutionary theory, rasps with sodden, florid-faced righteousness: "Well Hennery Withers, the dam little athyiss, says that men dissended offen monkeys, I have banged his head more'n oncet for that kind of wicked talk, it is a good thing this country has got men in it to bang the heads of all them athyisses."[10]

Rejection of the authoritarian in any form was one of the tenets of Marquis's individualism. One frequent object of his satire was the aplomb with which science and scientists set about explaining the universe. In an essay called "The Revolt of the Oyster" (1922), in which he showed his love for the fable as a satiric form, he described how Probably Arboreal, mankind's ancestor at an earlier stage of evolution, did battle with a giant oyster in order to decide which species would henceforth be supreme in the world. The oyster lost and became man's slave and food. In the collection of epigrams, anecdotes, and fables called *The Almost Perfect State* (1927) he outlined a whimsical utopia, which had to be projected three million years into the future since evolution is such a slow process.

Marquis turned from politics and history to a new aspect of American culture when he wrote a novel called *Off the Arm*, published in 1930, which grew out of his experiences in Hollywood. *Off the Arm* is set primarily in the kingdom of the film, and is a minor addition to the sparse literature inspired by that peculiar manifestation of American experience. Along with Van Vechten's *Spider Boy,* the novel looked forward to more substantial treatments of Hollywood in Fitzgerald's *The Last Tycoon* and West's *The Day of the Locust.*

Marquis persistently questioned and usually rejected organized religious authority. His book called *Chapters for the Orthodox* (1934) was both a condemnation of the hypocrisies of organized religions and a debunker's examination of Christian mythology. The fables and parables in this book are twentieth-century moralities, and predictably, some of them have allegorical figures. The ironies of the book are typical of the debunking wit and tone of the 1920s, and a reader today feels as distant from them as from the whimsical disaffection that must have produced them. In one parable Jehovah comes to New York, disguised as a member of the Union League Club. He decides to send another son to earth; as before, he settles on the device of a virgin birth. Only after a long and difficult search does he find a suitably mature virgin. She is a spinster who lives in an old house on Washington Square, and is a *Mayflower* descendant. But she flatly refuses the honor offered her, on the grounds that since she is a virtuous woman she cannot have a child out of wedlock.[11] In 1934 this wit was too dated to command an audience: orthodoxy was surely a significant subject for satire in the 1930s, but not the religious orthodoxy that Mencken had already so thoroughly and joyfully exorcised by evoking the enormous fictitious specter of puritanism in American life. Mencken, too, had lost his audience as more and more he revealed his unchanging prejudices, but here the similarity to Marquis ends. For in Marquis's *Chapters for the Orthodox* his interests in fable and allegory survived, and these modes of expression had been used to significant effect in the creation of Archy and Mehitabel. Within a fabulous world, through the character of a cockroach, Marquis discovered an original means of expression and approached the poetry and artistry to which he had always aspired.

The Archy and Mehitabel fables celebrate irrationality, which is a way of expressing misanthropy and hostility toward society. They point up

humanity's inadequacy before the terrors of both the known and unknown universes. They emphasize the foolishness of man's claim to
superiority. The fables are primarily vehicles for satire, and satire serves
at least two purposes. There is specific, topical satire: Archy's debunking of Prohibition, free verse, and theories of evolution, or Mehitabel's
eulogies on the Bohemian life. The purpose implied by such writing
would seem to be the reformation of a culture, in the great tradition of
Puritan satire, beginning with Bunyan and Defoe, or even Swift. But
there is also, paradoxically, more general, unspecified satire of the
structure and values of that same culture. Marquis seeks, and asks his
readers to share, release from the demands made by his world for coherence, logic, progress, and allegiance, through the glorification of what is
impulsive, anarchic, illogical, and disaffected. His best writing is generated out of the conflict between his impulses toward puritanical reformation on the one hand and anarchic dissolution on the other.

Archy the cockroach, biographer of Mehitabel the alley cat, first
appeared in the "Sun Dial" column of the *New York Evening Sun* in
1916. His creator took Archy and his other animal and insect friends and
enemies to the *New York Tribune* in 1922; some of the verses appeared
also in *Collier's*. The verses were collected into three books, *Archy and
Mehitabel* (1927), *Archy's Life of Mehitabel* (1933), and *Archy Does His
Part* (1935). The three were reissued in one volume, *The Lives and
Times of Archy and Mehitabel* (1950). The sources of the tales told
through the character of Archy are probably found in their earliest form
in animal fables and in the medieval beast epic. A more immediate
influence was Marquis's experience as editor of *Uncle Remus's Magazine* and his close exposure to the animal legends of Joel Chandler
Harris. But Harris's humor was usually a gentle, smiling humor: the
helpless and innocent always triumphed in one way or another. One
possible source for Archy's abilities as a cockroach philosopher, as well
as his bitterness, irony, and pessimism may have been the dialogues
between the Old Man and the Young Man in Mark Twain's *What Is
Man?* (in rejecting the theory of instinct, the Old Man shows that animals and insects have reasoning powers that are in many ways superior
to those of humans.) Another source of Marquis's appreciation for the
satiric possibilities of the animal story may very well be the bitter, ironic
fables and parables of Ambrose Bierce.

Archy has a dual nature, and thereby reflects his creator's sense of the
role of the artist. As an insect, Archy is an upsetting nuisance: he
threatens frequently to become an unsavory pest by drowning himself in
mince pies, stews, and soups. As a poet he is both an articulate, rational

creature and, like his master, driven by an inner, romantic intensity: "Expression is the need of my soul." Archy "was once a vers-libre bard." When he died, his "soul went into the body of a cockroach." As a result of this transmigration he finds that he has "a new outlook upon life," for he sees "things from the under side" (p. 20). Archy, we are told in the author's introductory explanation, expresses himself by laborious nighttime typing sessions upon Marquis's typewriter. He jumps headfirst onto the keys, slowly and painfully tapping out his verse in lower-case letters because he cannot work the shift key. The carriage return is also manipulated with great labor. When the inspiration has been literally pounded out of him, he crawls into a nest of discarded poems that clutter the floor and sleeps.

Marquis was continuing in the creation of Archy the ridicule of Bohemian affectation that had been his primary purpose in his pieces and verses about Hermione. The same sort of ridicule is present in aspects of his depiction of Mehitabel the alley cat, whose story Archy tells in bits and fragments. A manic lowbrow, slightly beat, somewhat faded, she is passionately committed to whatever is free and orgiastic: "There is a dance in the old dame yet" (p. 222). Usually her alliances with free-spirited tomcats are spoiled by the arrival of kittens. Mehitabel says she is "all maternal instinct" (p. 266), but kittens ruin her figure and are inconveniences to her career as a modern dancer. She abandons her offspring quickly and ruthlessly. If Marquis was debunking an aspect of American culture that could produce flamboyantly emancipated women like Mehitabel, cruelly indifferent to the middle-class values of family life, he also, through Archy, her creator, projected admiration for her glorious individualism. One of Mehitabel's favorite lovers is a highbrow and a poet, who sings of their times together:

we would rather be rowdy and gaunt and free
and dine on a diet of roach and rat
than slaves to a tame society
ours is the zest of the alley cat. (p. 31)

Most of the early verses by Archy, the bard of the animal and insect worlds, concentrate on ridicule of artistic affectation. In one of the fables Archy overhears an argument between a spider and a fly. The fly argues that he should not be eaten, for he serves "a great purpose / in the world." He says he is a "vessel of righteousness" because he spreads diseases that kill people who have led wicked lives (p. 40). The spider offers a higher argument. He says he serves "the gods of beauty" by creating "gossamer webs" that "float in the sun / like filaments of song"; he is

> busy with the stuff
> of enchantment and the materials
> of fairyland my works
> transcend utility
> i am the artist
> a creator and a demi god. (p. 41)

In order to create he must have food. The fly bows to this superior argument, but adds one final plaint against the futility of his existence; he says he "could have made out a case" for himself if he "had / had a better line of talk" (p. 41). The spider answers with the contempt of the predatory artist for mere utility:

> of course you could said the spider
> clutching a sirloin from him
> but the end would have been
> just the same if neither of
> us had spoken at all. (pp. 41–42)

There is an oblique satiric purpose in the poem: the creative imagination is seen as part of a world dominated by predatory instincts.

The world of Archy is struck through with the comic and the satiric; it is also a place of violence, terror, and sudden death. Archy is always in danger of annihilation. He is pursued by mice and even by his friend Mehitabel, when she is moved by hunger or playfulness. On one occasion he is stepped upon, but his soul enters the body of another cockroach. When, bored with being a cockroach, he decides to try suicide (he hopes to transmigrate into a higher form of life), he discovers that killing himself is no easy matter. He jumps from the top of the Washington Monument, but, too light, floats unharmed to the ground. He tries to hang himself with a thread, but again is too light; he just dangles. Violence also underlies the Bohemianism of Mehitabel. She can be a savage antagonist when love plays her false; she thinks nothing of slashing off a lover's ear or clawing out his eye.

Marquis ironically anthropomorphized the problem of survival in a world of predators in the fable called "The Robin and the Worm." A slow-witted angleworm is eaten by a robin before he can even "gather his / dissent into a wise crack." He finds that he is being digested:

> demons and fishhooks
> he exclaimed
> i am losing my personal
> identity as a worm
> my individuality
> is melting away from me (p. 65)

As he is assimilated by the robin, he begins to "swoon into a / condition of belief," which is that "a / robin must live" (p. 65). A beetle, who has just preceded him into the robin's stomach, agrees with him:

> is it not
> wonderful when one arrives
> at the place
> where he can give up his
> ambitions and resignedly
> nay even with gladness
> recognize that it is a far
> far better thing to be
> merged harmoniously
> in the cosmic all (pp. 65–66)

The robin, in his turn, is singing happily, singing praises to God and to his good digestion, when Mehitabel eats him. Mehitabel philosophizes:

> how beautiful is the universe
> when something digestible meets
> with an eager digestion
> how sweet the embrace
> when atom rushes to the arms
> of waiting atom
> and they dance together
> skimming with fairy feet
> along a tide of gastric juices
> oh feline cosmos you were
> made for cats (p. 67)

Sometimes Marquis brought horror, violence, and nonsense into even closer conjunction. "The Dissipated Hornet," a story told by Archy, is an ironic parable on "the corrupting / influence of the great / city." It partly debunks the militant prohibitionist's attitude toward strong drink by reducing the usually cautionary results of drunkenness to nonsense. But there is also a strong element of horror, and while the puritanical attitude is ridiculed, it is also confirmed: Marquis may have felt himself, on occasion, like the barflies in his verse. In the story, a happy, carefree, country hornet comes to the city in a crate of peaches. Wandering hungry and friendless, he meets a sophisticated city hornet who teaches him how to catch barroom flies. Staggering bemused with drink out of bars, these flies are easy to sting and consume. At first the country hornet only eats flies drunk on beer, but soon "the curse of drink" leads him to prefer flies who have taken stronger liquor. Then, confirmed in his wickedness, he trains six innocent young country hornets to do his fly-catching for him. The country hornets, corrupted in their turn, soon desert him; idle and dissipated, he finds that he can only catch flies that are "dead drunk." To Archy he bemoans the curse of drink and says:

i
have the gout in my stinger so bad
that i scream with pain every time i spear
a fly (p. 134)

Archy advises suicide, his usual remedy for worldly ills.

This is light verse, obviously, and as such it is playful. Nevertheless, it arises from an ironic sensibility that is defined on the one hand by impulses toward purification and renewal, and on the other by impulses toward disaffection and even apocalypse. The predatory instinct in Marquis's fables seems to be an objectification of his sense of original sin; it is both man's fate and, paradoxically, his glory: Marquis's creatures eat each other and die ecstatically or violently. In his underlying seriousness there are echoes of the ironic visions with which such near-contemporaries as Yeats and Frost contemplated apocalypse in the years immediately following the First World War.

During the 1930s much of Archy's commentary was topical and aphoristic. The Depression and the recovery schemes it spawned proved a rich source of comic material. But the tone was very different from that in the wilder fables of the first fifteen years. Archy became simply a mouthpiece who spoke gentle irreverencies in the manner of Will Rogers. He reported on his trips to Washington, he commented on recovery attempts, he held mock radio interviews on world affairs and current events, he climbed Mount Everest, he went flying, he deplored the waste of natural resources.

It was a time for reconstruction, not for debunking. Satire, it seemed, could entertain, but not radically criticize. Marquis made some unsuccessful attempts to introduce other animal and insect characters: there were Pete the Pup, Henry, another cockroach, and Lady Bug. None of them was the equal of Archy or of Mehitabel. The most notable character was Warty Bliggens, the toad who believed that the universe had been created for his pleasure and benefit. But he, too, was an early creation, and appeared only once. Archy remains the most enduring figure in the Archy and Mehitabel saga.

An undercurrent of hostility and disaffection formed the main stream of Archy's character. As an insect and commentator on humanity, he was, of course, superior and hostile in his attitudes toward human hypocrisies and ideals. Most of all he hated false optimism, which was epitomized for him in the vapid chirping of crickets. He says, in "The Cheerful Cricket,"

> i hate one of these
> grinning skipping smirking
> senseless optimists worse
> than i do a cynic or a
> pessimist. (p. 139)

In a much later poem called "The Sad Crickets," he decided that in spite of what "chas dickens believed" crickets sing a melancholy song:

> my love fell into a spiders web
> squeak squeak squeak
> and she screamed with pain as he
> crunched her bones into his
> bloody beak squeak squeak (p. 402)

Archy's insect world was a world of violence, terror, and sudden death, which he described with ecstatic intensity. And because the human world resembled his insect world, he viewed it with macabre humor and hostility. The essence of his hostility issued in an apocalyptic vision in which he declared

> and in the end i shall
> eat everything
> all the world shall come at
> last to the multitudinous maws
> of insects
> a civilizatiom perishes
> before the tireless teeth
> of little little germs
> ha ha i have thrown off the mask
> at last
> you thought i was only
> an archy
> but i am more than that
> i am anarchy (pp. 187–88)

He is both artist and predator. As artist, expression is the need of his soul; with passionate intensity he creates order and form. As predator he is a nuisance and a pest who nibbles constantly at order and form in what is imagined as a total attrition and descent back into anarchy, a return to Hell. Marquis similarly conceived of a dual role for himself as artist: a role as both poet and satirist, as both myth-maker and myth-destroyer. He was never comfortable with the knowledge of this division in himself, yet the artist in him created a memorable image for one of the tensions of American life in the twentieth century.

Marquis was a son of the Puritans who rejected the religious, secular, and artistic authority of his time and sought either to purify or destroy this authority. What he wanted was a kind of covenant of artistic grace for his own life and culture. He had a deep and frustrating sense of failure, a sense that he was not one of the elect, that he was the victim of something as pervasive as original sin. One of his responses was to glorify that awareness of damnation. The images of Archy's world arise out of Marquis's sense of a need for purification set against his impulses toward anarchic destruction. Marquis, like so many of his contemporaries, felt that the values of middle-class culture no longer made sense. His response was to create a fabulous world where hostility, violence, and the predatory instinct were the ordinary ingredients of existence, and thus were brought within a kind of tenuous artistic control. In his belief that mere anarchy was loosed upon the world, Marquis set loose an Archy of his own. He wanted somehow to counteract the mereness, the absurdity of existence as he viewed it, through an ironic glorification both of irrationality and of anarchy itself.

# Chapter Nine
## Out of the Underworld of Nonsense: Ring Lardner, Frank Sullivan, and E. B. White

ACTS II & III
(These two acts were thrown out because nothing seemed to happen.)

Ring Lardner, "Clemo Uti: 'The Water Lilies,' " 1925

narchic impulses ran deep in Lardner, too, although the decorum of his genteel surroundings usually concealed them. The *New Yorker,* which published Lardner's most anarchic writing— his nonsense plays—began in the mid-1920s as a magazine of dubunking humor, and thus came to emphasize what seemed nonsensical and whimsically urbane in American life. In the late 1920s and early 1930s it published several writers whose impulses were notably similar to Lardner's: Frank Sullivan, E. B. White and (later) S. J. Perelman. For all of them the deliberate abuse of sense seemed both to satirize and to offer respite from a world where language was misconstrued and misused. This tendency of satire toward the fabulous and toward nonsense had been present in nineteenth-century humor, in the extravagance of the tall tale, in the fables of Ambrose Bierce, in the tradition of buncombe oratory. The tendency became manifest in the twentieth-century debunkers: in Mencken's sustained burlesques and elaborate hoaxes, in Marquis's Archy and Mehitabel fables, in parodies by Corey Ford, Donald Ogden Stewart, and Hemingway, and in the *New Yorker* humorists. Like all the debunkers, Lardner, Sullivan, and White each had a purist's sense of how language should properly be used. As the *New Yorker* emerged in the 1930s from its debunking origins it gradually took unto itself a sacred and progressive mission to purify and conserve language. It sought to publish the finest of poetry and prose, and to establish high standards of style through meticulous editing.

Like Marquis, Lewis, and Mencken, Lardner was born (within a few years of the others) into an affluent middle-class family. All of them looked back to their early years with nostalgic recall, with a sense that an idyllic order lay behind them. These recollections posited places that had nurtured the potential for freedom, a kind of mid-nineteenth-century, Thoreauvian ideal.[1] While they rejected and ridiculed aspects of the world they remembered so tenderly, it never lost its sentimental hold upon them—whether it was Hollins Street in Baltimore, Sauk Centre in Minnesota, Walnut in Illinois, or Niles in Michigan. Lardner expressed his love and affection in a series of articles for the *Saturday Evening Post,* published in the early 1930s. Jonathan Yardley calls them "wonderful pieces of reminiscence, imbued with sunniness and gentle self-mockery and nostalgia."[2] Elsewhere in the lifelong accumulation of his writing he often had depicted this world as narrow, provincial, big-oted: his ambivalence toward the Midwest was very like that of Lewis and Marquis.

For all of them the emotional authority at the center of their pastoral sensibility was the mother or the mother-wife. Like Mencken and Lewis, Lardner's literary or artistic inclinations were encouraged originally by his mother, who prescribed the cultural values in his family. She encouraged him to write light verse, which he did all his life; some appeared in his newspaper columns, some in letters to friends. At the same time he seemed to want to be taken seriously as a poet—repeating the patterns of misplaced literary aspiration in Mencken, Marquis, and Lewis.

Another extension of literary aspiration in Lardner was his attempt to claim an audience and success as a playwright. As Yardley notes:

> It is the most puzzling contradiction of his life: that this man whose vision could be so acute and so dark should have poured so much of his energy into the most frivolous sort of theatrical endeavors. . . . He seems genuinely to have thought that success on Broadway was important, and he got more happiness out of the fleeting popularity of *June Moon* than he did out of any of his books or individual pieces.[3]

Lewis and Marquis enacted similar fantasies in their own personal lives, with equally notable lack of success. Perhaps for all three the theater held out the promise of instant, glamorous gratification, and seemed a natural, immediate outlet for their love of verbal play.

Central to the effect of Lardner's mature writing is his ambivalent attitude toward a diminishing pastoral way of life in America. The non-sense writings late in his life were both a reflection and a desperate ordering of this ambivalence. The First World War for Lardner, as for Marquis, Lewis, and Mencken, was comprehended as the shocking end of the order he remembered or imagined as central to his early life. That none of this generation fought in the war only increased its significance. Geoffrey Wolff has noted: "There would be only two classes of men after the war: those who went and those who did not."[4] This elitism served to intensify their senses of compensatory roles through their "combat" with the enemies at home: puritanism, provincialism, and Americanism. Lardner's actual experience of the war was peripheral and produced in him the vaguely unfocused feelings about the demise of a whole culture that were consistently to inform his writings of the 1920s.

He was sent to Europe by *Collier's* in 1917 as a correspondent. His dispatches were gathered and published in 1918 as *My Four Weeks in France*.[5] In this book the frustrations of the narrator-correspondent at his inability to obtain and communicate news of any significance are burlesqued. A baffling and meaningless bureaucracy emerges as a vaguely threatening presence. The war itself is omnipresent but so amorphous as to be unreportable. The setting in which these articles are enacted is a prefiguration of the settings for his writings in the 1920s and 1930s: a world near chaos where meaninglessness threatens sanity. The threat can only be comprehended and assuaged through the often hollow laughter evoked by parody, burlesque, and nonsense.

For a while before the war, Lardner found in baseball a miniature world of seemingly harmless heroic combat that embodied the values of a partly mythical America. Yardley describes the meaning of baseball to Lardner:

> It was a tough game played by tough men, yet for all its rudeness it also had humor and innocence. Its players had been raised on Georgia farms, in Pennsylvania coal towns and Chicago alleys, and they brought the individual character of their backgrounds to the game. There was no sameness, no conformity, and in its diversity baseball was, if not an exact microcosm of pre–World War I America, a reasonably faithful representation of a young nation still too close to its frontier to have lost its rough edge or its folk heritage.[6]

From his youth Lardner remembered, or perhaps in part imagined, a noble and honorable game that may never have fully existed in reality. What he remembered was changed irrevocably in the years that culminated in the war—years that reached their nadir in 1919 when the World Series was fixed by gamblers.

Baseball became a metaphor in Lardner's writing for an orderly, partly imagined world where, for a time, good confronted evil in predictable, meaningful ways. When he became disillusioned with baseball, his sense of it as a metaphor was enriched, deepened, and extended to incorporate all games in America. His attitudes reached an inverted extreme of contempt when he was asked to write on "Sport and Play" in a 1922 book of essays edited by Harold Stearns called *Civilization in the United States.* He wrote that Americans did not participate in sports "because (1) we lack imagination, and because (2) we are a nation of hero-worshippers." And he wrote that "hero-worship is the national disease."[7] This judgment of the American character, and therefore of American culture in the years after the war, was the negative factor in the contradiction so central to the effect of his writing—as it was in the writings of other debunkers.

Out of his sense of the nonparticipant whom he had condemned in 1922, Lardner created a new kind of character for most of his writings. His narrators speak in dialects that sound, as the *New Yorker* called it in Lardner's obituary, the "dim, sad music of America," but they were viewed with less and less sympathy as Lardner's vision of America became more cynical. The culmination of this pattern is the savage self-ridicule of narrator-author in the partly autobiographical *Story of a Wonder Man* (1927). The narratorless nonsense plays of his late writings are perhaps an index of Lardner's sense of having exhausted the device of the dialect narrators who had served his earlier fictions so well.

The narrator of *You Know Me Al* (first published serially in the *Saturday Evening Post,* and then as a book in 1916) is a complex character whose obsessions and attitudes are ridiculed yet who nevertheless has redeeming features. Lardner presents this narrator (his name is Jack Keefe) as an American type in the genre of Lewis's Babbitt and Mencken's boob. As a baseball "hero" we see that he is selfish, naive, stupid, and self-centered, but he has two redeeming human affections: his love for his baby son and for his loyal, silent friend, Al, to whom are addressed the letters through which the stories are told. His value system is defined by a terrible, sometimes vicious penuriousness, as if the petty manipulation of money has replaced all human values in his world. His obsession is ridiculed as we see him so easily duped and cheated.

Another fleetingly redemptive aspect of Jack Keefe appears in his moments of absorption as a baseball pitcher caught up in the intricacy and fascination of the game itself. His genuine skill emerges briefly through the overlay of arrogance, paranoia, and desperate lack of self-growth. Lardner clearly respects and cherishes the skill of the athlete-artist and implicitly, sometimes bitterly, laments its loss.

The Jack Keefe stories incorporated most of the effects that Lardner explored in other narrative structures after 1916. For example, the narrator in *The Young Immigrunts* is a child whose speech is a mixture of adult sophistication and childish naiveté, with both the wisdom and foolishness of Jack Keefe. However, another element in his narration emerges more clearly than in the Jack Keefe stories, an element that became dominant in Lardner's writing. The Young Immigrunt has a confused ear for the American language, a confusion manifested in many unconscious puns and in contexts that tend toward the nonsensical. They bear a similarity to the kind of exchanges exploited by the later nonsense plays (e.g., "I used the brains god gave me was my fathers posthumous reply").[8]

By 1920 Lardner was writing more and more out of a sense that the American language had deteriorated toward a condition of anarchic incoherence. He was fully aware that a long tradition of dialect narrators lay behind him in American humor. His tendency to burlesque the speech of his dialect narrator had become more explicit in *The Young Immigrunts*. Behind this burlesque was Lardner's growing, embittered sense of the dissolution, the near-chaos, the incoherence of American life. Marquis had written out of a similar apprehension, and it was an attitude that had to be concealed behind the mask of humor. Donald Elder has described the deceptive element in such Lardner narrators as Jack Keefe and the Young Immigrunt:

> In his broader outlines he appears to be the kind of man with whom the average reader can identify himself, in his innocence, shrewdness, and disregard for the niceties of discourse. But the character is deceptive. It is really a burlesque of all wise boobs, of all humorists and commentators; it is a burlesque of Ring himself.[9]

But Lardner's attitudes toward his narrators were not simple and were not fixed: he both loved and hated them. The stories in *The Big Town*[10] were narrated by a shrewd, wise fool named Finch, a middle American who, like Babbitt, speaks the aggressively independent language of middle America. The war is an important background factor in the stories, which have as their setting the kind of world more richly and novelistically textured in Fitzgerald's *Great Gatsby*. The stories depict Finch's newly rich family with its meretricious values and wealth accrued by wartime profiteering. Theirs is an ugly middle-class world where both sophisticates and provincials lead senseless, boring, migratory, conspicuous lives. The speech of the narrator, Finch, like that of other characters, is in one aspect aggressive, energetic, colorful. But it is also defective speech that in another aspect reflects a confusing world where traditional, ordinary English is inadequate.

This double attitude toward American language is implicit in what Lardner dramatizes as the speech of his narrators. We find it once again, for example, in a narrator called Gullible whose "Travels" were celebrated in a collection of stories published in 1925.[11] Gullible and his wife are lower-class Americans who aspire to middle-class respectability. Gullible is given the same capacity as other Lardner narrators: he can perceive and ridicule pretension, yet at the same time he succumbs to it. Once again, the war provides an ironic setting: in the title story we are shown a group of affluent midwesterners at a Palm Beach resort hotel, where they have gone because European travel would be impossible. We are given a picture of a gaudy environment where conspicuous consumption is the primary value. The war, it is implied, is being fought to preserve this manifestation of Western culture, and shortly, the reader knows, America will enter the war to make the world safe for the perpetuation of such a pretentious society. The real war for Lardner, the most important war, existed as a kind of implicit metaphor, in the conditions of American life. The world of Gullible is very like the world that Lewis created for Babbitt, but without novelistic depth. Gullible, like Babbitt, has a redeeming wit at times. While his speech is pretentious and ridiculous, it also can modulate into a graceful adroitness. His verbal dexterity is a natural part of his lower-class midwestern vernacular. There is energy in such language, and Babbitt has some of this energy, too. It is this same aspect of American speech that Mencken celebrated.

The abuse of language, especially its commercial and pornographic exploitation, incensed Lardner. Such abuse was to him both symptom and cause of the deterioration of a culture. Radio was its newest, most flagrant medium and Lardner poured much of its waning energy at the end of his life into a series of critical articles about radio written for the *New Yorker*.

Although Harold Ross, the editor of the *New Yorker,* was not a dedicated crusader—he shared Mencken's distrust of the reformer's moral bias—he did permit Lardner's campaign for better radio on the pages of his magazine. Lardner's column of commentary was called "Over the Waves," and was written in 1932 and 1933. Here Lardner produced some of his best satire; he also showed a tendency, like Sullivan and

White, to resolve humor into nonsense, a tendency apparent in his other *New Yorker* contributions (there were thirteen between 1927 and 1933). Nonsense was his final recourse both as a debunker and as a writer.

Lardner himself suggested to Ross that he write the radio columns. He was an invalid. For several years he had been in and out of hospitals and sanitariums, suffering from recurrent tuberculosis, with heart and stomach complications. When in 1932 he proposed to do the columns, he had only a year and a half to live. Because his illness did not permit him to read at length, he was part of radio's vast and rapidly expanding mass audience. He objected indignantly to what he heard; broadcasting companies promoted a lowbrow form of mass culture that was vulgar, sentimental, illiterate, and lacking in standards or taste. Moreover, the radio audience was a captive one. Lardner, flat on his back in bed, physically unable at times even to turn off the box with Gothic tracery decorating its speaker, was acutely aware of radio's flagrant invasion of privacy. He was also aware of the threat to individuality inherent in a medium of mass communication which could reach and perhaps per-suade nearly every citizen in the country. Radio's banality, its willing-ness to promote lowbrow culture, and its subservience to advertisers were a source of real distress to him. Satire was the natural vein of his protest; it was his way of reaching as large an audience as possible, and his way of bidding for the approval of that audience. At times, however, his indignation and disgust overwhelmed the satire. And at times he turned toward nonsense, since nonsense best expressed his frustration over what he knew, finally, was a futile crusade. In nonsense he could express and relieve his disgust at what mass culture seemed to promise for mankind.

The kind of low culture which radio produced had, of course, always existed, but for the first time this level of culture was being insistently and broadly disseminated. There was a horror in the realization that the radio waves were everywhere, invisible in the air, even if temporarily unheard: perhaps they caused tuberculosis? cancer? In his first column Lardner outlined his critical purpose in the columns to come, and also conveyed his indignation with its tinge of disgust. His attitude was sum-marized in what he wrote about a radio announcer, Tony Wons, a "sweet-toned side-kick" on the Camel cigarette show. Tony Wons had inspired in Lardner a special cheer: " 'Tony Wons! Tony Twice! / Holy, jumping ———' / and that was as far as I had progressed when the flash came that he was temporarily through and at present reciting Edgar Guest's poetry to an audience of helpless Wisconsin pickerel."[12]

Aspects of radio which offended him again and again were the lack of proficiency and the bad taste of many of the singers of popular songs. He commented on the ridiculousness of Bing Crosby's accusation to the effect that another singer, Russ Colombo, had imitated the Crosby style:

> Both are extremely proficient in the art of not hitting a note on the nose. They sneak up on it, or miss it entirely. . . . Russ can outsyllable Bing over a distance; for example, Russ, without apparent effort, sings "na-hight shall be fa-fa-filled with mee-hew-sic, na-hight shall be fa-fa-filled with luh-uh-uh-uhv," or whatever it is. Bing, however, is unbeatable in a sprint, such as the word "you."[13]

Among his other aversions were Morton Downey ("the male Lily Pons") and Kate Smith.

When they discovered he was a columnist, advertisers and their agencies, aided and encouraged by the broadcasting companies, bombarded Lardner with publicity releases that they expected him to disseminate in his columns. In one column he complained that he had been deluged by so much publicity from NBC and CBS that he had not had time to listen to any programs.[14] His comment on what the broadcasting companies seemed to expect of him was characteristically oblique: "When I asked my Latvian swineherd how I might repay in a measure the debt we Johnson disciples owe the Boswell family, he suggested that I might give some publicity to the Boswell Sisters. . . . They sing."[15]

Sexually suggestive singing always provoked his most vehement indignation. In the third column there is this comment on Ruth Etting: "When she sings you can't miss a word, and if ever there was a time in this country's history when song words needed a good missing, that time is (Bulova watch time) now. Ninety-nine and $^{44}/_{100}$ per cent of today's and yesterday's 'lyrics' should remain confidential between the lyricist and himself."[16] A few months later he was more explicit: "The lyricists . . . are polluting the once-pure air of Golly's great out-of-doors with a gas barrage of the most suggestive songs ever conceived, published, and plugged in one year. . . . Queer as it may seem, I don't like indecency in song or story, and sex appeal employed for financial gain in this manner makes me madder than anything except fruit salad."[17] He noted that words like "God," "hell" and "damn" were not permitted on the air, but comedians were allowed "gags running the gamut from vulgar to vile," and singers were allowed to make unmistakable off-color allusions. One taboo, however, comedians always observed: "It is permissible to joke about any relative except mother, who is still a Sacred Cow, to be used only as a snivel-song heroine, preferably dead."[18]

The vulgarity of tortured English offended him just as much as sexual vulgarity. He wrote that in "Night and Day" Cole Porter "not only makes a monkey of his contemporaries but shows up W. S. Gilbert himself as a seventh-rate Gertrude Stein and he does it all with one couplet, held back till late in the refrain and then delivered as a final, convincing sock in the ear." ("Night and day under the hide of me / There's an Oh, such a hungry yearning, burning inside of me.")[19]

Although some of the criticism in "Over the Waves" was constructive, in the next to the last column he wrote Lardner moved into whimsy and nonsense: the most fruitful ways to deal with the dreadful noises, vulgarity, and promotion schemes that had offended his sensibilities for so long. The column was a play called "Ricordi to the Rescue: A Radio Play in One Endless Act."[20] The setting is a "living room in the Clark's apartment. The room is comfortably furnished, the most expensive pieces being a combination radio-victrola-garage, and a lunch counter that gives the results of the Miami dog races." The action of the play parodies the miscellaneous panorama of radio fare: it is confused and meaningless.

Lardner's vision of the world could best be controlled by ridiculing what was rational, orderly, logical. All through his writing there is a tendency toward deliberate nonsense that becomes more and more pronounced as he grows older: an inversion of the child's attitude toward the adult world. Lardner's writing is intended to ridicule the kind of audience/reader who values reason, order, logic, rationality, and is pretentious about these staunch middle-class values. It is the same reader Mencken fooled in his bathtub-hoax essay.

The culmination of this tendency was the series of nonsense plays Lardner wrote in the 1920s, most of them for the *New Yorker*. In many of his other *New Yorker* contributions nonsense had been the humorous method. For example, in two stories published in 1929 and 1930 whimsy and illogical extravagance were used to objectify and project desperation, anxiety, and hopelessness. The attitude of despair was established in the beginning of the first story, "Large Coffee,"[21] which was to be "a human document of particular interest to men and women who, like the writer thereof, have been battered and broken by an insensate world." The story presents extracts as if from a writer's diary. We know at the beginning that "the body of a Mr. Lardner was found in a New York hotel room. . . . He was sprawled out on the floor, his head crushed in by a blow from some blunt instrument, probably another hotel." We learn that he has come to the hotel in order to get away from the social and alcoholic distractions of life at home. He tries desperately to write, but his anxieties, the hotel bureaucracy, and his interest in the sexual activities of people in the apartment building next door combine to defeat him. Caught here, in comedy that is both grotesque (in its sexual compulsion) and macabre (in its obsession with death) are the moods and frustrations of a writer-hero whose creative resources have been exhausted.

The second story, "Sit Still,"[22] is a sequence of loosely associated episodes narrated in the first person. Walking down Fifth Avenue, the narrator stops automatically "with the rest of the southbound traffic at Seventy-second Street to allow the crosstown traffic to move, though God knows what good it did them because it is a two-way street and there were just as many going one way as the other." He gets into a taxicab "that I had never seen before"; he jokes pointlessly with the driver, who drives aimlessly around for a while, then takes him to the Hotel Astor. In the lobby there is a crowd of people, all of whom are waiting for opportunities to sit down in the lobby chairs. These chairs, we learn, have been continuously occupied for periods of from eight to sixty-six years. Like those on the Stock Exchange, one of the chairs was sold for $125,000. After twenty-five years, Lardner tells us, a chair squatter "is privileged to get up and move around without jeopardizing his rights. He is privileged to get up and move around, but he can't. Because he can't."

In 1931, the *New Yorker* published a Lardner nonsense play called "Quadroon: A Play in Four Pelts Which May All Be Attended in One Day or Missed in a Group."[23] Half of the play is the author's prefatory note. For example: "The characters were all born synonymously; that is, in the 'Su'th,' they are know as half-castes"; "This play, as hinted in the subtitle, is actually four separate plays with four separate titles: 'Hic,' 'Haec,' 'Hoc,' and 'Hujus.' It can be seen that the original author was a born H lover." The play itself has two intermissions, one for lunch and the second for dinner; menus are helpfully included. The four "pelts" of the play are utter nonsense, with short spasms of logical dialogue. In the third "pelt" Mayor Jimmy Walker and the Prince of Wales dance together and trade platitudes about New York City: "New York is the richest market in the world"; "The theatre market is an unrivalled concentration of spending power." The mayor and the prince are interrupted by Frank Case ("proprietor of the Algonquin," played by Alice Brady) who asks: "Can either of you boys play a cellophane?" The last "pelt" finds Lavinia dancing with Fred Astaire; she says: "The minute you try Pebeco Tooth Paste you know by its 'bitey' tang that here is a tooth paste that really 'gets somewheres.' " The final program note is *"Leave your ticket check with an usher and your car will come right to your seat."*

In this play, as in the other nonsense writings, Lardner ridicules the orderly world by creating a confusing, illogical setting. Nonsense ridicules logic and order; it burlesques what is familiar by turning it upside down. Nonsense pointedly ignores human efforts to bring order out of what without these efforts would be the chaos of environment. Nonsense also is a way of temporarily dealing with anxieties about an environment that seems impossibly meaningless, cluttered, and valueless. Children in analogous fashion sometimes resort to nonsense as a way of ignoring and forgetting the difficult demands for coherent thought and rational behavior made upon them by adults. Nonsense is one way of meeting the need for relaxation from the persistent human search for order. When everything is deliberately made meaningless, one can, for a moment, relax.

Edmund Wilson has described the response to nonsense as being due to "the enfeeblement of the faculty of attention." He saw this enfeeblement as part of a general crisis—the intellectual chaos of the 1920s—and noted a parallel between European dadaism and the tendency of some American humorists of the 1920s toward the non sequiturs of nonsense.[24] Dada was nonsense codified and organized, and therefore a way of achieving relief from anxiety, a way of self-preservation. For the dadaists were supremely individualistic, with a little childishness in their antics and anguish. The movement arose in Paris, promoted chiefly by Tristan Tzara, in 1920. Dadaists were practical jokers; they were silly and sometimes obscene. They did not flaunt any specific authority, but rather abstractions such as logic, order, and authority itself. Underlying the deliberate enfeeblement of their faculty for attention was a spirit of progressive opposition: in the late 1920s and in the 1930s many of them joined various revolutionary or reformist groups.[25]

An underlying spirit of opposition is another dimension of Lardner's nonsense writing. Nonsense represented for him more than a withdrawal from the logical world, more than a release from anxiety through illogic and playfulness; it was also the expression of hostility. Some of this hostility issued in satire of the pomposities of radio and the theater, in ridicule of the vulgarity of mass culture, or in anxiety over the confusion of urban life. But a part of the hostility his nonsense communicated was directed at his primarily middle-class readers, an audience that included the perpetrators of chaos and pomposity in American life. Nonsense was his finally cynical way of commenting on the enfeeblement of people who were willing to believe such writing actually was funny. Nonsense is verbal play and in that sense evokes delight. It is also and at the same time the ultimate abuse of language.

Most of his nonsense writing came late in his life. Although he had been a successful humorist for years, no writer of humor had more of a sense of the jaded, cliché-ridden techniques to which as a humorist he was indebted for his success and popularity. His narrators ridicule pretension and at the same time undercut that ridicule by parodying themselves. The culmination of such parody was the mock autobiography, the *Story of a Wonder Man* (1927). It is an example of Lardner ridiculing autobiographical techniques, and the expression of his contempt both for himself as humorist and for his readers. In it he strained for comic effects. Published first in his syndicated column, it was journalistic hackwork by a humorist capitalizing on his reputation. Donald Elder's assessment is that Lardner "mimics the unctuous false modesty of many such memoirs, the egotistical complacency of Edward Bok, the revolting sentimentality of nostalgic recollections. He pictures the Wonder Man as a tireless exhibitionist, aggressive, conceited and hollow. In the almost repellent hospital jokes he reflects his own squeamishness and his own humiliation."²⁶ He refused to be coherent, and his frequent injections of nonsense reflect an attitude of contempt for his readers. He seemed to speak, like the dadaists, only to a coterie, a select group that in order to understand him must share his anguish and cynicism. At the same time he had contempt for an audience whose faculty of attention had become enfeebled, and that accepted his condition of enfeeblement with sophisticated despair.

One member of this sophisticated audience Lardner both pandered to and ridiculed must have been Hemingway. The *Story of a Wonder Man* echoes something of the tone of the kidding and debunking dialogues both in *The Torrents of Spring* and in *The Sun Also Rises*. There is the same ritual of irony shared with an elite audience through nonsense, non sequitur, and burlesque, with deflationary reference to contemporary figures, fads, and ideas. It is a tone echoed a few years later by West in his mock version of the American success story: *A Cool Million; or, The Dismantling of Lemuel Pitkin* (1934).

Hemingway, reacting to Lardner's ridicule of his audience, wrote an assessment of him in 1934, after his death, that cuts to the very heart of the narrative effect Lardner achieved again and again. Hemingway had turned against Lardner and repudiated his earlier sense of debt to him, following a pattern of rejection of literary influences that began with the debunking in *The Torrents of Spring*. But what Hemingway wrote in his hostility nevertheless reflected a sensitivity to something central in

Lardner: "Ring Lardner . . . with never a dirty word wrote of those who make it with their hands in the nightly tragic somewhere of their combat, distorting the language that they speak into a very comic diction, so there's no tragedy ever, because there is no truth."[27] Hemingway saw that Lardner's vision of America was a tragic vision, that the central metaphor for American experience in his time was combat, and that Lardner's characters talk a distorted, comic language, which destroys the sense of tragedy. What Hemingway also identifies is Lardner's perception that the very condition of American life and culture does not allow tragic resolution because both faith and a sense of reality in the world of the 1930s have been lost; I take it that Hemingway uses "truth" in this weighted, almost medieval way.

Wilson early identified the conflicting quality of Lardner's attitude about his culture. In a notebook entry of April 1924, Wilson described a drunken party that included the Fitzgeralds. Lardner read from a book of rules "put out by the local golf club. Lardner read these rules at length with a cold and sombre scorn that was funny yet really conveyed his disgust with his successful suburban life."[28]

Mencken was precise in locating Lardner's estimate of the American character:

> No writer in our history has ever done livelier or more life-like portraits of the nether American. . . . There is, indeed, an overwhelming reality in every detail of their clumsy and brutal behavior, in every tremor of their shabby souls, even in every grunt of their half-simian speech. Observing these dismal pugs, song writers, movie wenches, radio crooners and baseball players as they shuffle across the stage, it is quite impossible to doubt them. . . . If accurate character-drawing and adept plot-making were the whole of imaginative writing, then it would be difficult to think of even a pedagogue denying Lardner's high place in the trade.
>
> What makes him suspect, of course, is the nature of his philosophy. He offends by denying the doctrine that the purpose of literature is to spread sweetness and light.[29]

Like Mencken, Lardner both needed and attacked the culture that had nurtured him. In an essay on Lardner compiled from a review written in 1924, revised in 1926, and again in 1949, Mencken had seen that "Lardner concealed his new savagery . . . beneath his old humor." But of Lardner's characters Mencken wrote: "There is something far more than mere facile humor: they are all rigidly in character. . . . Lardner did not see situations; he saw people. And what people! They are all as revolting as so many Methodist bishops, and they are all as thoroughly American."[30]

In a comment on Lardner shortly after his death, there was a reference, in the *New Yorker*, not to Lardner the funnyman but to the Lardner who had an "ear for the dim sad music of America."[31] His crusade for cleaner and better radio on the pages of the *New Yorker* had been one of the last uses of satire in a sustained campaign, in an act of protest. His sense of the chaos of urban life as conveyed by some of his *New Yorker* writings was in sharp contrast to the glorification of urban sophistication explicit in the antiprovincial humor of many of the debunkers. It was as a writer of nonsense, however, that Lardner represented the culmination of a tendency in twentieth-century American satire away from the topical toward the more general expression of anxiety over the state of a whole culture.

Nonsense writing also was a culminating element of style in Lardner and reflected his extraordinary love of language for its own sake. He had a remarkable ear for the American language and could parody or mimic varieties of speech without effort. He loved verbal play. Dorothy Parker emphasized this power in a summary listing of his accomplishments as a writer: "Ring Lardner's unparalleled ear and eye, his strange, bitter pity, his utter sureness of characterization, his unceasing investigation, his beautiful economy." In an obituary, Fitzgerald's concern was that of a writer about writing: "Whatever Ring's achievement was it fell short of the achievement he was capable of, and this because of a cynical attitude toward his work."[32] But Virginia Woolf's assessment was that "he writes the best prose that has come our way." She was (in 1925) fascinated by the precision and evocative power of Lardner's language to describe the disorder and incongruity of American experience.[33]

Making order out of disorder and making the language adapt to their needs were also implicit concerns of White and Sullivan, *New Yorker* writers who, along with Lardner, shaped much of the special character of that magazine as it took on its present identity in the early 1930s. Through these three writers, satire of the debunkers reached its most consistent culmination, although it surfaced again in Perelman and West.

Underlying the satire of Lardner, Sullivan, and White was a similar apprehension of the triviality, materialism, and banality of mass culture in America. Although their styles and methods differed, all three tended toward the fable or nonsense-writing as characteristic ways of expression. Nonsense-writing was a way of relieving the anxiety produced by their hostility toward mass culture. And their audiences were invited to share with them the temporary release and relief from reality, order, and logic which immersion in nonsense offered.

All three, as well as some of the other debunkers (for example, Benchley, Thurber, and Perelman) were part of that tendency in American humor which had produced the wild extravagance and frequently satiric nonsense of the tall tale and buncombe oratory—the tradition to which Ambrose Bierce's "Swiftian satires" and fables belonged. Walter Blair has traced this tendency to Artemus Ward and has called its modern practitioners "Crazy Men."[34] The humor of Charles Farrar Browne, the creator of Artemus Ward, depended on his speaker's pose of uncertainty, of confusion, of bafflement before the logic and order of the adult, social world. Underlying this artful confusion were satiric intentions.

Although Sullivan's best writing was published by the *New Yorker,* he did his earliest debunking and comic writing for the daily and Sunday editions of the *New York World.* His byline began to appear in 1924. He shared the feature page and the Sunday "Metropolitan Section" with, among others, Lardner, Mencken, Franklin P. Adams, Will Rogers, and Broun. In 1926 he stepped up the volume of his comic writing by appearing also under the pseudonym "Martha Hepplethwaite." "Miss Hepplethwaite" was an addled, long-winded, middle-class lady very like Marquis's Hermione. His own column "Out of a Clear Sky" began to appear regularly in the daily editions of 1927. Sullivan was one of the earliest contributors to the *New Yorker,* and wrote regularly for that magazine from 1925 on.

Frequently Sullivan's writing deals with bureaucratic pomposity, legal obfuscation, pedagogic stiffness, or, simply, mannered pretentiousness, by reducing them to nonsense. He uses the familiar satiric device of exaggeration, or, that oldest device of them all, the world turned upside down. Much of his humor has its roots in close observation of language; he has written a series recording the statements of cliché experts on such cliché-saturated topics as the atom, politics, Christmas, health, football, baseball, and the drama. This series must have owed some of its narrator's character to Lewis's Lowell Schmaltz, "The Man Who Knew Coolidge," as well as to the nineteenth-century parodies of the buncombe orators, and to the fabricated confusion of Artemus Ward and other comic lecturers. Although Sullivan has made fun of the man from the provinces and has debunked persistent Americanisms, his natural subject is more in the broad area of middle-class culture and pretensions to culture.

In some of his best work he gets part of his effect through parody: the deflation of affected style through ridicule of the subject matter that normally would accompany the style. In "Dear Old Paris: Memories by One Who Has Never Been There but Has Heard and Read Plenty about

It," he spoofed the breezy kind of reminiscences about the good old Bohemian days to which some aging artists were prone:

> Milwaukee stifled me. I felt that there was something in me that was very precious that Milwaukee would kill unless I escaped. I had to be free. . . . I left, and went to Paris. But Mother sent me plenty of money. . . . Marie and I would go to Foyot's in the Place Pigalle just off the "Boul Mich," for *escargots*. Gad, when I think of those *escargots* at Foyot's in the old days, prepared as only Pierre could pierre them, with that heavenly sauce that only he could conjure. . . . He would place it near the snails. Entranced by the magic concoction, they would troop out of their shells and pop one by one into the sauce, willing martyrs in the cause of good cuisine.[35]

In one of the many footnotes to "A Garland of Ibids for Van Wyck Brooks," he parodied Brooks's humorless thoroughness and also debunked his sometimes breathless sense of the sacredness of New England's literary flowering:

> Henry David Thoreau, philosopher who lived at Walden Pond for two years on carrots, twigs, nuts, minnows, creek water, and, as Margaret Fuller suspected (booming it out at Brook Farm in that full, rich voice of hers, to the dismay of William Ellery Channing, Henry Wadsworth Longfellow, Edward Everett Hale, John Lothrop Motley, Charles Eliot Norton, and William Lloyd Garrison), sirloin steaks and creamery butter smuggled to him by Emerson.[36]

Sullivan's humor had its special modern appeal not only in the realm of satire and parody (the cliché-expert writings are good examples), but also in the way he used nonsense to express and to deal with more profound feelings about the modern environment. His parodies of nostalgia frequently used nonsense as an expressive device. He often chose to write of what he variously called the Machine Age, the March of Civilization, the Cellophane Age, or Our Vaunted Civilization by creating a narrator whose voice parodied the sentimentally nostalgic, reminiscent attitude and style. This tendency persisted in his writing until after the Second World War. He began one essay written near the end of the war with a reminder to himself to gird his loins "in preparation for the Postwar Era. I went through the last Postwar Era ungirded and have not been the same since." He had, for instance, been unprepared for New York's elaborate and frenzied building projects during the 1920s, and wrote about them in a tone that skirts the edge of nonsense, nonsense which assesses his experience in the 1920s and conveys an underlying attitude of desperate fear: "I remember the other Postwar Era in Manhattan when the *rat-ta-ta-tat* of the rivet sounded far into the night and you had to pick your way along the streets lest a skyscraper shoot up under you, skewer you on its pinnacle, and boost you forty-two stories into the cerulean."[37] In an elaborate spoof of nostalgia itself ("The Night the Old Nostalgia Burned Down") he offered up a nonsensical hodge-podge of memories and anecdotes set in the framework of a New York childhood. He caught the pattering, inconsequential tone of reminiscence when he jumbled facts, dates, and geography in a parody of a kind of writing that the *New Yorker* was overly fond of printing (as early as 1928 there had been a *New Yorker* series by Russel Crouse called "That Was New York"):

> When I was a boy, Fourteenth Street was where Twenty-Third Street is now, and Samuel J. Tilden and I used to play marbles on the lot where the Grand Opera House still stood. . . .
> Mike Horan's place was at Minetta Lane and Washington Mews, and I clearly remember my father telling a somewhat startled Walt Whitman that old Mike Horan could bend a banana in two—with his bare hands! But I never saw him do it. . . . Then the Civil War came and the property of the Loyalists was confiscated. I still have some old Loyalist property I confiscated on that occasion. . . .
> I was six when the riots occurred. No, I was *thirty*-six. . . . Well, that was New York, the old New York, the New York of gaslit streets, and sparrows (and, of course, horses), and cobblestones. The newsboy rolled the *Youth's Companion* into a missile and threw it on your front stoop and the postmen wore uniforms of pink velvet and made a point of bringing everybody a letter every day.
> *Eheu, fugaces!*—[38]

Less and less in the 1940s and 1950s did the tensions of urban life inspire Sullivan, and he reverted to a gentler re-creation of those sophisticated attitudes that he had earlier debunked. *A Moose in the Hoose* (1955) bears witness to this mellowing of tone, which was not entirely of his own choosing. Thurber has noted that when Sullivan wanted to do a piece about his cliché expert and McCarthyism, Ross wrote to him: "I don't think so. I'd think twice about it. I can't see it myself."[39] But Sullivan's earlier writings, especially in the first years of the 1930s, were powerful in their breathless extravagance, and also profound in their ridicule of some of the absurdities of American culture. The carefully wrought incongruities of much of his work (especially the cliché-expert writings and the parodies of nostalgia) were expressive of a concern about the misuse of language. Underlying his ridicule of American clichés was his indignation at a culture pompous enough to want to codify and perpetuate its absurdities in repetitively ordinary patterns of verbal expression. Yet at the same time there was an affection for the clichés and for the pomposities: they were the stuff of his humorous artistry. Underlying his parodies of nostalgia was a vague horror—made even more acute by its very vagueness—at a culture with a tendency to look backward with maudlin and inconsequential sentimentality rather than forward. Yet this horror in his best nonsense writing is the controlled attitude through which he contrived his satiric effects. His skill at mimicry was like that of Lewis and his ear for the varieties of American speech was as keen. Like Lewis's writing, his prose often contained a tension between scorn and affection—the attitude typical of this generation of satirists.

White's work has reflected some of the same attitudes as Sullivan's. White sustained the *New Yorker* as editor, editorialist, and humorist from its beginning. He collected his best essays of the late 1920s and '30s, most of which appeared originally in the *New Yorker,* in a book he called *Quo Vadimus?* A satiric commentator on American culture, manners, and morals, he is less savage on the surface than Mencken or Marquis: his compassion and optimism are more overt. He dedicated *Quo Vadimus?* to "Walt Whitman, of Paumanok"; invoking Whitman suggests an attempt to rediscover both cultural direction and optimism. The attitude of the speaker who tells the stories in *Quo Vadimus?* is that of a disillusioned adult in search of a lost innocence. This adult has been forced into whimsy and irony by his sense that there is not enough room in the modern world for either innocence or optimism.

White can be acerbic and direct in his contempt and hostility, but in much of his writing he tends toward the nonsensical and the fabulous as his most comfortable modes of expression. The "Parables and Prophecies" in *Quo Vadimus?* illustrate this tendency. One fable was called "The Wings of Orville."[40] Orville is a sparrow, who nests with his family in Madison Square near the Farragut Statue. He is a pretty good father "as cock birds go," but he has "a quirk in his nature." Like many American males of the type here satirized he imagines himself as a hero-adventurer. A new Charles Lindbergh, he sets out to achieve a couple of "firsts" in the realm of air travel. In his first adventure he proves "the practicability of a round-trip flight between Madison Square and Hastings-upon-Hudson carrying a bottle-cap." In his second adventure he sets out to "prove the feasibility of towing a wren behind a sparrow." He cracks up, tangled in the tow-string on his first attempt, but he has succeeded in winning his wife's admiration after her original skepticism; she is a twentieth-century Pertelote. Orville, of course, is a fool, but like Chaucer's Chauntecleer, he elicits some admiration for his foolishness.

There is satire in White's fables, but there is also comic playfulness and a mood of relaxation. The attitude in many of his parables is quite different. Here, as in the world of Archy and Mehitabel, there is an animating anger. For example, in "Irtnog"[41] White traces the ultimate results of America's mania for digests, outlines, and reading short-cuts, as exemplified by the *Reader's Digest,* Wells's *Outline of History,* and *Time* magazine. The step beyond the digest is "the idea of digesting the digest." The first digest of the digests is *"Pith,"* followed by *"Core,"* *"Nub,"* and *"Nutshell": "Nutshell* folded up, because, an expert said, the name was too long." But soon there were hundreds of digests of digests, and "again readers felt themselves slipping." Then a mathematician worked out an "ingenious formula" whereby "he could take everything that was written and published each day, and reduce it to a six-letter word." The first day he produced the word "Irtnog," the second "Efsitz," and so forth. People were "thoroughly satisfied," for they were assured that, knowing the "Word of the Day," "they were not missing anything." Other debunkers had laughed at the abusive simplicity of digests. Always, underneath their ridicule, was their outrage as writer-artists, for they were reacting to the wanton, mindless misuse of the English language.

White incorporated into the fable and the parable controlled nonsense that expressed both his sense of the complexity of, and his most pessimistic feelings about, American culture. In one 1933 *New Yorker* series he invoked Lewis Carroll's *Alice in Wonderland* in order to give his comic method a special coherence. This series was called "Alice Through the Cellophane."[42] In it he ridiculed America's confusion during the first years of the Depression. There were, he suggested, great changes and movements in the air. Civilization had "momentum" and "complexity." Momentum and complexity had been revealed for the first time by "the transparency of cellophane." In fact, he wrote, "the social revolution began with cellophane, which allowed people to see what they were buying instead of simply going ahead and buying it anyway." Momentum, complexity, and social revolution had brought about changes in values. Most profoundly affected by these changes was the consumer, who, a loyal American and a faithful, if baffled capitalist, took his responsibility to his way of life seriously. White posed as the whimsical, confused epitome of this consumer: "Sometimes I wake in the middle of the night, thinking about the country's emaciation, and throwing on my shirt and trousers and coat, I trudge out to the corner drugstore to make a small purchase from patriotic motives. Some aspirin tablets or a Tootsie Roll."

White moved in the 1930s through the fabulous and the nonsensical toward the more and more overt expression of outrage at some of the manifestations of mass culture. His parable called "The Crack of Doom"[43] pictured a world dominated and finally destroyed by radio waves, and hence by the superficiality and vulgarity of the mass culture which radio glorified and perpetuated. Lardner's sensibility, too, had been offended severely by the same awareness. Both, on the pages of the *New Yorker,* fought a desperate battle against the sentimental, sloppy, superficial culture that abusive speech reflected and created. Both fought under the guise of comedy and satire, but everywhere in what they wrote despair and disgust were present.

Lardner's sensitivity to the potential of American language is what defined the moral perspective behind his debunking, and this sensitivity was shared by Sullivan and White, as it was by Marquis, Lewis, and Mencken. They all recognized both the banality and the vigor of American speech. They sought in their own styles an enactment of that vigor. They sought, sometimes desperately or cynically, always romantically, a world elsewhere through their visions of themselves as artists. There could be no return even to the imagination of an ideal place: that was a nineteenth-century pastoral vision lost. As it was for Archy the cockroach, expression was the need of their souls.

For a while, for several of them, the *New Yorker* became a kind of sanctuary, a place where expression was possible.

# Chapter Ten

## The New Yorker

To describe, to unify, to make order out of all these severed parts,
a new art is needed and the control of a new tradition. That
both are in process of birth the language itself gives us proof.
For the Americans are doing what the Elizabethans did—they
are coining new words. They are instinctively making the
language adapt itself to their needs.

Virginia Woolf, "American Fiction," 1925

**D**eveloping the energy of American English into a distinctive American style became an implicit mission for the *New Yorker* as it grew in the 1930s into a magazine of unusual cultural significance and achievement. The *New Yorker* began as a magazine of debunking satire and wit, but prior to 1930 its satirical tone was uneven and its facetiousness unsure. During the years between 1925 and 1930 there were some exceptions, some prefigurings of the comic spirit it was to display in the 1930s, but its initial success came primarily during the years of the Depression, and grew out of the comic way in which it treated Depression-related subjects.

In the late 1920s and the early 1930s the *New Yorker* was publishing debunking commentary by some of America's best satirists. These few years were also the years of the *New Yorker*'s greatest success as a magazine of humor. This humor was not of the sort that celebrated the smiling aspects of American life. It was debunking humor: urbane, witty, satiric. Its subjects were those identified and worked by the debunkers: provincialism, Puritanism, Americanism, Philistinism, and the defective language that was the common vehicle of such subjects.

Other ingredients contributing to the success of the magazine's humor were brevity, simplicity of format, and topicality. The principle that humorous articles and facetious commentary must be brief had been learned from the venerable comic weeklies, *Puck, Judge,* and *Life.* *Time* magazine, three years older than the *New Yorker,* had also demonstrated that capsule treatment of contemporary events was effective. The relationship among humor, satire, and contemporary events was one that was understood by the editors of the older comic weeklies; it was a relationship exploited by journalists throughout the nineteenth century, and it had been proved, in the 1910s and 1920s, by the popularity of the feature pages of newspapers such as *New York World,* the *New York Evening Sun,* and the *New York Tribune.* The *New York World* had featured Adams's "The Conning Tower," Broun's "It Seems to Me," Sullivan's "Out of a Clear Sky" and the writings of Benchley. Marquis had written "The Sun Dial" column for the *Evening Sun* and "The Lantern" for the *Tribune.* For most newspaper humorists the shift from the feature page of the newspaper to the pages of comic weeklies was easy and natural. The *New Yorker* preserved the brevity and topicality necessary to the writing of the journalist. It used the narrow newspaper column as an aid to rapid reading, and in so doing imitated *Puck, Judge,* and *Life,* all of which had begun to imitate newspaper layout around 1916.

More indirect influences on the *New Yorker* were some of the "little" magazines that had preceded it. Like them, the *New Yorker* was able with assurance, almost from the very beginning, to represent and project an attitude and point of view. Its attitude flattered the urbane reader; its point of view was satiric. Such a combination of characteristics had not figured prominently in American humor before the advent of debunkers such as Mencken and Marquis. Satire, with a few exceptions (Bierce is one), had been possible in the nineteenth century only for those American humorists who assumed an unsophisticated comic mask. Usually the satire was delivered in a rustic dialect by a wise fool from the provinces. The twentieth-century shift of comic posture, to which the *New Yorker* responded, was from the provincial to the urbane. Two late nineteenth-century journalistic prefigurations of the shift were magazines briefly published in metropolises on opposite sides of the country: *M'lle New York* and, in San Francisco, the *Lark.* With them the *New Yorker* shared simplicity of format, the effective use of drawings and cartoons, and the planned appeal to a limited readership. The *Lark* and *M'lle New York* did not survive into the new century. Obviously, the *New Yorker* conceived of a different audience. Nevertheless, it accepted from the beginning the principle that the satiric attitude could be at once entertaining and effective.

*Puck* magazine, begun in 1877, was the immediate progenitor in the field monopolized by the *New Yorker* after the early 1930s. *Puck* had conceived of itself as a comic and satiric magazine; it was also an instrument of partisan political commentary, leaning heavily toward the Democratic Party. A survey of issues in the late 1870s and the early 1880s shows satiric treatment of some of the subjects which the debunkers of the twentieth century handled in similar fashion. There was the "Puck's Sensational Novels" series, which parodied tales of adventure and sentimental fiction. The "Puck's Essential Oil of Congress" series spoofed activities and inactivities in Washington. Mock histories of the United States prefigured Stewart's historical parodies in the 1920s. There was also a series called "Fitznoodle in America," in which the impressions of a traveling Englishman were recorded in comic fashion. The affected, snobbish, and effeminate Fitznoodle was depicted as ridiculous and pathetic as he confronted the masculine crudities of American life. The twentieth-century debunkers' hostility was an inversion of this, for theirs was directed not at the Englishman or European but at the provincial American. *Puck* in the depression of 1893 expressed antipopulist attitudes which also pointed toward the comic antiprovincial hostility that was a persistent attitude and an important ingredient of the *New Yorker*'s early success. British mannerisms and traditions continued to be a source of *Puck*'s material in the 1890s. H. C. Bunner wrote a series called "The People in the Fog—Being Desultory Dips into the Gray Matter of the British Brain." The debunkers, especially writers for the *New Yorker,* borrowed this satiric tone to ridicule Americans who lived in what they took to be the provincial fog of the Midwest.

There was a good deal of antipapist sentiment in *Puck,* satire of papal politics and of the doctrine of papal infallibility. *Puck* insisted that it was ridiculing the way the church was administered, not Catholicism itself, but genteel Protestant readers must have assumed otherwise. The tendency of the debunkers was to ridicule organized religion in general, with the emphasis on the Puritan roots of American culture, since the middle class in America was primarily Protestant. In 1893 and 1894 *Puck* initiated an antipuritanism campaign, aimed at those who wanted to force blue laws on the Chicago World's Fair—such restraints as Sunday closing and art censorship. The debunkers, many of them in the pages of the *New Yorker,* continued to deride the Puritan minority which tried with frequent success to impose its morality on everyone else.

In the twentieth century *Puck* continued very much as it had in the 1890s. There was little change in format until 1916, when the neater, easier-to-read, three-column page was introduced. With the change in format, the magazine promised that it would develop a "new school of satire."[1] To that end it called for contributions from newspapermen; perhaps it hoped for debunking material from journalists such as Marquis and Mencken. During the prewar years the tenor of its humor was much the same as it had always been. Women's rights movements were ridiculed (as they had been in the 1870s). Special targets for comic treatment were the tycoons J. P. Morgan, Andrew Carnegie, John D. Rockefeller, and Theodore Roosevelt, with his quadrennial presidential aspirations. The Armory Show of 1913 provoked satiric commentary about modern art. Most of the debunkers, the *New Yorker* writers among them, continued to be offended by the avant-garde in art; here was an easy way to elicit the hostile laughter of middle-class citizens whose tight moral attitudes the debunkers, paradoxically and inconsistently, attacked in so many other areas. *Puck,* always Democratic, gave its vehement allegiance to Woodrow Wilson, and its comic tone was lost in pro-American, antialien, prowar polemics. After 1916 it did try to bring itself up to date by publishing some of the younger satirists. There were cartoons by John Held, Jr., and Ralph Barton, both *New Yorker* contributors. Among the writers appearing in issues during its last two years of publication were Samuel Hoffenstein and George S. Chappell, parodists who wrote frequently for *Vanity Fair.* But *Puck* was hopelessly outdated, in spite of the addition of numerous photographs of enticingly draped female models. After being sold to Hearst's International Magazine Company in 1917 it reverted to the kind of gentility it had once debunked, and the last issue appeared in September 1918. The comic weekly field was left to two very similar *Puck* imitators, *Judge* and *Life.*

Like *Puck, Judge* and *Life* had for years been the repositories for homespun humor which relished the cheerful character of American life. Thomas L. Masson was a typical early twentieth-century contributor to both magazines. There were many he-she jokes: early issues of the *New Yorker* did not disdain this venerable comic affliction either. There were pictures of handsome, healthy young women, suitable for admiration in the parlors of the American home. That the *New Yorker* scorned such pictures was a sure sign of sophistication and of an attempt to appeal to emancipated feminine readers, who saw themselves as something other than attractive parlor centerpieces. There was some political commentary in *Judge* and *Life,* frequently on presidential candidates. In 1912 *Judge* ran a cartoon which showed "Wouldgrow Wilson" trying to get into Bryan's oversize presidential suit. *Judge* also in each 1912 issue devoted a page to "The Modern Woman," spoofing the energetic enthusiasms of the militant female suffragists. The *New*

*Yorker* discovered that women, who paid their advertisers, were no longer suitable comic material; like it or not, a magazine that aspired to a general readership in America had to take women seriously.

By 1925 *Judge* and *Life* had adjusted somewhat to the times. Keeping their national circulations in mind, they made fun of the frantic lives of hard-drinking urbanites, but tried to maintain their urban appeal at the same time by printing jokes and cartoons about quaint life in the provinces. The *Judge* cover girls wore less clothing and thus revealed more of their wholesomeness, but their pulchritude was never especially suggestive. Nevertheless, that they were present at all was evidence of *Judge's* bias toward the masculine reader. The magazine displayed a fatal disregard for the tastes and interests of a female America that had just been given the right to vote. The advertisements, which were national in scope, contrasted sharply with what was to appear in the *New Yorker;* the somewhat unsophisticated emphasis was on trusses, health cures, and how-to-be-a-success-in-love-and-business books. *Judge* did see the humorous possibilities of all this nonsense when, on 11 April 1925, it published a burlesque advertising issue, which debunked the elaborate claims of manufacturers. Norman Anthony, the editor responsible for the issue, left *Judge* to become editor of *Life* in 1929.

Anthony had tried as editor of both *Judge* and *Life* to find a formula that would maintain the reputations and circulations of these magazines. Both of them foundered in the 1930s. The title *Life* was sold to Time, Incorporated, in 1936, while *Judge* lingered on uncertainly and unsuccessfully. Anthony himself, upon leaving *Life* after a year, produced a new humorous magazine that had brief but spectacular fame. The magazine, *Ballyhoo,* first appeared in 1931. *Ballyhoo* used the burlesque technique which Anthony had developed in 1925 as editor of *Judge.* Advertisements were flamboyantly parodied. Sex was used freely both as a weapon for parody and as a circulation booster in itself. The appeal of the magazine was primarily to New Yorkers; one printing in 1931 exceeded two million copies. It seemed at first that Anthony had found a formula which could rival the *New Yorker's.* Advertisers, discovering that derogatory burlesques of their products led to increased sales, frequently paid for *Ballyhoo* advertisements which satirized their products. Such a peculiar inversion of standards led to the further deterioration of *Ballyhoo's* original debunking intentions.[2] The novelty soon wore off; burlesque advertisements were not enough to sustain a general-circulation magazine. The fad died quickly, although *Ballyhoo* did not expire completely until 1939. The *New Yorker* in the 1930s had little left in the way of competition.

Some competition at the start came from Mencken's and Nathan's *American Mercury*. While the early *New Yorker* was much more flippant in appearance and style, it borrowed Mencken's antiprovincialism so thoroughly that at first there seemed to be little else. It looked and sounded much like the *Smart Set* because its initial appeal was to "cleverness" and to "minds that are not primitive."

While the *Smart Set* continued as a Hearst publication, it was radically changed from a magazine of cleverness and satirical wit. Probably the *New Yorker* acquired some of the *Smart Set*'s subscribers, although many must have followed Mencken and Nathan to the *Mercury,* which appealed to much the same audience. After 1927 the circulation of the *Mercury* decreased while the *New Yorker* enlarged and consolidated its readership. Initially its subjects for satire were the same as the *Mercury*'s: provincialism, puritanism, Americanism, and the pretentions of aesthetes. It imitated the *Mercury*'s "Americana" section by using as column fillers self-parodying excerpts from the American press. Its "Profiles" were shortened forms of the *Mercury*'s biographical essays. Like the *Mercury,* the *New Yorker* was able to demonstrate successfully that Americans had come of age, that there were in America enough aspirers to a native urbanity and wit to support a magazine which both flattered and directed their sense of superiority.

Another magazine that was aimed at some of the same circulation the *New Yorker* hoped to attract was *Vanity Fair*. Begun in 1914 with Frank Crowningshield as editor, *Vanity Fair* made its suave and glossy appeal to those elements of society who were flattered by the reassurance that their artistic tastes were at once catholic, avant-garde, and European in flavor. *Vanity Fair* provided vignettes of, and writings by, the people who mattered in society, sports, drama, and the visual arts. It also sought out for ridicule the unknowing Philistines and those newly arrived in the outer parlors of high culture. Its most effective weapons in these campaigns were parody and the two departments of the magazine that with equal assurance made nominations for the "Hall of Fame" or for "Oblivion."

Humorists who appeared regularly in *Vanity Fair* during the 1920s were Benchley, Ford, Stewart, George S. Chappell, Nancy Boyd (Edna St. Vincent Millay), Samual Hoffenstein, and Edgar Dalrymple Perkins. Stewart wrote often from the point of view of the Ivy League socialite giving facetious hints to young ladies from the Midwest who were about to attend Eastern schools. Chappell was perhaps best remembered for his "Rollo" series: Rollo was the young son of a family, recently come from the provinces to live in New York, whose efforts to become cultured urbanites were hampered by the hayseed which clung to them. Millay, under the pseudonym "Nancy Boyd," wrote many "he-she" dialogues, which chronicled the manners and problems of young, urban married couples. Ford was the most persistent contributor, frequently appearing under his own name and a pseudonym in the same issue. *Vanity Fair,* like the *New Yorker,* depended primarily on satire for its success during the 1920s. There were, of course, other departments, but satire made up the bulk of each issue.

*Vanity Fair*'s decline began around 1930. Cleveland Amory and Frederic Bradlee blame this decline on the Depression.[3] It is true that *Vanity Fair* changed very little during the Depression years. There was the same flamboyance, the same features, and with Prohibition dying a natural death the magazine nevertheless campaigned vigorously for its repeal, as if the issue were still fresh. The satiric tone of the magazine in the 1930s was upheld almost entirely by the glib ironies of Clare Boothe Brokaw (whose addition to the staff as a satiric writer had been hailed in 1930), and by Ford's astonishing productivity. But the main reason for the decline and fall of *Vanity Fair* was that the *New Yorker* was a far better magazine, both in its humor—which remained predominantly debunking humor in the 1930s—and in its other offerings. *Vanity Fair* tried to change the trend by becoming a picture magazine (color photography and reproduction became commercially feasible in the early 1930s) and by frankly imitating the *New Yorker* in some respects. There were many short biographies of prominent people, in imitation of the *New Yorker*'s series of "Profiles." Perhaps both magazines were responding to *Time* magazine's capsule technique in the news field. In December 1932 and thereafter, *Vanity Fair* acknowledged the *New Yorker*'s potency by imitating its format: the narrow column, three to a page, was used. Even the covers began to look like the *New Yorker*'s. But these cosmetic alterations were to no avail, since the *New Yorker* had the advantage over *Vanity Fair* in the quality of its satire. Often *Vanity Fair*'s satiric commentary rambled and became tedious, but the *New Yorker* insisted on brevity, whether in humor or features. *Vanity Fair,* more expansive and flamboyant, was less carefully edited. And the *New Yorker* provided an American, New York-centered sense of sophistication, whereas *Vanity Fair*'s orientation was more European.

The *New Yorker* had, however, begun by trying to imitate some of the mannered superiority of *Vanity Fair.* It was trying to be a reliable, worldly, amusing guide for the social, cultural, and material needs of well-to-do New Yorkers. Bringing these elements into harmony was not easy. For the first few years the magazine was an uneven comic hodge-podge. The format of the pages was cluttered. The effect was a little like that of the feature pages of the *New York World* and *New York Evening Sun*. But gradually the *New Yorker* cleaned up its pages, simplified its format, established its weekly departments, and drastically reduced the number of drawings and cartoons, as well as the many inane and gossipy jokes about its friends and enemies. In 1935 and 1936 the old *Life*, just before it was taken over by Time, Inc., acknowledged the *New Yorker*'s success, as had *Vanity Fair*, by imitating its format, layout, covers, and typeface.

The *New Yorker* began in 1925 as a magazine of debunking humor; there were other departments and kinds of writing in the first years, but it was primarily through satiric writing that Ross hoped to reflect the urbanity and vitality of New York. Jokes, short anecdotes, and humorous "casuals" were the meat of the early issues. It was not until the 1930s that short, nonhumorous stories began to appear with regularity. Gradually longer and longer contributions were printed; the climax of this tendency was the one-issue Hiroshima article by John Hersey in 1946. The tendency toward length has also led away from humor; the essence of the humorous piece is brevity. Thus (disregarding weekly features, which have remained nearly unchanged) the *New Yorker* has changed over the years from a humor magazine with occasional articles and stories to a magazine of articles, stories, and poetry which occasionally prints humor. But in the early 1930s it was not unusual to find satiric writing in each issue. These pieces almost invariably were produced by several of the same group of writers: Ford, Stewart, Davis, Parker, Benchley, Lardner, White, Thurber, Gibbs, Sullivan, and Perelman. Other writers appearing less frequently as humorists were Fillmore Hyde, Thomas Beer, Stephen Leacock, Nunally Johnson, and Heywood Broun. The *New Yorker* conceived of urbanity in terms of humor and wit; there were other ingredients, but humor came first. The success and tone of the magazine depended upon a combination of editorial policy and the kind of contributions available.

Ross had no talent as a writer, but as editor of the *New Yorker* his first and lifelong interest was in comic writing. Satire and burlesque were the modes of expression that appealed to him, and in these preferences he was like the writers he most appreciated, one of them being Mencken. He was like Mencken in his professed rejection of the genteel, and in his need for the recognition and applause of sophisticated people. Both were outspoken in their prejudices. Ross's ignorance of culture and literature appalled those who thought that the editor of the *New Yorker* should have been more obviously cultured, like *Vanity Fair*'s Frank

Crowningshield. Ross said loudly and in public that he distrusted the female and femininity in general, but his own mother and later his daughter were important exceptions (he was married three times). In a book which admiringly perpetuated Ross's carefully contrived aura of the enigmatic, Thurber wrote that he was plagued by a "truly severe Momism." Ross said, "Men don't mature in this country, Thurber. They're children. . . . I think it's the goddam system of women school teachers."[4] Ross insisted that he was surrounded and oppressed by women and children; he claimed that he looked constantly and unsuccessfully for a superman who could run his magazine smoothly. In his vague, comic, and half-nostalgic public statements about an ideal masculinity he was very like Mencken. In fact, the writers who surrounded him were men—Dorothy Parker was one of the exceptions—but Ross must have realized that many, perhaps most of the readers of his magazine were women. Like Mencken, he must have sensed that relationships between male and female in America were changing gradually but irrevocably.

Part of Ross's nature was captured in a parody *New Yorker* cover; it was drawn for a burlesque issue which was privately printed on the magazine's first anniversary in 1926. The figure of Eustace Tilley, the dapper dandy who adorns all the anniversary issues of the *New Yorker,* was given the scowling features of Ross. In the perennial cover by Rea Irwin, Eustace strikes the pose of Walt Whitman in the famous photograph, but the butterfly he is examining has the head of Alexander Woollcott. Woollcott and Ross were both friends and enemies all their lives. Woollcott typified the kind of cultured superiority that Ross both longed to emulate and hated for its snobbishness.

The magazine that Ross created in 1925 conformed to his rather limited concept of urbanity. His concern for precision of language echoed the sensibilities of all the debunkers who ridiculed inflated, abusive rhetoric everywhere around them. Ross has been frequently pictured as a perfectionist, and it is true that he developed a mania for fact-checking, clarity of expression, and conformity to Fowler's *English Usage.* Perfectionism may have been a belligerent defense that he developed after his magazine had been laughed at by some of the urbane readers he wanted most to impress. It was also a sign of his anxiety for his magazine's success and a compensation for his general cultural naiveté. He responded as an editor especially to parody and to writing that ridiculed excessive pompousness both in language and in attitude.

Ross had been a wandering reporter before the war, and during the war was editor of *Stars and Stripes* in Paris. Just before beginning the

*New Yorker* he worked briefly for *Judge* magazine. *Judge,* and to a lesser extent, *Life,* were previews of what he hoped to do with the *New Yorker.* Ross thought he could publish a successful magazine by aiming directly at middle-class New York readers; to this end he sought advertising material which would have local appeal. *Life* and *Judge* differed: both were magazines that tried to be national in scope.

From its superior vantage point in the citadel of New York, the *New Yorker* persistently in its early years deprovincialized the rest of America through ridicule and satire. In the first issue (21 February 1925), the magazine announced "that it is not for the old lady in Dubuque. By this it means that it is not of that group of publications engaged in tapping the Great Buying Power of the North America Steppe region by trading mirrors and colored beads in the form of our best brands of hokum."[5] Some of the other voices in the early issues, however, were not as sure of their sophistication. Certain anecdotes and gossip items had a hometown flavor which was not quite appropriate to the big city, and which betrayed a naiveté more often found in college humor magazines. For example: "Don Marquis sort of satisfied a boyhood dream when he playacted as a bartender at a 'pope night' down at the Players. Don's just been seriously noticed by 'Doc' S. P. Sherman, but it don't seem to have gone to his head much yet."[6] In the "Washington Notes" of the same issue there was a comment on Henry Cabot Lodge which began: "He wasn't so darned high-hatty."[7] Even at its most facetious the mature voice of the *New Yorker* was never guilty of such lapses in its assured tone and meticulous English usage. Nevertheless, the rest of the "Washington Notes" in which the comment on Lodge appeared was a devastating, deadpan indictment of Coolidge's provincialism—a clear imitation of subject and attitude found in issue after issue of the *American Mercury.*

During 1925 many other subjects which became perennial *New Yorker* topics were fondly introduced: taxis and their drivers, smog, flamboyant building projects that changed the face of the old town, Prohibition, suburban life, commuter life, Hollywood, the problems encountered while weekending in the country. Also making their debut in 1925 were some writers and artists of note, or who would shortly become noteworthy: there were, for example, sketches by Reginald Marsh, and writings by Sullivan, White, Stewart, Benchley, Maxwell Bodenheim, and Elmer Davis.

The most persistent debunking campaign of the early years involved ridicule of those regions of the country so unfortunate as to lie outside of New York. The urban sophisticate seemed never to get enough reassurance of his superiority. Davis, who came from Indiana, was a contributor in this vein: in "On the Banks of the Wabash," he borrowed both Menckenian hyperbole and Menckenian scorn. The piece was

the first installment of the report of *The New Yorker's* expedition to explore the Unexplored Area lying southeast of Chicago and northwest of Cincinnati, known to the ancient cartographers as Indiana. . . . The principal hazard encountered by the inexperienced traveller is the streams of tobacco juice which spurt geyserlike in all directions on the streets of Indianapolis. . . . Threading my way through a crowded corridor, I found myself about to step on a citizen who looked pretty much like a cockroach. "Don't do that!" cried my companion in horror. "It may be a Grand Dragon."[8]

Provincialism as a subject was practically inexhaustible. In 1932 there was this in the "Notes and Comments" department: "A lot of people in Darke County, Ohio, and in Kansas, Louisiana, Oregon, etc., think that one of the candidates for President this fall is the late Theodore Roosevelt, a man who, they feel, is greatly needed at the helm of State in these times."[9]

Other familiar debunking subjects appeared frequently. Morris Markey, who wrote the weekly feature variously titled "In the News," "The Current Press," and finally "A Reporter at Large," borrowed the burlesque tone of Mencken's polemic and at least one of Mencken's favorite subjects. He wrote on the origin of Prohibition that "a group of tightwad puritans: hard-fisted, greedy—more deeply concerned in the end with their wads than their morals—that vast body of the vulgate lying to the South and West of us, precipitated the calamity."[10] The first sustained issue against which the *New Yorker* measured its superiority was fundamentalism. Throughout 1925 there were jokes, anecdotes, and "casuals" about William Jennings Bryan, and also a profile of him. The Scopes trial took place that year in Dayton, Tennessee.

Many pretensions to culture and urbanity were debunked. In "Up the Dark Stairs—" Benchley wrote that the trouble with journalism "began about ten years ago when the Columbia School of Journalism began unloading its graduates on what was then the *New York Tribune.* . . . Every one of the boys had the O. Henry light in his eyes, and before long the market report was the only thing in the paper that didn't lead off with 'up the dark stairs at ———.' "[11]

Corey Ford provided many burlesques in the early years; one series in 1925 was on creative art in New York. Some of the sources of "the native art that springs untrammeled from the heart of a free people" were billboards ("every subway station shows this craving for expression"), blotters, laundry bills, sand, and shattered glass ("observe what a devastating effect the unknown artist has achieved by the simple process of pasting a horsehide baseball against the pane of glass").[12] Published frequently in *Life, Judge,* and *Vanity Fair* (under the pseudonym "John Riddell"), Ford did not appear very often in the *New Yorker* after 1930. His humor eventually (in the 1950s) was found suitable by the *Saturday Evening Post* and by *Reader's Digest.* His most notable writings were parodies and burlesques of heroic tales of adventure and exploration; his spoofs of the adventurer June Triplett[13] had a wild ebullience borrowed from the burlesque theatre, and in them one finds both the monotony and hilarity of burlesque. When the *New Yorker* around 1930 ceased to print Ford's writings, it seemed to be rejecting the kind of humor that had sustained *Life* and *Judge* for years. Yet it had been Ford to whom Ross had turned in 1925 when he was looking for a writer who could give substance to the *New Yorker's* sense of cosmopolitanism. Ford, using Rea Irwin's first-issue cover picture for his inspiration, had created Eustace Tilley in a series called "The Making of a Magazine," which was begun on 3 August 1925 and was printed on the insides of the covers of the magazine.[14]

Davis was another frequent early contributor whose offerings dwindled as the *New Yorker* became surer about its attitudes and style. Davis had learned a great deal from Mencken, especially from the bathtub hoax. One of his pieces was a burlesque profile of the typical, successful American novelist. This attack on aestheticism presented a composite portrait: "He began his literary career, in the approved manner, with a spiritual Autobiography. . . . It was casual; and the critics called it the authentic voice of tortured and groping youth." Then the novelist went to war and wrote a novel "spelling out for the benefit of etymologists certain Anglo-Saxon terms often heard but rarely written, except with chalk." Picture rights were sold; when Hollywood drastically altered the plot of the novel (which was pro-Communist), the novelist "called in the reporters and denounced the smug vulgarians of Hollywood who had Falsified His Artistic Concept, and a thousand editorials praised him." Next he "discovered that the curse of America was the conspiracy of silence about Sex. Fearlessly he broke the taboo in a novel which the critics called searching and masterly." He began to have trouble with his wife, "so his next book dealt with the hopeless situation of the artist with a Rotarian wife, in a Rotarian civilization. . . . He went abroad, and from his villa in Capri wrote an article for *Vanity Fair* explaining that life in America is impossible for the artist."[15]

By 1928, the *New Yorker* had developed enough of a manner and style to be ridiculed by one of its ablest contributors. Lardner wrote and published in the *New Yorker* a parody of one of its favorite departments—a bit of frivolity probably only possible in the more carefree days of the *New Yorker*'s youth. He wrote a mock profile entitled "Profiles: Dante and ———." The thin thread of logic in the piece had to do with Beatrice Kaufman's pursuit of and marriage to George S. Kaufman. Beatrice was also referred to as Lotta Fairfax, who had in turn assumed the name of Beatrice Lillie. As in the typical *New Yorker* profile, there was deliberate violation of logic and of normal biographical sequence: Beatrice-Lotta-Beatrice is described as having "written many plays under the sobriquet of Owen Davis, and in 1926 she won the women's national tennis championship as Mrs. Bjurstedt." She had arrived in the United States as a stowaway on a Gaelic ship and her first glimpse of New York was from the steeple of a church in South Orange, New Jersey. On seeing New York she says: "Oh, mumsey, (mother) . . . please take me to New York so I can marry a Kaufman."[16]

Also ridiculed here was the *New Yorker*'s method of reporting, a method which even in 1928 had become characteristic. The method, a modification of the satiric catalog, hinges on the facetious effect produced when unrelated facts, names, or ideas are telescoped and presented to the reader in juxtaposition. Mencken was a master of such catalogs. The style, actually highly contrived, gives the impression of casual yet articulate sophistication; there is usually a hint of irony suggested by the carefully balanced incongruity in the sequence. There was a close parallel to, and perhaps source of, this development in the concurrent growth of *Time* magazine's condensed style, particularly in its creation of portmanteau words. Both magazines thought they had similar journalistic problems: *Time* strained mightily to hold the interest of the tired executive, who did not have the time or ability to read more eloquent English; the *New Yorker* struggled to flatter its readers with the illusion that they were bored literati who had read too much. *Time* had set an iconoclastic pattern for journalistic English and the *New Yorker* in its probably unconscious way followed where Henry Luce had led, although at some unlocatable point imitation may have become parody. It is a striking testimony to the sharpness of Lardner's ear and eye for language and to his sensibilities as a humorist that he, as early as 1928, recognized that the *New Yorker* was developing a style which could be parodied. And it is to the credit of the editors that they were willing to print this spoof of what became a central affectation. However, one *New Yorker* contributor did not completely concur; in 1929 Woollcott wrote his own mannered profile of Kaufman. He commented on Lardner's effort: "In it, for the first time in this series of Profiles, the spirit of whimsy reared its ugly head."[17] Woollcott's own spirit and temperament were usually better suited to the pages of *Vanity Fair*.

Insofar as the *New Yorker* has had an editorial voice, the "Notes and Comments" section has been that voice, and White was the most consistent writer of the section. He came to the *New Yorker* in 1926; even in the early issues the "Notes and Comments" showed the style of writing and imagination that he was to bring to them for years. The comments covered a wide range of attitudes and subjects. They could be serious, facetious, whimsical, satiric, indignant, nostalgic. Frequently White's commentary was on subjects which had been given wide and overly serious treatment in the week's news. During the early 1930s there was a great deal of subject matter exactly suited to the *New Yorker's* pointed commentary. These were the years when the *New Yorker* solidified its success, because it recognized in the Depression and in the administrations in Washington rich sources of comic material. Certainly, too, it was not above catering to the gentility of its middle-class readers, many of whom were Republicans. Yet at the same time it avoided any overt political commitment. Thus it was able to appeal to both liberal and conservative elements in its middle-class audience. It chose not to be solemn about America's embarrassment as the home of free enterprise, and this attitude was exactly right for the intelligent readers in whose existence Ross had always believed.

In the late 1930s the *New Yorker* began to take on what Thurber has described as "matronly girth." The quality and tenor of its humorous writing changed. Lardner, a frequent contributor in the early 1930s, had died in 1933. Sullivan turned more and more to reminiscences for his comic effects. Thurber wrote about life in the provincial city of Columbus, Ohio, with nostalgic affection. Toward the end of the war White took up the United Nations as a cause and used the *New Yorker* as an editorial rostrum. The days for relentlessly debunking life and manners in the provinces were over; too many *New Yorker* readers lived in them (by 1958, 80 percent of the *New Yorker's* circulation was outside of New York.)[18] Parody continued as the main form of satiric writing; but there was less and less comic hyperbole of the sort leveled at the provinces, or like that shaped as a weapon in Lardner's short crusade against radio. Gradually during these years the *New Yorker* attracted and published America's best writers of fiction, a function which in the *Mercury* had deteriorated in the early 1930s under the dictatorial editorship of Mencken. For example, it published Thurber and Kay Boyle after they were rejected by the *Mercury*.[19] Initially the *New Yorker* had fallen heir to the prestige of the *Mercury* in the 1920s by reflecting more success-

fully a spectrum of interests in satire, literature, politics, manners. Later, its humorists not only entertained but provided an accurate expression of the anxiety of sensitive Americans about the serious economic,
political, and social problems of the 1930s. Finally, the *New Yorker*'s
initial success depended on a combination of editorial direction and the
quality of the satiric writing that was available to it.

The *New Yorker* conveyed the most central concern of all the debunkers: again and again, the feelings of the mimics, parodists, and
satirists about the abuse of language ranged from amusement to outrage. The *New Yorker* accepted this concern for the purity of language
as its own. In the nonsatiric writing, in the expository prose, fiction, and
poetry that it published more and more after the early 1930s, the *New
Yorker* developed rigorous standards of usage and style. Its enhancement of the art of writing in America has been of far-reaching effect.
One aspect of that enhancement has been its emergence as one of the
most significant journals for the publication of contemporary poetry and
fiction. In retrospect we can look back on the satire it published in its
formative years as a kind of crusade for the preservation of the medium
sacred to all writers. The *New Yorker* writers and editors of these years
were not purists or traditionalists, but they were responsive to the vitality and potential of American English. Perhaps more consistently than
any other twentieth-century journal, the *New Yorker* has preserved and
promoted that vitality and potential. The active, participatory concern
of its writers had an aloof scholarly counterpart in Mencken's *American
Language* and its supplements; several articles by Mencken on the
American language were first published in the *New Yorker*.[20]

# Chapter Eleven
## Nathanael West

Although dreams were once powerful, they have been made
puerile by the movies, radio and newspapers. Among
many betrayals, this one is the worst.

Miss Lonelyhearts, 1933

The culture that had so horrified Lardner as it emanated from the
speakers inside his radio was the same culture that the debunkers
had exorcised for fifteen years. They had identified its perpetrators, its institutions, its flimsy values, and its lack of style with
what had at first been a kind of outraged joy. More and more that joy
changed into scorn, into variations of Lardner's cynicism and despair,
for a hideous victory was in their hands: they had shown the horror for
what it was, but it seemed to make no difference.

The production in Hollywood of films that pandered to the sentimental tastes and prurient interests of the boobs and yokels was another sign
that the war with banality had been lost. As Hollywood added sound to
its capacity for affecting culture, there were few debunkers left with the
energy to engage the enemy on new ground. The literature of the 1920s
that satirized Hollywood was sparse and ineffectual in the face of what
was emerging as an overwhelming phenomenon. Van Vechten in *Spider
Boy* (1928) and Marquis in *Off the Arm* (1930) tried to identify Hollywood's grossly inflated sense of its importance as an American institution. But their satire in these books was random and obscure. It was not
until the 1930s that objectifications of Hollywood's significance were
achieved in novels by Fitzgerald and West. Fitzgerald's unfinished novel
*The Last Tycoon* centered around Hollywood as the culmination of
tragic tendencies in American culture. West, the spiritual son of the
debunkers, produced a major achievement in his Hollywood novel, *The*

*Day of the Locust* (1939). His satiric vision showed the significance of Hollywood as an emblem for the deterioration of elements central to American mythology. In his vision, innocence and the promise of pastoral fulfillment come to an apocalyptic end.

Van Vechten's *Spider Boy*[1] was superficial in its satire of Hollywood manners and appearances. Horror at a culture that Hollywood seemed to epitomize, a horror that is the underlying moral tone of *The Day of the Locust,* was conspicuously absent. In satirizing a writer's success in New York and Hollywood, *Spider Boy* repeated many of the attitudes and situations already overworked by the debunkers. Absent from Van Vechten's description of Hollywood's flamboyance and of its manners was West's later insight, that the movie-viewing public fosters the Hollywood image in order to relieve its boredom and frustration. The frivolous stuff of *Spider Boy* is as slack as Woodward's novels. There is none of the intensity that West incorporated into the structure of *The Day of the Locust* ten years later. Clifton Fadiman wrote at the time that "Mr. Van Vechten is a mediocre reporter of the smart cracks of five years ago and a fairly good purveyor of the appetites of the upper-class fourteen year olds."[2]

Nevertheless, the subject-matter for satire was overwhelmingly present, and two years later Marquis came closer to locating what was bizarre, banal, and frightening about Hollywood. The big studios frantically lured writers there by giving them large salaries, the promise of inflated status, and, perhaps, the green hope of an orgiastic future. Marquis, along with Fitzgerald and West, took the bait. Like *Spider Boy,* much of the satirical material in *Off the Arm*[3] was drawn from Hollywood's attempts, in the late 1920s, to make the transition from silent films to talkies. The novel is also partly successful in objectifying in a convincing way, through satire, some of the problems confronting the creative writer during the late 1920s in a literary world that had three shifting centers—Paris, New York, and Hollywood—although the novel is set primarily in Hollywood.

In *Off the Arm* the satire ranges from the expression of Marquis's hostility toward pseudoartists and Bohemians to his awareness of Hollywood's synthetic and fraudulent elements. There is in the Hollywood scenes something of the nightmare quality that West so vividly evoked a few years later. The novel is resolved in a comic situation that, in its melodrama, borders intentionally on the nonsensical. The hero, Hugh Cass, does battle with the movie tycoon, Bertram Rose, to prevent his wife from divorcing him and marrying Rose. The battle is fought to the accompaniment of the exhortations of a radio preacher, who warns them to repent before the day of destruction. The hysterical tenor of this scene is like that in the mob scene that is the climax of *The Day of the Locust*. It has something also of the dreamlike grotesqueness of some of Lardner's nonsense writings.

Marquis conceived of Hollywood as a travesty of American culture, and West had a similar concept in *The Day of the Locust*.[4] But West's descriptions underline Hollywood's grotesqueness to greater effect than those of either Van Vechten or Marquis. Even the natural landscape seems contrived and artificial. West's narrator speaks in a detached, matter-of-fact way that nevertheless evaluates through startling diction and figurative language. He describes the evening light in California as "violet piping, like a Neon tube." This light outlines "the tops of ugly, hump-backed hills." Everywhere in nature there is ugliness, contortion, and distortion: "the canyon twisting down to the city below," "a cactus garden in which a few ragged, tortured plants still survived," "through a slit in the blue serge sky poked a grained moon that looked like an enormous bone button." The natural world reflects the tinseled, human-corrupted atmosphere: a blue jay chased by a hummingbird "flashed by squawking with its tiny enemy on its tail like a ruby bullet. The gaudy birds burst the colored air into a thousand glittering particles like metal confetti." The call of the quail "was not like the cheerful whistles of the Eastern bobwhite. It was full of melancholy and weariness." It is as if these descriptions of the natural world were written upon a palimpsest. Visible underneath the debunker's deliberate distortion is a contrasting, romantic view of nature. Against this distorted natural background, and a reflection of it, looms the artificial Hollywood. "Only dynamite," West writes, "would be of any use against the Mexican ranch houses, Samoan huts, Mediterranean villas, Egyptian and Japanese temples, Swiss chalets, Tudor cottages, and every combination of these styles that lined the slopes of the canyon." These buildings are made of "plaster, lath, and paper," which "know no law, not even that of gravity."

Hollywood manners—the manners of the successful at a screen writer's party—are debunked in a description in which realism, surrealism, and fantasy are combined. The screen writer lives in an enormous house "that was an exact reproduction of the old Dupuy mansion near Biloxi, Mississippi." He greets his guests by doing an impersonation that complements the southern colonial architecture: "He teetered back and forth on his heels like a Civil War colonel and made believe he had a large belly." To help keep his guests amused, he has placed a life-size reproduction of a dead horse in the bottom of his swimming pool. The main part of the evening's entertainment is provided by a trip to an elegant house of prostitution, where the guests are shown pornographic movies.

The climactic representation of Hollywood's grotesque nature occurs in chapter eighteen, which describes a movie studio and the filming of the battle of Waterloo. West's satiric writing is at its best here, as he penetrates and mocks Hollywood's creation of illusion. Like the satires of Horace and Juvenal, the scene he describes is cluttered, chaotic, and absurd. West's hero wanders through the studio lot looking for the location where the battle of Waterloo is being filmed. He sees "an ocean liner made of painted canvas with real life-boats hanging from its davits." He has to cross a desert which is being made "by a fleet of trucks dumping white sand." He rests for a while on the porch of the "Last Chance Saloon" from where he can see "a jungle compound with a water buffalo tethered to the side of a conical grass hut." He sees "a truck with a load of snow and several malamute dogs." He walks through the swinging door of the saloon and finds himself in a Paris street; at the end of the street is a Romanesque courtyard. He comes across a group of men and women who are picknicking on a lawn of fiber: "They are eating cardboard food in front of a cellophane waterfall." He sits down "on a rock made of brown plaster" and looks at

> bridges which bridged nothing, sculpture in trees, palaces that seemed of marble until a whole stone portico began to flap in the light breeze. And there were figures as well. . . . A man in a derby hat leaned drowsily against the gilded poop of a Venetian barque and peeled an apple. Still farther on, a charwoman on a stepladder was scrubbing with soap and water the face of a Buddha thirty feet high.

Wandering lost in this maze, he comes to "the final dumping ground," where old sets, flats, and props are discarded. He views it as a Sargasso Sea, "a dream dump," which tells the history of civilization: "A Sargasso of the imagination! And the dump grew continually, for there wasn't a dream afloat somewhere which wouldn't sooner or later turn up on it, having first been made photographic by plaster, canvas, lath, and paint."

The filming of the battle of Waterloo is a fittingly farcical climax for this dreamlike setting. A great plain is covered with troops, all elaborately costumed. An assistant director orders the French troops to attack Mont St. Jean. But he makes "a fatal error. Mont St. Jean was unfinished. The paint was not yet dry and all the struts were not in place. Because of the thickness of the cannon smoke, he had failed to see that the hill was still being worked on by property men, grips and carpenters." The result is chaos as Mont St. Jean collapses:

Nails screamed with agony as they pulled out of joists. The sound of ripping canvas was like that of little children whimpering. Lath and scantling snapped as though they were brittle bones. The whole hill folded like an enormous umbrella and covered Napoleon's army with painted cloth. . . . The victors of Bersina, Leipsic, Austerlitz, fled like schoolboys who had broken a pane of glass. "Sauve qui peut!" they cried, or, rather, "Scram!"

In the imagery of this description there are echoes of Lardner's and Sullivan's perceptions of urban landscape.

Finally, there is the cinematic illusion and the effect it has on the public. The illusion itself is a compound of newspaper, radio, and movie images that project the myth of California as a sun-drenched, orange-laden, wave-washed, earthly paradise where movie stars live orgiastic lives. Van Vechten, Marquis, and West all ridiculed this illusion. But West was not superficial where the first two were. He was profoundly concerned with California's meretricious distortion of an older pastoral myth. His point of view was governed by pity and ultimately, transmuting his satiric methods, it was quite serious. He wrote: "It is hard to laugh at the need for beauty and romance, no matter how tasteless, even horrible, the results of that need are. . . . Few things are sadder than the truly monstrous." The monstrosities that both horrified and fascinated West, and that were the subjects of his satire, were generated by both middle-class Philistinism and the pretensions to the avant-garde of middle-class aesthetes. These monstrosities were the prolific emanations from a segment of American culture that either knew what it liked or pursued grotesque imitations of what was deemed fashionable. Both attitudes were opposite faces of Mencken's booboisie, whether Philistines or aesthetes.

West published three other books in his lifetime, all in the 1930s (he was killed in 1940 in an automobile accident at the age of thirty-four). All were preparations, in a sense, for his major achievement in *The Day of the Locust*. He was direct heir to the attitudes, subjects, and methods of the debunkers, bringing them to bear on the art of the novel, uniquely drawing them into novelistic coherence. West was a little like Mark Twain, who fifty years before had similarly transmuted the rich, diffuse traditions of American humor into his two best novels, *Huckleberry Finn* and *The Tragedy of Pudd'nhead Wilson*. Although their talents and accomplishments differed greatly, both Mark Twain and West stood in a similar relationship to the traditions of American humor immediately available to them in their times.

West's biographer, Jay Martin, shows that satire was "his way of adjusting to society."[5] The patterns of his middle-class upbringing were very like those in the lives of most of the debunkers, who could have been his fathers or in some cases older brothers. There was the same reserve in sexual matters. There was the same adoration of mother and idealization of women. There were efforts on the part of his family to push him toward a profession or business. There was his sense that in the art of writing alone he might find a mode of salvation in the face of the feeling that things were falling apart, that the center would not hold. As was true of the other debunkers, some aspect of pastoral order worked a contrasting, mollifying effect on West. West's pastoral fantasies led to the purchase of a farm in Pennsylvania. However, in his fiction such fantasies were undercut; in *Miss Lonelyhearts* the natural world is seen as vicious, ugly, terrifying. Martin observes that "life was West's fiction, an illusion—his tough reality was in his books."[6] Hunting became another element of his pastoral dream, an activity in which he fled from the pressures and disappointments of the depressed world of the 1930s. Like Lewis, Lardner, and Marquis, he tried for popular success as a playwright. He proposed a musical review based on American folklore; he collaborated on a play with Perelman; he wrote an antiwar play with Joseph Shrank that closed after two performances. It is as if he belonged to the generation that immediately preceded his, as if he had been born too late. Yet that generation of satirists gave his writing its astonishing energy. He was able, it seemed, to begin where they had left off.

West's first book, *The Dream Life of Balso Snell* (1931),[7] debunked art in general, and thus owed much to the antiaestheticism of earlier debunkers. West shared Mencken's attitude toward the divine afflatus, Boyd's scorn for the aesthete, and Marquis's distrust of Bohemianism. The method of the book was closest to Hemingway's in *The Torrents of Spring;* it was a young writer's act of defiance toward the whole artistic tradition that had nurtured him. There is as in *The Torrents of Spring,* a fantastic, dreamlike setting, an incongruous chain of events, topical satire, parody, and deliberate nonsense. The hero, Balso Snell, a lyric poet, sets out on a mock-epic quest to discover the meaning of art. Marquis's idea of the artist as predator who feeds upon and violates the stuff of reality, who wears it down by constant attrition, reappears in West's notion that "art is not nature, but rather nature digested. Art is a sublime excrement." Therefore, the setting for Balso Snell's quest is the alimentary canal of the Trojan horse, which he has entered through its posterior opening. He discovers that the horse is inhabited mostly by writers in search of an audience. This narrative structure is used to present a series of parodies. There is a parody of a saint's life, followed by a parody of Dostoyevsky's *Crime and Punishment* and by a parody of a schoolteacher-biographer's complex and ridiculous metaphor-making compulsion. There are also briefer parodies of Stein and Joyce. All of these are examples of art as "sublime excrement."

One of the writers in search of an audience (a twelve-year-old boy who writes stories with the hope that they will help him seduce his English teacher) expresses hatred for an aspect of the middle-class public which virtually all the debunkers had ridiculed. This public is made up of the "the smart, sophisticated, sensitive, yet hard-boiled, art-loving frequenters of the little theatres. . . . School teachers who adore the grass-eating Shaw, sensitive young Jews who adore culture, lending librarians, publisher's assistants, homosexualists and homosexualists' assistants, hard-drinking newspaper men, interior decorators, and the writers of advertising copy."

For all of them—the noncreative art lovers—art is a form of solace, a substitute for unsatisfied sexual desires. And all true artists (invariably men, West ironically declares) are like the twelve-year-old boy who wants to seduce his English teacher. Their primary motive is "the attraction of the female." For the artist the object of art is sexual conquest. Balso Snell's quest for the meaning of art ends, explicitly, in orgasm. Underlying Balso Snell's sense of the function of art is his distrust of women except as grotesque sexual enticements (he is made "sick with passion" by a girl-cripple). This misogyny was dramatized in the writings of other debunkers, too, although West is much more explicit in representing the strange mixture of aversion for and attraction to the female. In *Miss Lonelyhearts* and *The Day of the Locust* he equates the mixture with puritanism. Both heroes of these novels have New England backgrounds; one of them is the son of a Baptist minister.

Mencken especially had identified and tried to come to terms with the radically shifting role of women in American life. Militant aspects of the women's movement were but obvious manifestations of a pervasive, usually sublimated warfare between traditional, masculine, patriarchal assumptions about sex roles and a sense that the attitudes of female toward male were shifting, unfixed, changing. One response on the part of debunkers like Mencken was a kind of jovial joking (as in sections of *In Defense of Women*) that acknowledged even while concealing a feeling of disorientation. West reflected anxiety about these changes, too, and it was shared in some degree by all the debunkers.

Parts of *Balso Snell* were printed in *Americana,* a magazine of satire published for a year in 1932. The name of the magazine probably derived from Mencken's "Americana" section of the *American Mercury;* certainly their purposes were similar. The *Americana* editors (who included George Grosz and Gilbert Seldes) characterized themselves with Menckenian extravagance: "We are Americans who believe that our civilization exudes a miasmic stench and that we had better prepare to give it a decent and rapid burial. We are the laughing morticians of the present."[8] In *Balso Snell* West experimented with parodies and nonsense writings like those of the debunkers. Like Lardner, West was learning to use the cliché-dominated speech of Americans. He was to shape it into a style that expressed both mockery and pity.

West's attitude of savage negation and dissent took political form in another book of satire, *A Cool Million; or, The Dismantling of Lemuel Pitkin.*[9] West was here directly in the tradition of the satirists and debunkers who had attacked Americanism and the processes by which heroes and demagogues were created. *A Cool Million* also involved parody of that type of American success story in which meager, simple beginnings, adversity, and temptation are crucibles for the formation of the virtues and characteristics of leaders and heroes. The Horatio Alger boys' books of the 1860s and 1870s followed this pattern.

West's Lemuel Pitkin is an American boy of Alger's Ragged-Dick type. Lemuel is born and raised on a farm near the Rat River in Ottsville, Vermont. As a youth he sets out in the world to earn enough money to pay off the mortgage on his mother's farm. He is sent on his way by "Shagpoke" Whipple, ex-president of the United States. Shagpoke compares Lemuel with John D. Rockefeller and Henry Ford, because, like them, he was "born poor and on a farm." Lemuel leaves Ottsville with unshakable faith in the American way of life; he is naive and honest to the point of imbecility. In his quest for success in the America of the Depression he is afflicted by appalling and grotesque adversity. His girl friend, also from Ottsville, is frequently raped by villains and is forced by white slavers to become a prostitute. Lemuel is easy prey for confidence men; he is robbed, beaten, and thrown in jail. He fails utterly in saving his mother's house; it is sold to a New York interior decorator. During the course of his adversity he is literally dismantled: he loses his teeth, an eye, a thumb, his scalp, a leg, and finally he is shot to death. But after his death he becomes a hero. Shagpoke Whipple has organized the National Revolutionary Party, a fascist, hyper-American organization whose Storm Troopers dress in leather shirts and coonskin caps, and carry squirrel rifles. Lemuel's dismantling and death are attributed to the Communists on the one hand and to "International Capitalism" (the Wall Street Jew bankers) on the other. He becomes a martyr to the rampantly successful National Revolutionary Party, which takes over the country with Shagpoke Whipple as its dictator. West, following the debunkers in his satire of the simple, provincial American virtues, developed an ultimate, terrifying irony, for in *A Cool Million* these ridiculed "virtues" are made the basis for fascist political action.

Some of West's comic effects are achieved through mock oratory. Although characters in all his books occasionally deliver comic perorations struck through with the tone of burlesque, this device is used extensively in *A Cool Million*. Shagpoke Whipple, for example, never simply speaks, he orates. In assuring Lemuel that the world is his oyster "that but waits for hands to open it" (preferably bare hands), he spouts platitudes and success-story exempla:

> America is the land of opportunity. She takes care of the honest and industrious and never fails them as long as they are both. . . .
> Let me warn you that you will find in the world a certain few scoffers who will laugh at you and attempt to do you injury. They will tell you that John D. Rockefeller was a thief and that Henry Ford and other great men are also thieves. Do not believe them. The story of Rockefeller and of Ford is the story of every great American, and you should strive to make it your story.

In an effort to recruit a group of vagrants and unemployed for his National Revolutionary Party Shagpoke mounts a soapbox, and begins by flattering them:

> We of the middle class are being crushed between two gigantic millstones. Capital is the upper stone and labor the lower, and between them we suffer and die, ground out of existence. . . .
> Who but the middle class left aristocratic Europe to settle on these shores? Who but the middle class, the small farmers and storekeepers, the clerks and petty officials, fought for freedom and died that America might escape from British tyranny?
> This is our country and we must fight to keep it so. If America is ever again to be great, it can only be through the triumph of the revolutionary middle class.
> We must drive the Jewish international bankers out of Wall Street! We must destroy the Bolshevik labor unions! We must purge our country of all the alien elements and ideas that now infest her!
> America for Americans! Back to the principles of Andy Jackson and Abe Lincoln!

At the end of the book, on Pitkin's birthday, the dictator Shagpoke explains the meaning of Lemuel's martyrdom to 100,000 of his Leather Shirts: "Through his martyrdom the National Revolutionary Party tri-

umphed, and by that triumph this country was delivered from sophistication, Marxism and International Capitalism. Through the National
Revolution its people were purged of alien diseases and America became again American." Shagpoke is the ultimate provincial and demagogue: he triumphs on a platform of hatred and contempt for the
scoffers and debunkers, the sophisticates who ridiculed the simple
American virtues.

West's method—his re-creation of buncombe oratory— derived from
Lewis, especially from *The Man Who Knew Coolidge*. The platitudes
mouthed by Lowell Schmaltz are the same as the ones that become a
basis for Shagpoke Whipple's fascism. Sullivan's cliché-expert writings
were also analogous comic representations of the pompous American
capacity for phrase and slogan making. And Mencken relentlessly
gathered such phrases and slogans in the "Americana" section of the
*Mercury*. West's attitude toward provincial Americans—those Americans who became a fascist mob—was Mencken's attitude toward the
booboisie and the yokels; the only difference is that West pushed
beyond contempt and ridicule to a depiction of their potential for mob
action. A similar, although vaguer, awareness had been an aspect of
Lardner's ridicule of mass culture in America. Most of the debunkers
sensed a crisis in American life, but they were not precise or articulate
in defining the sources of crisis. They ridiculed its manifestations: provincialism, Americanism, cultural pretensions, Prohibition, fundamentalism. Mencken's idea that Puritanism was the root of all evil in
America was one attempt at profundity which all the debunkers seized
upon. West's sense of horror at what mass culture in America had
become was much more explicit than Mencken's, or, indeed, than that
of any of the other debunkers, except for a prefiguration in Lardner.
West's kind of savage disaffection was only approached in America by
the occasional misanthropy of much earlier satirists: DeForest, Mark
Twain, Bierce.

Parody is the mode of *A Cool Million*. While the structure of the book
seems random, its discursiveness is deliberate and carefully designed. It
was as if West was including in his wide-ranging satire a parody of what
had come to be called the Great American Novel (originally so named
by DeForest). The tradition, if it can be called that, included among its
masters Henry James and William Dean Howells, where complex but
coherent structures are conceived to celebrate American virtues seen in
contexts of diversity, conflict, and irony. The Great American Novel
was in the 1920s a cliché, something to joke about, and West's attitudes
derive from this background. According to Martin,

In 1923, Contact Press published William Carlos Williams's *The Great American Novel,* which Williams described as "a satire on the novel form in which a little (female) Ford car falls more or less in love with a Mack truck." In his first letter to Williams, in July 1931, West mentioned this sketch, and the idea for carrying out a full-scale reversal of the form seems to have been part of the impetus for *A Cool Million.*

At the very center of West's intention in *A Cool Million,* which Martin calls a "dark comedy," is "the even darker suggestion that the primary use of language in modern America is deception."[10] This discovery had been made earlier by the debunkers, especially Lardner.

West's two other books, *Miss Lonelyhearts* and *The Day of the Locust,* were novels in which satire, parody, and debunking were methods contributing to their effects as novels, not the main vehicles of their effects. These novels represent the successful aesthetic culmination of the debunking point of view that had characterized the era of West's upbringing and that he had assimilated so completely. In both, West further isolated his sense of a crisis in his culture. This culture, we are told explicitly in *Miss Lonelyhearts,* is dead (the setting is the early 1930s, the low point of the Depression). This culture—again, we are told explicitly—can only be brought to life through faith. But such is the nature of the deadness that faith can only be expressed through hysteria. In *Miss Lonelyhearts* a newspaperman who functions as a twentieth-century priest tries to reawaken in America a traditional faith in Christ. He is misunderstood and he fails. *A Cool Million* (which was written after *Miss Lonelyhearts*) examined another kind of faith, Americanism, and the fascist hysteria which it had produced. *The Day of the Locust,* the last book West wrote, complemented *A Cool Million* in its exploration of the promised land and life that had become the twentieth-century American version of paradise. Like *A Cool Million* and *The Day of the Locust, Miss Lonelyhearts* ends in hysteria: the only possible expression for the kind of faith of which Americans in the mass were capable.

The hero of *Miss Lonelyhearts*[11] is a twentieth-century priest because he is "capable of dreaming the Christ dream." He is a newspaperman who is assigned to write the "Miss Lonelyhearts" column of a New York newspaper. He realizes that "men have always fought their misery with dreams," with faith. But he sees that in America, "although dreams were once powerful, they have been made puerile by the movies, radio and newspapers." This conspiracy, he feels with puritanical conscience, amounts to a betrayal. He tries to help his readers and redress his own sense of complicity by preaching in his column the healing power of Christ's love. To preach thus he must overcome his own cynicism and sophistication, for he has discovered that the intense feelings aroused by faith in his time can only issue in hysteria. Thus faith is, in part, for West's hero, what it was for Mencken: a benign booziness. It is also, as it was for Lewis's Elmer Gantry, an emotion confounded by sexuality. All of the appeals for help made to Miss Lonelyhearts have as their basis some form of sexual frustration. West's hero exhibits an innocence and simplicity against which other characters are evaluated.

One character in *Miss Lonelyhearts* is a caricature of the debunker. Shrike (his appearance is that of the vicious bird whose name suggests both a blow and a scream), the feature editor for whom Miss Lonely-hearts works, is unremittently the cynic, the disillusioned wit who bur-lesques and tries to destroy feeling in whatever form it appears. Like Shagpoke Whipple he is one of West's oratorical characters. Every word he speaks is part of a mock oration. He substitutes rhetoric for feeling, in order to hide his own emptiness and torment. He persistently and maliciously debunks all of Miss Lonelyhearts's attempts at escape, or strivings for a meaningful faith: " 'My friend, I know of course that neither the soil, nor the South Seas, nor Hedonism, nor art, nor drugs, can mean anything to us. We are not men who swallow camels only to strain at stools. God alone is our escape. The church is our only hope, the First Church of Christ Dentist, where He is worshipped as Preventer of Decay.' " Sometimes Shrike sounds like Mencken, in the rolling, bombastic assurance of his intonation. Sometimes his oratory frays to-ward nonsense and the threshold of hysteria that is present in Lardner's late writings. The element of anguish in his voice echoes the fishing-trip orations of Bill Gorton in Hemingway's *The Sun Also Rises*.

Miss Lonelyhearts sets out to overcome Shrike's influence, for he, too, has inherited something of the Shrikean cynicism and disaffection. He, too, is incapable of projecting genuine emotion into his own personal relationships. When he becomes aware of the suffering of those who write to him as Miss Lonelyhearts, his conscience is touched; he feels person-ally responsible for the emotional dis-ease of a whole segment of his culture. The panacea he tries to offer his readers is the most powerful emotion he has ever known: complete immersion in an all-embracing love. Part of this love has been evoked for him by Father Zossima in *The Brothers Karamazov,* and part by his experiences as the son of a New England Baptist minister. There is, however, a terror for him in the emotion, because of its extremity: "As a boy in his father's church, he had discovered that something stirred in him when he shouted the name of Christ, something secret and enormously powerful. . . . He knew now what this thing was—hysteria. . . . He wondered if hysteria were really too steep a price to pay for bringing it to life." He can conceive of no other solution, so he offers Christ's love to his readers. But he is misunderstood (one of his female readers meets and seduces him) and he succeeds only in evoking an incontrollable sexual hysteria. The book ends in violence, as do all of West's books. Miss Lonelyhearts is killed—crucified—by one of those he had attempted to save.

In *The Day of the Locust*, West continued to explore the crisis of faithlessness in American life. The implicit conclusion of *Miss Lonely-hearts* is in *The Day of the Locust* made explicit: the most powerful emotion of which Americans individually or in the mass are capable is sexual hysteria. Hollywood, the setting for the novel, had made possible the atmosphere in which this hysteria could be easily expressed. There are two aspects of *The Day of the Locust* that can be illuminated in a special way by isolating West's debunking point of view. One of these is the satire of Hollywood, and has already been considered at the beginning of this chapter as a culminating aspect of a more general attack by the debunkers on American mass culture. The other is West's description of the people who have been lured to Hollywood by the romantic, cinematic illusion.

These people have come out of the vast midland of America into the California of West's novel where, as a segment of society, they form a stark, naturalistic background for the action of the novel. "Every day of their lives," West writes of them, "they read the newspapers and went to the movies. Both fed them on lynchings, murder, sex crimes, explosions, wrecks, love nests, fires, miracles, revolutions, war. This daily diet made sophisticates of them. . . . Nothing can ever be violent enough to make taut their slack minds and bodies." These people are "savage and bitter, especially the middle-aged and the old, and had been made so by boredom and disappointment." They are Mencken's booboisie and yokels, the people from the provinces of America. They are Lewis's Lowell Schmaltz, Marquis's Old Soak, and Lardner's Jack Keefe. "All their lives they had slaved at some kind of dull, heavy labor . . . saving their pennies and dreaming of the leisure that would be theirs when they had enough." Inevitably many of them go to California to die, to "the land of sunshine and oranges" and tinsel romance. Once there, "their boredom becomes more and more terrible. They realize that they have been tricked and burn with resentment."[12] They are provincials who have been cheated by Hollywood's travesty of sophistication. West writes of them with the debunker's blunt realism, as he displays the comedy of their grotesqueness, individually and in the mass.

At the end of *The Day of the Locust* the frustrated and bitter provincials, cheated by the false promises of the Hollywood version of American life, coalesce into a hysterical, violent, sex-crazed mob. Packed outside of Kahn's Persian Palace Theatre, where they have massed to view the arrival of celebrities at the world premiere of a new picture, their hatred and resentment are suddenly released into violence. The disillusioned and frustrated find as a ravening mob a substitute for the orgies and the romance which the films in their prurience and sentimentality had promised them. Hollywood becomes a grotesque American paradise in which hysterical mob action is the ultimate glory.

Some of West's sources and resources as novelist, then, were in the immediate debunking tradition. His rhetorical method (in oratorical speeches of his characters) derived from Mencken and Lewis; he also had Lewis's, Hemingway's, and Lardner's ear for American speech in his own time. His attitudes were closest both in time and nature to Lardner's, while he was like Marquis in his comic sense of art as predatory, and in his compassion. He had, of course, sources and resources other than American humor (as had all the debunkers); he was closely familiar with nineteenth- and twentieth-century French and Russian literatures, especially with Voltaire and Dostoyevsky.[13] He must have known about the European dadaist movement through his friend George Grosz.[14]

West wrote in his first book a description of one aspect of his satiric writing: "I always find it necessary to burlesque the mystery of feeling at its source. . . . The ritual of feeling demands burlesque."[15] For West, as for the debunkers who fathered him, the authority of feelings ritualized and codified in institutions such as family and church was disappearing along with other forms of authority. And it was no longer fashionable in a liberated, post-Freudian world to repress one's feelings. Yet West, like the debunkers, was still enough of a Puritan not to be able to make his deepest feelings the direct, matter-of-fact currency of his writings. Some of those feelings were hostile and rebellious; some were compassionate. Burlesque was often his instinctive mode of expression and in that he was like the debunkers. Humor was an acceptable way of venting and at the same time concealing hostile and subversive feelings. Especially in his first book, this humor took the form of intentional nonsense. As for the debunkers, nonsense could both express and relieve anxiety about a culture that seemed to have become chaotic and meaningless.

In all of West's books there is the dramatization of hysteria. He had the double vision—the sense of indignation set off against compassion—

of the satirist. Debunking tended in the 1930s to lose focus and fray off into nonsense without any specific satiric effects. But unlike most of the debunkers, West discovered a coherent structure for dealing with fantasy and hysteria as subjects. He identified what Auden called "West's Disease," a malady of the spirit that leads to a rejection of self:

This is a disease of consciousness which renders it incapable of converting wishes into desires. A lie is false; what it asserts is not the case. A wish is fantastic; it knows what is the case but refuses to accept it. All wishes, whatever their content, have the same and unvarying meaning—"I refuse to be what I am."[16]

In his analysis of this sickness of the American spirit West had, more explicitly than any of the debunkers upon whose shoulders he stood, realized that in laughter, even in hysterical laughter, there was a kind of relief. This kind of laughter in West, as Norman Podhoretz has written, was "almost un-American in its refusal to admit the possibility of improvement, amelioration, or cure."[17]

However, at the end of his life, which was also the end of the 1930s, West seemed to have achieved a sense of personal identity and assurance very like that of Mencken in his prime, ten years earlier. He seemed to have transcended the frustrations and bitterness of his other progenitors among the debunkers. Recently married, he was extravagantly happy; he was nearly secure financially as a sought-after screenwriter in Hollywood, and he had two books in progress that would reflect a new sense of purpose and assurance. One was to be a novel that would take a Shrike-like character and involve him in a world of human need and anguish, although he had not yet worked out the effect of such a change of identity on his archetypal debunker. The other book was to be a collection of "loosely related sketches of the American scene." There would be a central, "uninvolved character plunged time after time into experience of all kinds." The organizing theme of these sketches "would deal with the flight from indifference," but most would involve "a sense of terror, a metaphysics of doom, the condition and nature of human separateness."[18] Then, suddenly, he was killed along with his wife in an automobile accident, and that new sense of coherence in his life was never to be tested. He had himself epitomized in the 1930s the two previous decades that had so precisely defined him. With his death, with America moving out of the Depression into a war, it was as if the late flowering his work seemed to represent ended, too. Only the day before he was killed Fitzgerald had died. Martin has shown that West and Fitzgerald were as intimately connected, both personally and as artists, as in the closest of father-son relationships: "Fitzgerald had been the incarnation of the twenties . . . and West was the last American novelist to be deeply affected by that spirit."[19] Part of the spirit of the 1920s was reflected in the satire of the debunkers—in the loving anguish of their dissociation from their past and in their instinctive remediation through the curative power of laughter. West was animated by the spirit of the debunkers, too.

# Afterword

**W**est's four books chronicling the metastasizing banality of mass culture did not attract many readers until 1957, when the *Complete Works* was published. It may be that West could only be reconsidered during an era in which it was perfectly clear that his dark vision had been prophetic: the mass culture that he described had not only survived depression, world war, and cold war, but was complacently flourishing. With the exception of the *New Yorker,* the decline (but not the extinction) of the literature of debunking began in the early 1930s and continued until the return of war to the Western world. Some of the debunkers, notably Mencken, who had both absorbed and satirized the mood of resurgence in America in the decades surrounding the First World War, were older and more inclined to be moved by nostalgia than by disaffection. And some had died: Lardner in 1933, Marquis in 1937, West in 1939. Woodward, who named the phenomenon, was busy denying that he had ever been a debunker at all. The long period of war, hot and cold, extended from the late 1930s into the 1950s. A time of unusual affliction, it spawned the black humor that flourished in the 1950s and 1960s. The debunkers, with West as their main transmitter, were progenitors for the wild, perverse satire through which these writers sought strange, sometimes hysterical relief.

During the Depression era one of the most popular funnymen, until he died in 1935, was Will Rogers. His popularity illustrates the decline of the satiric perversity that had characterized the wit of the debunkers in the 1920s. Rogers, whose career began around 1915, was enormously successful as a topical satirist. He became a popular hero in the 1920s, when so many hero-entertainers emerged. He expanded his popularity in the 1930s by continuing to develop the posture of a homely philosopher and by becoming more and more a commentator on the smiling aspects of American life. He rose to fame through vaudeville, the lecture circuit, then the newspaper syndicates and radio. He shared some of the subjects and targets of the debunkers: Bryan, Ford, Prohibition, Harding, Coolidge. He also toured in Europe and other parts of the world. He did not pose as a worldly sophisticate, as had Mencken, but as an innocent abroad, in the nineteenth-century manner of Mark Twain. He was in the tradition of the satirist performers who spoke or wrote in dialect, who carefully preserved an illusion of casual, off-hand commentary, and who cultivated a pose of simplicity. Most of his humor was based on mild exaggeration and deflation. If they failed to amuse, he did rope tricks. His popularity as an entertainer depended on his simple honesty and on his overt faith in American institutions. He managed his talent carefully and set a high cash value on it; many Americans admired him because he was successful. In their hero-worship his audiences were responding in part to the myth of the simple man who had made good and who could thus dine with kings and dictators.[1]

A vivid contrast to Rogers's gentle, smiling irony is the wit of Perelman, one of the mainstays of *New Yorker* humor since its golden age, through the 1930s and beyond. The wild perversity of his style echoed Lardner's deliberate irrelevance: "What the hookless fastener people are selling, of course, is nothing as crass as zippers for pants, but spiritual regeneration, a commodity made famous by one Feodor Dostoievski about 1866."[2] Something of the debunking perspective was sustained in his writing, although he was not in the 1930s nearly as popular as Rogers. Perelman's euphoria, wildness, and verbal disjunctions had counterparts in the films of the Marx Brothers.

Ridicule of the American middle class continued in the 1930s, often from a point of view inspired by Communist ideology. Typical of this sort of writing were the essays by Kyle Crichton for the *New Masses* in 1934 and 1935, published under the pseudonym "Robert Forsythe." His debunking commentary in the Menckenian tone and style on manners, morals, politics, and culture alternated with party-line polemic. Although his writing was ostensibly for the furtherance of the Communist cause, like Mencken he could not be contained by any ideology. There was here and there in his essays an attitude of nostalgia for the earlier days of America's cultural resurgence. In his essay "In Defense of Mr. Mencken," he was moved by both affection and disillusionment. The young men who had fled to Paris after the war, he observed, had been able to leave "with the consciousness that Mr. Mencken remained behind to stand off the enemy." Now all that was over, and there only remained the spectacle of Mencken writing for *Liberty* magazine: "When one has digested Mr. McFadden's editorial in the front and Mr. Mencken's article in the middle and the crossword puzzle at the end, there is really little additional that one may ask of American letters." Although Crichton saw that Mencken could not be reincarnated, he looked back with nostalgia and tried to infuse his own writings about Communism with the same breathless emotion that had so recently liberated America from its genteel past. He was capable of both Mencken's rhythmic bellicosity and Lardner's misanthropic irony. But readers must have been startled by such polemic as: "They may kill Communists and imprison and torture them, but they never can kill Communism. It is ingrained in the bones of life; it is inevitable because the collapse of capitalism is inevitable."[3] For a time, in the 1930s, the fervid muckraking attitude of reform that Mencken had come to deplore for its extremist orientation was again in the air.

At the beginning of the Second World War it became fashionable, following the lead of MacLeish and Brooks, to look back on many of the writers of the previous two decades as irresponsibles.[4] In 1942 Philip Wylie, the angry polemicist of *Generation of Vipers,* condemned the American public in general for having acquiesced to world chaos and war. He brought together the attitudes of the muckrakers, along with all of the subjects and some of the methods of the debunkers. *Generation of Vipers* was both popular and notorious in the sense that Mencken's books had been fifteen years earlier. A revised edition was published in 1955, with annotations of the I-told-you-so sort. There had been nothing quite like it since Mencken's decline; yet Wylie held Mencken's hand, he did not stand on Mencken's shoulders. Much of Wylie's polemic is, like Mencken's, in a Juvenalian tradition of satire, but his Juvenalian pose is not consistent and his books, while using satiric devices, break down frequently into irascible bombast. He vacillates between satire and denunciation.

Wylie's appeal was considerable partly because he set out, in 1942, to explain why America was involved in the catastrophe of a world war, and in 1955, to explain the cold war. In an arraignment of the debunkers' subjects he argued in effect that, because of their provincialism, their puritanism, their narrow Americanism, and their Philistinism, Americans acquiesced in the conditions that spawned Hitler, fascism, and the cold war. His popularity also depended upon the encyclopedic extravagance of the manner in which he addressed these dilemmas. Wylie must have been at least partly conscious that his appeal to a large audience depended not only on the apparent relevance of his inquiry— why did America come to be in its twentiety-century predicament?—but also upon the voice with which he addressed that audience, the voice of the satirist-entertainer. He was working in and gaining popularity from a long tradition of satirists, with the debunkers his immediate predecessors. His antifeminism was like the debunker's ridicule of feminist extremists (the "Cinderella myth" and "momism") without the underlying and partly concealed sympathy that often complicated it. Mass culture, as it had been for the debunkers, was the Grendel of America, and "Mom" was Grendel's mother. Wylie's sense of puritanism in America had mostly to do with attitudes toward sex; for a culture which was about to produce the Kinsey reports, he was franker than any of the debunkers had been. His "common man" was the provincial or boob more euphemistically labeled.

Where Mencken's heroes had been Darwin, Nietzsche, and Shaw, Wylie's were Christ, Freud, and Jung. His treatment of Christ was like Woodward's treatment of George Washington. He debunked what he took to be the myth of Christ's humanitarianism, and revealed the "real" Christ, the preacher of inner integrity and individualism—a somewhat Dionysian Christ. He looked to psychology, the scientific inquiry into man's nature, as the redeeming faith of the future; he ridiculed the prevailing science of America as one that had gadgetry as its main aim (culminating in the better mousetrap of the atomic bomb, which, writing in 1955, he claimed he had prophesied in 1942).

Wylie, like Mencken, found himself accused of self-indulgence. He denied the charge, for it was part of his pose as a satirist-entertainer to present himself as a simple, truth-loving man whose moral indignation could not be repressed. Like Juvenal, he created a narrator who is gripped by a mysterious compulsion: anger, the muse of satire, is his inspiration. Writing in 1952, Auden noted that satire could not flourish in the years immediately following the Second World War because "in public life, the serious evils are so importunate that satire seems trivial and the only suitable kind of attack prophetic denunciation."[5] In *Generation of Vipers* the satirist's pose is unevenly maintained. There are long passages of hyperbolic invective, where the voice we hear is the voice of a muckraker who has succumbed to hysteria. There is no relief and little humorousness in this posture. Wylie, who saw himself as a prophet, was not so much a writer of satire as of prophetic denunciation.

Debunking, i.e., topical satire that derived from the attitudes of the progressive movement, did have some liberalizing effects. Some repressive, genteel attitudes had been laughed away. Popular histories and biographies capitalizing on the debunker's calculated pose of irreverence offered a refreshingly new appraisal of the American past, of American mythology, and especially of American puritanism. Some demagogues had been discredited. Maudlin glorification of life in the American village had been ridiculed. The debunkers were successful in making it difficult for rural America henceforth to revel in its provincialism. In his speech accepting the Nobel Prize in 1930, Lewis identified himself as only one of many American writers who had escaped and come to ridicule "the stuffiness of safe, sane, and incredibly dull provincialism." He thought that the way had been cleared for a group of younger writers who "refused to be genteel and traditional and dull."[6] Although he did not name any, the characterization is general enough to fit West and the diverse black humor that followed West.

In their success the debunkers lost their original and most fundamental subject. As the distinction between rural provincialism and urban sophistication broke down, so too did the tension upon which the debunkers had depended for the articulation of much of their satire. The increasing importance of the New Yorker as a magazine of cultural and literary significance rather than as a magazine of sophisticated wit illustrates this change most dramatically.

Legislation as a means of promoting private moral attitudes and aims had received a setback: Prohibition was repealed in 1933. A climax in the campaign for the freedom of subject-matter in literature came also in 1933 with the legal admission of Ulysses into the United States. Although none of the debunkers was notoriously outspoken in sexual matters, nevertheless their general irreverence helped promote greater sexual freedom in and out of books. Sentimentality and prudishness were no longer respectable in sophisticated circles.

One implicit vision of a reality of American life, shared by many of the debunkers, was the sense that relationships between men and women were changing radically and that these changes were affecting in only vaguely perceived ways many aspects of American culture. Mencken articulated these not quite focused perceptions. He saw that a kind of civil war was in progress between male and female and that while neither the conditions nor results of battle were clearly definable, the effects would be as profound as those of the actual war in Europe. Lewis used warfare as an underlying metaphor in Main Street, where, by making Carol Kennicott his heroine, he sought to dramatize the tension between male and female as a condition central to American life.

In Mencken, twentieth-century American prose satire following mainly in the tradition of burlesque oratory found a practitioner as able as any of the nineteenth-century humorists. Satire in the tradition of the tall tale had one of its twentieth century expressions in Marquis. He was most successful as a fabulist whose fables had satiric intent, but there was also the more general satire of order and logic implied in the tendency of his writing toward nonsense. Lardner moved even closer to nonsense, sometimes losing completely the thin thread of sense needed for coherence as he responded to the afflictions of his time. Hemingway made dramatic use of the debunking attitude—here and there in the *The Sun Also Rises* and extensively in *The Torrents of Spring*. West was the precocious offspring of the debunkers. He used their methods for novelistic purposes and tried to objectify by wild humorousness his anxiety about American culture. Burlesque for West became a necessary and compulsive dramatic method.

The debunkers had ridiculed the values and self-congratulatory language of a more and more commercially and technologically oriented culture. The word *debunking* is expressive of the assumptions about language held by these satirists: remove the bunk and the truth will remain. As they discovered during the 1920s, satire caused little to change. Their ridicule therefore shifted from the exposure of particular absurdities, fraudulent values, or false ideologies to ridicule of logic and order and of human attempts to create logic and order. Topical satire became more and more fantastic: in fantasy the divisive realities of American life could be allegorized, and thus, in the forms of a minor art, be subjected to a kind of tenuous control. The extremes of this satire were the improvised, incoherent theatrics of the dadaists. But some of this satire did record and codify a sense of a culture on the edge of madness. In the early 1930s Lardner especially heard in American speech the sounds of hysteria and brought them to articulation.

Lardner is one writer who was able to go beyond the revelation of hysteria and madness to an objectification of the disorientation at the roots of American life. Similarly, Mencken's exorcism of puritanism—however simplified and exaggerated as a thesis—had moments of confrontation with one of the root elements of American culture, and the act of exposure was healthy in its way. Hemingway's strongest response to the disorientation of American life was in *The Sun Also Rises,* but that he had been moving toward this response, discovering the diction for expressing it, is shown by the focus of *In Our Time.* The very insistence that a writer's subject is our time was important. In *The Torrents of Spring* Hemingway took the bunk out of those literary progenitors by whom he had been educated. He was trying to decontaminate his language by laughing at his mentors; thus *Torrents* is primarily parody. At the same time he was writing *The Sun Also Rises,* where he was not a debunker, but at several points he re-created the language and attitudes of the debunkers. He wanted to express the anguish of a generation who had discovered that God was dead and who responded with flippancy and satire as a way of remaining sane and gaining tenuous relief. They were looking for the values and the modes of survival in their own contemporary world—not in tradition or the past—that would sustain them. They apprehended the unusual afflictions of their time. They were not, Hemingway insisted, a "lost generation," because their despair was as natural and cyclical as the rising of the sun. To express despair and fear in the flippant, joking tones Hemingway so accurately incorporated within some of the dialogues of *The Sun Also Rises* was somehow to control and modify the anguish. We hear the same tones in Lardner, Lewis, Marquis, and others: we hear these tones given a pomp and dignity by Mencken.

Nevertheless, it is the wild perversity of the debunkers that is our special heritage from them, not their role in liberating their culture, through satire, from some of its genteel affectations—although they did that, too. The black side of debunking, its toying with chaos through the deliberate creation of nonsense and irrelevance, had always been a significant element in American humor. That element flourishes in many of our major writers: Melville, Hawthorne, Poe, Mark Twain, Frost, Faulkner, as well as Hemingway and West.[7] The immediate predecessor of the debunkers had been Ambrose Bierce. As Martin has observed, Bierce used satire not mainly for moral purposes but as a psychologically stabilizing mode of artistic expression. Through Bierce there emerged much of what had always been present in American humor: a sense of the grotesque; a wild extravagance that threatened—and ridiculed—form, stability, and convention; and savage invective that released pleasurable hostility toward "deluded contemporaries and the institutions delusions created and perpetuated," as Martin puts it.[8] Bierce consciously rejected the tolerance and tenderness of smiling-aspects humor and celebrated the iconoclasm of what he called wit. His ironic response to conflict and division in American life was very much within the central tradition of American humor. Therefore his transmigration, as it were, into Mencken's body was in some sense inevitable.

Mencken is the central and defining figure for American humor from roughly 1910 to 1930. He located the subjects—provincialism, Americanism, cultural pretentiousness—for that humor, and his deliberate mediating extravagance had its tonal echoes everywhere in American letters during this period. The *New Yorker* humorists exploited his subjects. Lewis and Lardner attacked the stupidity and aridity of village life. It was especially Lardner who, in his extravagance, pushed toward a point where language dissolved into nonsense, particularly in his plays and radio columns for the *New Yorker*. This use of language was also the tendency of so-called light verse, at least from the 1890s down through the 1920s. Resolution in nonsense or abuse of sense is the writer's final way of ridiculing the middle-class values of logic, order, and decorum. Light verse easily can become middleweight or heavy, as the lyrics of Marquis bear witness.

The black side of debunking that West responded to so profoundly is a source for the black humor of much of the literature of the 1950s and 1960s. Brom Weber, whose *Anthology of American Humor* (1962) demonstrates the origins of black humor in the whole range of American literature, has this to say about it:

> Black humor violates sacred and secular taboos alike without restraint or compunction. It discovers cause for laughter in what has generally been regarded as too serious for frivolity: the death of men, the disintegration of social institutions, mental and physical disease, deformity, suffering, anguish, privation, and terror. For anyone steeped in the dominant traditions of Anglo-American culture, which since the eighteenth century has believed that humor is intrinsically good-natured, trivial, and kindly, the unpredictable, topsy-turvy, often hostile and sadistic character of black humor may well appear to be perverse and intolerable.[9]

What Weber defines was also the tendency of the debunking humor of the 1920s. There was an analogue in the mad playfulness of dada in Europe, as both moved into nonsense and the surreal, or at least toward resolutions where logic, decorum, and ordinary rational or artistic processes are ridiculed. Some examples are Hemingway (in *The Torrents of Spring*), Lewis (in *The Man Who Knew Coolidge*), and Lardner (in his dadaist-surrealist nonsense plays). The immediate inheritor of this dark comic tradition was West, who displayed it in all four of his novels. It flourished next in the 1950s and 1960s, especially in the fiction of Vladimir Nabokov, William Burroughs, J. P. Donleavy, Terry Sothern, Joseph Heller, Ken Kesey, Thomas Pynchon, Walker Percy, John Barth, and others. Barth is typical, because in Barth the play of language and the evocation of a pleasurable ironic response to the absurd view that nothing is of value are more important than moral resolution or content. The resolution of Barth's "Night-Sea Journey," for example, is explicable only by considering its style. Barth is playing a game. His narrator's voice combines the extravagance of southwestern humor with the understated ironic tonal modulations of the debunker as creator of a hoax: we discover that his narrator is a sperm on a romantic journey to an ecstatic consummation. We respond to the sustained comic characterization much as we respond to the mock-serious voice of the historian in Mencken's "A Neglected Anniversary."

Another element in the vision of American culture that has animated fiction since the 1950s is the imagery of clutter and junk. The artifacts of mass culture, as Philip Stevick has shown,[10] are prominently in the foreground of writings by such as Barthelme, Vonnegut, Elkin, Coover, Pynchon. Images from radio, film, television, advertising slogans, and brand names animate fiction. Often there is no coherent context. Such images express something of the disconnectedness, disconcertedness, and irrelevance of much of contemporary life. They are part of the shared experience of an audience that has in common its awareness of mass culture, and very little else—unlike the audiences for Victorian novels or for the realistic and naturalistic fiction of the modernist period, which often shared moral and aesthetic values. It was in the nonsense writings of Lardner, then in Sullivan, White, and, later, West and Perelman, that the images of clutter and junk were used to project the absurdity of much of modern life.

Sometimes in our own hours of unusual affliction we draw upon the stylistic heritage left us by the debunkers and those fiction writers with black visions. We echo them in the rhythms and diction of American speech: we make fun of what we fear most. In these hours we reexperience what to the debunkers was a common perception. It is the abuse of language that expresses the deterioration of the authority of such institutions as family, church, government, and business. The debunkers loved language with the special commitment of poets. To say the-thing-that-is-not was more abusive, they felt, than any action by any figure or institution in authority. As they came of age they realized the failure of the moral commitment of the muckrakers. That discovery was as distressing as the death of the idea of progress, for the muckrakers were their fathers and mothers. The universal sign of moral disarray was the abuse of language. Propaganda and advertising were obvious manifestations, but so were the distortions, inflations, and deceptions of ordinary discourse. One alleviating mechanism was to mock such language. That is why the 1920s produced so much parody, and why parody is a major element in fiction since West.[11] Behind the mockery there was an unshakable anguish and the puritanical sense that such a response was not entirely suitable. Language was sacred to the debunkers, if it was put to its proper use. But to mock an element of what one most profoundly believes is a profoundly disorienting experience—although the mockery brings relief.

# Notes

## Introduction.

1. Ernest Gruening, ed., *These United States,* first series (New York: Boni and Liveright, 1923). I shall cite pp. v, 1, 12, 17, 56, 372, 320.
2. H. L. Mencken, *Prejudices: Second Series* (New York: Knopf, 1920), pp. 136–54. First printed in the *New York Evening Mail,* 13 November 1917, p. 6.
3. Gruening, *These United States,* p. 12.
4. Henry F. May, *The End of American Innocence* (Chicago: Quadrangle Books, 1964), pp. 3–51.

## Chapter One. Rejection of the Past: Foreground and Background

1. *New York Times,* 20 May 1919, p. 14. See also J. N. Leonard, *The Tragedy of Henry Ford* (New York: Putnam's, 1932), p. 140.
2. *Smart Set* 67 (April 1922): 45.
3. *Nation* 117 (October 1923): 398.
4. William E. Woodward, *Bunk* (New York and London: Harper, 1923), pp. 206, 2, 134, 229.
5. Ibid., pp. 9, 47–48, 278.
6. William E. Woodward, *George Washington: The Image and the Man* (New York: Boni and Liveright, 1926), pp. 9, 224, 454.
7. *Saturday Review of Literature* 3 (11 December 1926): 415.
8. *International Book Review* (November 1926): 753.
9. William E. Woodward, "The World and Sauk Centre," *New Yorker* 10 (27 January 1934): 25.
10. *New York Times,* 30 September 1950, p. 17.
11. See Eleanor Flexner, *Century of Struggle* (New York: Atheneum, 1974), pp. 308, 280–81.
12. See F. J. Hoffman, Charles Allen, and C. F. Ulrich, *The Little Magazine: A History and a Bibliography* (Princeton: Princeton University Press, 1947).
13. *The Seven Arts* (November 1916): 52–53.
14. Waldo Frank, *Our America* (New York: Boni and Liveright, 1919), p. 132.
15. *Forum* 67 (May 1922): 371–75.

16. *Forum* 79 (February 1928): 161–76.

17. Lewis P. Simpson, "The Satiric Mode: The Early National Wits," in Louis D. Rubin, Jr., ed., *The Comic Imagination in American Literature* (New Brunswick, N.J.: Rutgers University Press, 1973), pp. 49–61. See also essays by Louis B. Wright, "Human Comedy in Early America," pp. 17–31; and Lewis Leary, "Benjamin Franklin," pp. 33–47, in the same volume.

18. George M. Roth, "American Theory of Satire, 1790–1820," *American Literature* 29 (January 1958): 399–407.

19. James M. Cox, "The Humor of the Old Southwest," in Rubin, ed., *Comic Imagination,* pp. 101–12.

20. Constance Rourke, *American Humor* (New York: Harcourt, Brace, 1931), p. 64.

21. Brom Weber, "The Misspellers," in Rubin, ed., *Comic Imagination,* pp. 127–37.

22. Rourke, *American Humor,* pp. 130–31.

23. John William DeForest, *Honest John Vane* (New Haven: Richmond & Patten, 1875), pp. 46, 251, 245.

24. Jack London, *The Iron Heel* (New York, London: Macmillan, 1907), pp. 177, 79–80, 72, 297.

25. See Larzer Ziff, *The American 1890s* (New York: Viking, 1966); and May, *The End of American Innocence.*

26. James M. Cox, "Mark Twain," in Rubin, ed., *Comic Imagination,* pp. 139–48.

27. H. L. Mencken, *A Book of Prefaces* (New York: Knopf, 1917), p. 202.

28. Ambrose Bierce, *Collected Works,* 12 vols. (New York: Neale, 1909), 1:87.

29. Ambrose Bierce, "The Devil's Dictionary," ibid., vol. 7.

30. Ambrose Bierce, "Wit and Humor," ibid., 10:98–102.

31. Quoted in Paul Fatout, *Ambrose Bierce* (Norman: University of Oklahoma Press, 1951), p. 194.

32. Ambrose Bierce, "The Passing of Satire," in *Collected Works,* 10:281–84.

33. *Lark,* 1, 2 (1 May 1895 to 1 April 1897); *Epi-Lark* (1 May 1897); Ziff, *The American 1890s,* pp. 120–45.

34. *M'lle New York* 1 (August 1895): 14–15.

35. "Foreword," 1 (August 1895): 1.

36. "Leader," 2 (November 1898): 1.

37. "Foreword," 1 (August 1895): 1.

38. "Polite Letters," 1 (August 1895): 14–15.

39. "Foreword," 1 (August 1895): 1.

40. "Leader," 1 (October 1895): 41–42.

41. Carl R. Dolmetsch, *The Smart Set: A History and Anthology* (New York: Dial, 1966), pp. 34–35.

42. May, *The End of American Innocence,* pp. 69–71.

43. Richard Hofstadter, *The Age of Reform* (New York: Knopf, 1950), pp. 210, 212; Louis Filler, *Crusaders for American Liberalism* (Yellow Springs,

Ohio: Antioch Press, 1950), pp. 359–78. Also, John M. Harrison and Harry H. Stein, eds., *Muckraking* (University Park: Pennsylvania State University Press, 1973), especially essays by Stein and Harrison and by Jay Martin.

## Chapter Two. The Ordeal of H. L. Mencken

1. Murray Kempton, "Saving a Whale," *New York Review of Books* 28 (11 June 1981): 8–14.
2. H. L. Mencken, *Prejudices: Fourth Series* (New York: Knopf, 1924), pp. 139–40.
3. Carl Bode, *Mencken* (Carbondale: Southern Illinois University Press, 1969), pp. 23–26.
4. Ibid., pp. 30–31.
5. William Manchester, *Disturber of the Peace: The Life of H. L. Mencken* (New York: Harper, 1950), p. 58; Douglas Stenerson, *H. L. Mencken: Iconoclast from Baltimore* (Chicago: University of Chicago Press, 1971), pp. 134–37; Bode, *Mencken*, p. 44.
6. Manchester, *Disturber of the Peace*, p. 70. See also Burton Rascoe, "*Smart Set* History," in *The Smart Set Anthology of World Famous Authors*, ed. Burton Rascoe and Groff Conklin (New York: Reynal, 1934), pp. xxv–xxviii; Dolmetsch, *The Smart Set*, pp. 3–94; and Bode, *Mencken*, p. 69.
7. I first tried to describe this conflict in "The Ordeal of H. L. Mencken," *South Atlantic Quarterly* 61 (Summer 1962): 326–38. I have used elements of that essay in this chapter. See also Norris Yates, "The Two Masks of H. L. Mencken," in *The American Humorist* (Ames: Iowa State University Press, 1964), pp. 142–54; and Guy J. Forgue, *H. L. Mencken* (Paris: Minard, 1967), pp. 423–31.
8. Philip Wagner, *H. L. Mencken* (Minneapolis: University of Minnesota Press, 1966), p. 10.
9. Hofstadter, *The Age of Reform*, pp. 134–48.
10. Mencken, *Prejudices: First Series* (New York: Knopf, 1919), pp. 181, 183, 186, 188, 189.
11. H. L. Mencken, *George Bernard Shaw: His Plays* (Boston: Luce, 1905), pp. vii, ix, ix–x, x, xii, xvi, xviii, xxvi.
12. Charles A. Fecher, *Mencken: A Study of His Thought* (New York: Knopf, 1978), pp. 64–65; William H. Nolte, *H. L. Mencken: Literary Critic* (Middletown, Conn.: Wesleyan University Press, 1966), pp. 30–34.
13. Fecher, *Mencken*, p. 135.
14. H. L. Mencken, *The Philosophy of Friedrich Nietzsche* (Boston: Luce, 1908), pp. x, 72, 105.
15. "Fifteen Years," *Smart Set* (December 1923), quoted in William H. Nolte, ed., *H. L. Mencken's Smart Set Criticism* (Ithaca: Cornell University Press, 1968), pp. 333–34.
16. Nolte, *Literary Critic*, pp. 37–42.

17. Mencken, *A Book of Prefaces*, pp. 177–83.

18. H. L. Mencken, "Ambrose Bierce," in *A Mencken Chrestomathy* (New York: Knopf, 1949), pp. 492–96.

19. Quoted in Fatout, *Ambrose Bierce*, p. 109.

20. J. V. Ridgely, "Ambrose Bierce to H. L. Mencken," *Book Club of California Quarterly News Letter* 26 (Fall 1961): 27–33.

21. Mencken, *Prejudices: First Series*, pp. 236–39.

22. Mencken, *Prejudices: Second Series*, p. 45.

23. Mencken, *Prejudices: Fourth Series*, p. 20.

24. H. L. Mencken, *Prejudices: Third Series* (New York: Knopf, 1922), p. 35.

25. Mencken, *Prejudices: Second Series*, p. 65.

26. Fecher, Mencken, p. 99n.

27. Sara Mayfield, *The Constant Circle* (New York: Delacorte, 1968), p. 195.

28. Dolmetsch, *The Smart Set*, pp. 243, 244.

29. Nolte, ed., *Smart Set Criticism*, p. 322.

30. Dolmetsch, *The Smart Set*, p. 247.

31. Unpublished materials originally written for *Minority Report*, two boxes, Enoch Pratt Free Library, Baltimore, Maryland.

32. Letter to Paul Patterson (publisher of the Baltimore *Sunpapers*) 9 September 1922, "Letters and Documents Relating to the *Baltimore Sunpapers*," vol. $1_1$, Enoch Pratt Free Library, Baltimore.

33. Guy J. Forgue, "Myths about Mencken," *Nation* 193 (16 September 1961): 163–65. Gwinn Owens makes a similar point in "Mencken and the Jews, Revisited," *Menckeniana* 74 (Summer 1980): 6–10.

34. Forgue, *Mencken*, pp. 142–43; Charles Scruggs, *The Sage in Harlem* (Baltimore: Johns Hopkins University Press, 1984).

35. Fecher, *Mencken*, p. 102; pp. 200–207.

36. "Un complexe de contraires: securité et liberté, nord et sud, ville et campagne." See Forgue's *Mencken*, p. 26.

37. Bode, *Mencken*, pp. 10, 19–20.

38. H. L. Mencken, *The Days of H. L. Mencken* (New York: Knopf, 1947), pp. vii, viii, 248, 249, 250; Bode, *Mencken*, p. 13.

39. Quoted in Fecher, *Mencken*, p. 54.

40. Leslie Fiedler, *Love and Death in the American Novel* (New York: Criterion Books, 1960), p. 556.

## Chapter Three. H. L. Mencken and Equal Rights for Women

1. *Smart Set* 38 (December 1912): 154.

2. H. L. Mencken, "Portraits of Americans," *A Book of Burlesques* (New York: Lane, 1916), p. 233.

3. Manchester, *Disturber of the Peace*, p. 126.

4. Stenerson, *H. L. Mencken*, p. 53.

5. Alistair Cooke, "The Public and Private Face," *Six Men* (New York: Knopf, 1977), p. 92.

6. Mencken, *Nietzsche*, p. 177.

7. Quoted in Cooke, *Six Men*, p. 92. Fecher also cites Mencken's celebration of intelligent women in *Mencken*, pp. 123–27.

8. Ann Douglas, *The Feminization of American Culture* (New York: Knopf, 1977), p. 13.

9. Forgue, *Mencken*, p. 443.

10. Mencken, *The Days of H. L. Mencken*, p. 3.

11. Bode, *Mencken*, pp. 16–20.

12. Ibid., p. 17.

13. Mencken never expressed his affection in public ways, but such expression was not the style of his class or time.

14. Bode, *Mencken*, p. 151. Fecher, *Mencken*, p. 120, makes a similar observation. Anita Loos, *A Girl Like I* (New York: Viking, 1966), pp. 211–20.

15. Bode, *Mencken*, p. 153.

16. H. L. Mencken, "Books to Read and Books to Avoid," *Smart Set* 30 (February 1910): 153–54.

17. H. L. Mencken, "A 'Doll's House'—with a Fourth Act," *Smart Set* 29 (December 1909): 153–54.

18. *Smart Set* 33 (January 1911): 163–64.

19. *Smart Set* 35 (November 1911): 153–64. Guy L. Forgue, ed., *The Letters of H. L. Mencken* (New York: Knopf, 1961), pp. 12–14.

20. *Smart Set* 50 (October 1916): 139.

21. *Smart Set* 64 (January 1921): 139.

22. For example, "The Free Lance" columns of 1, 3, 6 February 1912 in the *Baltimore Evening Sun* were devoted to the suffrage movement.

23. H. L. Mencken, *In Defense of Women* (New York: Goodman, 1918; Knopf, 1922). Page references are to the 1922 edition.

24. Quoted in Betty Adler, *The Mencken Bibliography* (Baltimore: Johns Hopkins University Press, 1961), p. 8.

25. Mencken, *Women*, pp. 3, 10, 158.

26. Mencken, *Women*, pp. 206–9. Yates, *The American Humorist*, p. 163, describes this scene as a "parody of the language of sentimentality and morality." Forgue recognizes the complexity of *In Defense of Women*, and its unique effect, although he sees Mencken's own misogyny as an underlying factor: "La thèse misogyne que nous trouvons ici correspond probablement au tempérament de l'écrivain." *Mencken*, pp. 131–32.

27. The most extensive misperception of Mencken in print is Charles Angoff's *H. L. Mencken: A Portrait from Memory* (New York: Yoseloff, 1956). Angoff, who assisted Mencken as editor of the *American Mercury*, never seemed to understand that Mencken delighted in kidding him. He was a consistent straight man to Mencken's ingenious and irrepressible extravagance. For example, he believed Mencken's boisterous invention of male locker-room talk

about his sexual exploits, and did not comprehend the almost prudish reality of Mencken's relations with women.

28. Mencken, *Women*, pp. 181, 8.

29. Mencken's writings about his years as a journalist and editor contain very little about his private life, and nothing about his relationships with women. His published letters, including those he wrote to women close to him, observe the same strict, even rigid, sense of aloof propriety.

30. *Smart Set* 38 (December 1912): 154.

31. Mayfield, *The Constant Circle*, p. 111.

## Chapter Four. The Progressive H. L. Mencken.

1. Stuart Sherman, "H. L. Mencken and the Jeune Fille," *New York Times*, 7 December 1919, p. 718. Sherman was showing how bright single women perceived Mencken.

2. Carl Bode, ed., *The Young Mencken* (New York: Dial, 1973), pp. 117–18.

3. W. H. A. Williams, *H. L. Mencken* (Boston: Twayne, 1977), p. 53.

4. H. L. Mencken, *Newspaper Days* (New York: Knopf, 1941), pp. 37–38.

5. Stenerson, *H. L. Mencken*, p. 71.

6. H. L. Mencken, *Treatise on Right and Wrong* (New York: Knopf, 1934), pp. 318–19.

7. Mencken, *George Bernard Shaw*, p. xvi.

8. H. L. Mencken, *Prejudices: Fifth Series* (New York: Knopf, 1926), pp. 64–74.

9. Mencken, *Prejudices: First Series*, p. 177.

10. My reading of Mencken's *Sun* contributions was done in his own clippings files, which are available in volumes bound by year in the Enoch Pratt Free Library, Baltimore. These clippings are not always dated, although many have penciled dates, apparently in Mencken's own hand. Since these files are available, I have not confirmed the dates by searching through originals or microfilms of the *Sun* papers. Subsequent references are to these volumes, identified by year, with month and day included when available.

11. Reprinted in H. L. Mencken, *The Bathtub Hoax and Other Blasts and Bravos from the Chicago Tribune* (New York: Knopf, 1958), pp. 4–10.

12. "Mencken Diary," vol. 1 (1930–1941), 15 February 1935, Enoch Pratt Free Library, Baltimore.

13. M. K. Singleton, *H. L. Mencken and the American Mercury Adventure* (Durham, N.C.: Duke University Press, 1962), p. 153; Scruggs, *The Sage in Harlem*.

14. Theo Lippman, Jr., ed., *A Gang of Pecksniffs* (New Rochelle: Arlington House, 1975), p. 41.

15. H. L. Mencken, *Minority Report* (New York: Knopf, 1956), pp. 189–90. The book was conceived in 1931 and written in the early 1930s.

16. "Letters and Documents Relating to the *Baltimore Sunpapers*," vol. 1₁ (28 July 1931), Enoch Pratt Free Library, Baltimore.

17. Reprinted in Bode, ed., *The Young Mencken*, pp. 119, 126.

18. Reprinted in Lippman, ed., *A Gang of Pecksniffs*, pp. 47, 54.

19. Ibid., p. 59.

20. Ibid., p. 67.

21. Ibid., p. 110.

22. Walter Lippmann, *A Preface to Politics*, reprinted as an Ann Arbor Paperback (Michigan, 1962). Page references are to this edition, and are given parenthetically where they occur.

23. *Smart Set* 40 (August 1913): 154.

24. Ibid., 34 (August 1911): 156.

25. Ibid., 46 (August 1915): 150–55.

26. Louis D. Rubin, Jr., "That Wayward Pressman Mencken," *Sewanee Review* 86 (Summer 1978): 474–80.

## Chapter Five. H. L. Mencken: Dancing with Arms and Legs.

1. Mencken, *Prejudices: Fifth Series*, p. 64.

2. H. L. Mencken, "On Breaking into Type," *Colophon* 1 (February 1930): 29–36; reprinted in Elmer Adler, ed., *Breaking into Print* (New York: Simon and Schuster, 1937), p. 141.

3. Two typical stories are "On the Edge of Samar," *Criterion* 4 (July 1903): 17–18; and (with Leo Drane) "The Passing of Sam Ching," *Criterion* 6 (September 1903): 18–22.

4. H. L. Mencken, *Ventures into Verse* (Baltimore: Marshall, Beek and Gordon, 1903), p. 10.

5. *New England Magazine* 22 (May 1900): 275. Reprinted in *Ventures into Verse*, p. 36, with "city's" in line four changed to "alley."

6. *New England Magazine* 33 (October 1905): 133.

7. Mencken, *Prejudices: Third Series*, pp. 146–70.

8. H. L. Mencken, "Authors and Other Fauna," *New York Evening Mail*, 21 June 1918, p. 8.

9. H. L. Mencken, "Hymn to the Truth," *Prejudices: Sixth Series* (New York: Knopf, 1927), pp. 194–201.

10. H. L. Mencken, "A Neglected Anniversary," *New York Evening Mail*, 28 December 1917, p. 9; reprinted in *The Bathtub Hoax*, pp. 4–10.

11. Vilhjalmur Stefansson, *Adventures in Error* (New York: McBride, 1936), pp. 279–99, has recorded evidence that the bathtub-hoax essay was accepted by some as authentic history.

12. H. L. Mencken, "Hymn to the Truth" and "Melancholy Reflections," *Chicago Tribune*, 25 July and 23 May 1926; reprinted in *The Bathtub Hoax*, pp. 10–19.

13. Edmund Wilson, "H. L. Mencken," *New Republic* 27 (1 June 1921): 10–13.

14. H. L. Mencken, "Suite Americane [*sic*]," *Prejudices: Third Series*, pp. 320–24.

15. Fecher, *Mencken*, p. 348.

16. Rourke, *American Humor*, pp. 59–60.

17. Forgue, *Mencken*, pp. 421, 425, 426: "Le masque de Mencken n'est le plus souvent que la caricature de ses traits réels."

18. Quoted in Fecher, *Mencken*, p. 97.

19. Henry David Thoreau, *Walden*, ed. Walter Harding (New York: Washington Square, 1963), p. 245.

20. H. L. Mencken, "The American Language," in *Literary History of the United States*, ed. Robert E. Spiller et al., 3 vols. (New York: Macmillan, 1948), 2:675.

21. Lippmann, *A Preface to Politics*, pp. 86–87.

22. James K. Kilpatrick, "The Writer Mencken," *Menckeniana* 79 (Fall 1981): 4.

## Chapter Six. What Mencken Wrought: The Debunkers at Work.

1. Mencken, *Prejudices: Fourth Series*, p. 156.

2. Fred C. Hobson, Jr., demonstrates the effect of Mencken's antiprovincialism in the South: *Serpent in Eden: H. L. Mencken and the South* (Chapel Hill: University of North Carolina Press, 1974).

3. Owen Hatteras [pseud.], "Seeing the World," *Smart Set* 41 (November 1913): 65–68; reprinted in *A Book of Burlesques*, pp. 105–32.

4. Donald Ogden Stewart, *Mr. and Mrs. Haddock Abroad* (New York: Doran, 1924), p. 19.

5. Ernest Hemingway, *The Sun Also Rises* (New York: Scribner's, 1926), pp. 115–24.

6. H. L. Mencken, *A Little Book in C-Major* (New York: Lane, 1916), pp. 53, 76.

7. Mencken, *Prejudices: Fifth Series*, pp. 10–11.

8. Mencken, *Prejudices: Third Series*, pp. 213, 219.

9. Mencken, *Prejudices: Fourth Series*, p. 232.

10. Heywood Broun et al., *Nonsenseorship* (New York: Putman's, 1922), p. 94.

11. Ibid., p. 11.

12. H. L. Mencken, *Damn! A Book of Calumny* (New York: Goodman, 1918), p. 65.

13. Mencken, *Prejudices: Fourth Series*, p. 159.

14. Broun et al., *Nonsenseorship*, pp. 28, 29–30.

15. Manchester, *Disturber of the Peace*, pp. 187–207; Bode, *Mencken*, pp. 270–75.

16. Mencken, *Prejudices: Fifth Series*, p. 19.

17. James Thurber and E. B. White, *Is Sex Necessary?* (New York: Harper, 1929), pp. 1, 6, 8, 30, 83.

18. Mencken, *Prejudices: Fifth Series*, p. 13.

19. Ben Hecht, *Erik Dorn* (New York: Putnam's, 1921), p. 109.

20. Matthew J. Bruccoli, *Some Sort of Epic Grandeur* (New York: Harcourt Brace Jovanovich, 1981), pp. 160–61, 163–64, 221.

21. See Singleton, *H. L. Mencken and the American Mercury Adventure* and Dolmetsch, *The Smart Set*.

22. Arthur Schlesinger, *New Viewpoints in American History* (New York: Macmillan, 1922), pp. vii–x.

23. H. L. Mencken, "Portrait of an Immortal," *American Mercury* 16 (February 1929): 251–53; reprinted in *A Mencken Chrestomathy*, pp. 223–26; Van Wyck Brooks, review of *Meet General Grant*, *Outlook* 151 (January 1929): 72.

24. William W. Woodward, *The Gift of Life* (New York: Dutton, 1947), pp. 245, 246.

25. Mencken, *Damn! A Book of Calumny*, p. 7.

26. Mencken, *Prejudices: Second Series*, p. 103.

27. *American Mercury* 1 (January 1924): 31–38.

28. Mencken, *Prejudices: Fifth Series*, pp. 147–8.

29. Merle Curti, *The Roots of American Loyalty* (New York: Columbia University Press, 1946), p. 240.

30. [Clinton W. Gilbert], *The Mirrors of Washington* (New York: Putnam's, 1921), pp. 3–4, 7–8.

31. Warren G. Harding, *Our Common Country* (Indianapolis: Bobbs-Merrill, 1921), pp. 1, 20, 39, 160, 230, 254.

32. In Calvin Coolidge, *Calvin Coolidge, Foundations of the Republic* (New York: Charles Scribner's Sons, 1926), pp. 194–95.

33. Clinton W. Gilbert, *You Takes Your Choice* (New York: Putnam's, 1924), p. 18.

34. Corey Ford, "The Pole at Last," *New Yorker* 2 (22 May 1926): 11–12.

35. John R. Tunis, *$port$: Heroics and Hysterics* (New York: John Day, 1928), pp. 23, 35.

36. Mencken, *Prejudices: Second Series*, pp. 155–71.

37. Ibid., p. 21.

38. Ibid., pp. 100, 12–13.

39. Mencken, "Puritanism as a Literary Force," in *A Book of Prefaces*, p. 203.

40. Mencken, *Prejudices: Second Series*, pp. 30, 31.

41. Ben Hecht, *A Child of the Century* (New York: Simon and Schuster, 1954), p. 220.

42. *American Mercury* 1 (January 1924): 51–56. Reprinted in Ernest Boyd, *Portraits, Real and Imaginary* (New York: Doran, 1924), pp. 11–25.

43. Boyd, *Portraits, Real and Imaginary,* pp. 36–46.

44. Ibid., pp. 153–61.

45. In a note attached to a copy of *Aesthete, 1925,* in the Princeton University Library.

46. Carlos Baker, *Hemingway: The Writer as Artist* (Princeton: Princeton University Press, 1952), p. 41.

47. Ernest Hemingway, *The Torrents of Spring* (New York: Scribner's, 1926), pp. 37, 116, 123–24.

48. Donald Ogden Stewart, *Aunt Polly's Story of Mankind* (New York: Doran, 1923), pp. 28, 34, 277.

49. H. G. Wells, *Outline of History* (New York: Macmillan, 1920), p. 7.

50. Hector B. Toogood [pseud.], *The Outline of Everything* (Boston: Little, Brown, 1923), pp. 5, 7, 89, 121–22.

51. "A Parody Interview with Mr. Van Loon," *Vanity Fair* (November 1927): 90.

52. Dolmetsch, *Smart Set,* p. 90.

## Chapter Seven. The Mimic as Artist: Sinclair Lewis.

1. Mark Schorer, *Sinclair Lewis: An American Life* (New York: McGraw-Hill, 1961), p. 20. Subsequent citations are in the text.

2. Ernest Hemingway, *Across the River and into the Trees* (New York: Scribner's, 1950), p. 87.

3. Letter to Mencken, January 1922; quoted in Schorer, pp. 290–91.

4. Mencken, *A Little Book in C-Major,* p. 55.

5. Angoff, *H. L. Mencken,* pp. 142–46.

6. Mencken, *Damn! A Book of Calumny,* p. 101.

7. Mencken, *Prejudices: Fifth Series,* pp. 104–5.

8. Ibid., pp. 221, 228.

9. Ibid., p. 54.

10. Sinclair Lewis, *Elmer Gantry* (New York: Harcourt, Brace, 1927), pp. 197, 175, 214.

11. Ibid., p. 432.

12. Paul Fussell, *The Great War and Modern Memory* (New York: Oxford, 1976).

13. Sinclair Lewis, *Main Street* (New York: Harcourt, Brace, 1920), p. 1. Further citations are in the text.

14. Edith Wharton, *The House of Mirth* (New York: Scribner's, 1905), pp. 101, 117, 498.

15. Sinclair Lewis, *Babbitt* (New York: Harcourt, Brace, 1922), p. 234. Further citations are in the text.

16. Rourke, *American Humor,* p. 286.

## Chapter Eight. A Puritan's Satanic Flight: Don Marquis, His Archy, and Anarchy.

1. Don Marquis, *The Lives and Times of Archy and Mehitabel* (New York: Doubleday, 1950), p. 231. Further citations are in the text.

2. H. L. Mencken, *Happy Days* (New York: Knopf, 1940), p. 79.

3. Quoted by Christopher Morley in "O Rare Don Marquis," *Saturday Review of Literature* 17 (8 January 1938): 14.

4. Don Marquis, *Sons of the Puritans* (New York: Doubleday, 1939), pp. 37, 83–84, 199–200.

5. Edward Anthony, *O Rare Don Marquis* (New York: Doubleday, 1962), pp. 210–12, 422–23, 26.

6. *Dictionary of American Biography*, s.v. "Marquis, Don."

7. Don Marquis, *The Cruise of the Jasper B.* (New York: D. Appleton, 1916), pp. 67, 98, 97–98, 276.

8. Don Marquis, *Hermione and Her Little Group of Serious Thinkers* (New York: D. Appleton, 1916), p. 16. Further references are in the text.

9. Don Marquis, *Prefaces* (New York: D. Appleton, 1919), pp. 9, 64, 86, 206, 209.

10. Don Marquis, *The Old Soak's History of the World* (New York: Doubleday, Page, 1924), pp. 35, 81.

11. Don Marquis, "Miss Higginbotham Declines," in *Chapters for the Orthodox* (New York: Doubleday, Doran, 1934).

## Chapter Nine. Out of the Underworld of Nonsense: Ring Lardner, Frank Sullivan, and E. B. White.

1. Schorer, in *Sinclair Lewis*, p. 811, makes this observation about Lewis.

2. Jonathan Yardley, *Ring: A Biography of Ring Lardner* (New York: Random House, 1977), p. 354.

3. Ibid., pp. 304, 368.

4. Geoffrey Wolff, *Black Sun* (New York: Random House, 1976), p. 76.

5. Donald Elder, *Ring Lardner* (New York: Doubleday, 1956), pp. 146–49.

6. Yardley, *Ring,* p. 9.

7. Harold Stearns, *Civilization in the United States* (Connecticut: Greenwood Press Reprint, 1961), p. 461.

8. Ring Lardner, *The Young Immigrunts* (Indianapolis: Bobbs-Merrill, 1920), p. 71.

9. Elder, *Ring Lardner,* p. 169.

10. Ring Lardner, *The Big Town* (New York: Scribner's, 1925). These stories were first written in 1919.

11. Ring Lardner, *Gullible's Travels* (New York: Scribner's, 1925).

12. *New Yorker* 8 (18 June 1932): 34. Quoted in Elder, *Ring Lardner,* p. 352.

13. 8 (25 June 1932): 30.

14. 8 (1 October 1932): 34–38.

15. 8 (17 September 1932): 55.

16. 8 (2 June 1932): 27.

17. 8 (19 November 1932): 53–54.

18. 9 (8 July 1933): 27.

19. 9 (6 May 1933): 38.

20. 9 (5 August 1933): 43–44.

21. 5 (28 September 1929): 26–27.

22. 6 (19 April 1930): 17–18.

23. 7 (19 December 1931): 17–18.

24. Edmund Wilson, "Gilbert Seldes and the Popular Arts," *The Shores of Light* (New York: Farrar, Straus and Young, 1952), p. 163.

25. See Tristan Tzara, "Some Memoirs of Dadaism," *Vanity Fair* 28 (July 1922): 70, 92, 94; reprinted in Edmund Wilson, *Axel's Castle* (New York: Scribner's, 1931), pp. 304–12.

26. Elder, *Ring Lardner,* p. 299.

27. Quoted in Yardley, *Ring,* p. 183.

28. Ibid., p. 257.

29. *American Mercury* 29 (June 1933): 254–55.

30. H. L. Mencken, "Ring Lardner," in *A Mencken Chrestomathy.*

31. "Notes and Comments," *New Yorker* 9 (7 October 1933): 5.

32. Quoted in Yardley, *Ring,* pp. 330, 5.

33. Quoted in Elder, *Ring Lardner,* p. 120.

34. Walter Blair, *Horse Sense in American Humor* (Chicago: University of Chicago Press, 1942), pp. 274–80.

35. *New Yorker* 8 (17 September 1932): 15–16; reprinted in Frank Sullivan, *A Rock in Every Snowball* (Boston: Little, Brown, 1946), p. 65.

36. Sullivan, *A Rock in Every Snowball,* p. 65.

37. Ibid., p. 41.

38. Reprinted in Frank Sullivan, *The Night the Old Nostalgia Burned Down* (Boston: Little, Brown, 1953), pp. 3–10.

39. James Thurber, *The Years with Ross* (Boston: Little, Brown, 1959), p. 172.

40. E. B. White, *Quo Vadimus?* (New York: Harper and Brothers, 1939), pp. 3–8.

41. Ibid., pp. 44–49.

42. 9 (6 May 1933): 22–24; 9 (20 May 1933): 21.

43. White, *Quo Vadimus?* pp. 50–57.

## Chapter Ten. *The New Yorker.*

1. *Puck* 59 (5 February 1916): 3.

2. Norman Anthony tells the *Ballyhoo* story himself in *How to Grow Old Disgracefully* (New York: Duell, Sloan, and Pearce, 1946).

3. See Cleveland Amory, and Frederic Bradlee, *Vanity Fair: Selections from America's Most Memorable Magazine* (New York: Viking, 1960).

4. James Thurber, *The Years with Ross,* pp. 226, 4–5. See also Dale Kramer, *Ross and the New Yorker* (New York: Doubleday, 1951); Walter Blair and Hamlin Hill, *America's Humor* (New York: Oxford University Press, 1978), pp. 417–59.

5. *New Yorker* 1 (21 February 1925): 2.

6. Ibid. p. 18.

7. Ibid., p. 24.

8. 2 (26 June 1926): 13–14.

9. 8 (23 June 1932): 5.

10. 1 (12 September 1925): 17.

11. 1 (19 December 1925): 7–8.

12. 1 (2 May 1925): 20; 1 (6 June 1925): 16.

13. See Corey Ford, *Salt Water Taffy* (New York: Putnam's, 1929); and idem, *Coconut Oil: June Triplett's Amazing Book Out of Darkest Africa* (New York: Brewer, Warren and Putnam, 1931).

14. Kramer, *Ross and the New Yorker,* p. 85.

15. "Portrait of an American Author," 1 (6 February 1926): 24.

16. 4 (7 July 1928): 16–17.

17. 5 (18 May 1929): 29.

18. For a detailed analysis of the *New Yorker's* financial success, see J. H. Rutledge and P. B. Bart, "Urbanity, Inc.," *Wall Street Journal,* 30 June 1958, pp. 1, 6.

19. Singleton, *American Mercury Adventure,* pp. 182, 211.

20. He wrote occasionally for the *New Yorker* from 1934 on. The first installment of his memoirs appeared in 1936.


## Chapter Eleven. Nathanael West.

1. Carl Van Vechten, *Spider Boy* (New York: Knopf, 1928).

2. Quoted in Bruce Kellner, *Carl Van Vechten and the Irreverent Decades* (Norman: University of Oklahoma Press, 1968), p. 236.

3. Don Marquis, *Off the Arm* (New York: Doubleday, Doran, 1930).

4. Nathanael West, *The Complete Works of Nathanael West* (New York: Farrar, Straus and Cudahy, 1957). I am quoting in my discussion of *The Day of the Locust* from pp. 262, 297, 274, 328, 330, 262, 271, 350–56 (passim), and 262.

5. Jay Martin, *Nathanael West: The Art of His Life* (New York: Farrar, Straus and Giroux, 1970), p. 38.

6. Martin, *West,* p. 199.

7. The discussion of *The Dream Life of Balso Snell* quotes from West, *The Complete Works,* pp. 8, 10, 30, 26.

8. Quoted in Martin, *West,* p. 215.

9. The quotations in the discussion of *A Cool Million* are from West, *The Complete Works,* pp. 149–50, 188, 255.

10. Martin, *West*, pp. 239–40.
11. The discussion of *Miss Lonelyhearts* cites West, *The Complete Works*, pp. 115, 110, 75.
12. The quotations from *The Day of the Locust* are from West, *The Complete Works*, pp. 411–12.
13. Edmund Wilson has stressed the influence of postwar French writers on West: see "The Boys in the Back Room" in *Classics and Commercials* (New York: Farrar, Straus and Giroux, 1950), pp. 51–56. Also see Martin, *West*, especially chapters 5 and 6.
14. See George Grosz, *A Little Yes and a Big No* (New York: Dial, 1946) for an account of his connection with dada in the 1920s.
15. West, *The Dream Life of Balso Snell*, in *The Complete Works*, p. 27.
16. Quoted in Martin, *West*, p. 161.
17. Norman Podhdoretz, "A Particular Kind of Joking," in Jay Martin, ed., *Nathanael West: A Collection of Critical Essays* (Englewood Cliffs, N.J.: Prentice-Hall, 1971), pp. 154–60.
18. Martin, *West*, p. 397.
19. Ibid., p. 386.

## Afterword.

1. Donald Day, *Will Rogers: A Biography* (New York: D. McKay, 1962), passim, for an account of both the man and the legend.
2. Reprinted in S. J. Perelman, *The Dream Department* (New York: Random House, 1943), p. 166.
3. Robert Forsythe [Kyle Crichton], *Redder than the Rose* (New York: Covici, Friede, 1935), pp. 2, 240.
4. Archibald MacLeish, *The Irresponsibles* (New York: Duell, Sloane and Pearce, 1940); Van Wyck Brooks, *On Literature Today* (New York: E. P. Dutton, 1941); idem, *Opinions of Oliver Allston* (New York: E. P. Dutton, 1941), chapters 18, 19. The issue was further argued in the *Nation*, 1940, and *Partisan Review*, 1941–1942; also see Bernard De Voto, *The Literary Fallacy* (Boston: Little, Brown, 1944).
5. W. H. Auden, "Notes on the Comic," in *The Comic in Theory and Practice*, ed. J. J. Enck, E. T. Forter, A. Whitley (New York: Appleton-Century-Crofts, 1960), p. 115.
6. Sinclair Lewis, "The American Fear of Literature," *Why Sinclair Lewis Got the Nobel Prize: Address by Eric Axel Karlfeldt . . . and by Sinclair Lewis* (New York: Harcourt, Brace, 1931), pp. 22, 23.
7. Richard Boyd Hauck discusses the element of the absurd in some of the major American fiction writers. See *A Cheerful Nihilism* (Bloomington: Indiana University Press, 1971).
8. Jay Martin, "Ambrose Bierce," in Rubin, ed., *The Comic Imagination*, pp. 195–205.

9. Brom Weber, "The Mode of Black Humor," ibid., pp. 361–71.

10. Sarah Blacher Cohen, ed., *Comic Relief: Humor in Contemporary American Literature* (Urbana: University of Illinois Press, 1978), pp. 263–80.

11. For the importance of parody as a central mode in contemporary fiction see essays by Max F. Schulz, Richard Pearce, and Stanley Trachtenberg in Cohen, ed., *Comic Relief.*

# Works Cited

Adler, Betty. *The Mencken Bibliography*. Baltimore: Johns Hopkins University Press, 1961.

Adler, Elmer, ed. *Breaking into Print*. New York: Simon and Schuster, 1937.

Amory, Cleveland, and Frederic Bradlee. *Vanity Fair: Selections from America's Most Memorable Magazine*. New York: Viking, 1960.

Angoff, Charles. *H. L. Mencken: A Portrait from Memory*. New York: Yoseloff, 1956.

Anthony, Edward. *O Rare Don Marquis*. New York: Doubleday, 1962.

Anthony, Norman. *How to Grow Old Disgracefully*. New York: Duell, Sloan, and Pearce, 1946.

Auden, W. H. "Notes on the Comic." In J. J. Enck, E. T. Forter, and A. Whitley, eds., *The Comic in Theory and Practice*. New York: Appleton-Century-Crofts, 1960.

Babbitt, Irving. "The Critic and American Life." *Forum* 79 (February 1928): 161–76.

Baker, Carlos. *Hemingway: The Writer as Artist*. Princeton: Princeton University Press, 1952.

Barnes, Harry E. "The Drool Method in History." *American Mercury* 1 (January 1924): 31–38.

Benchley, Robert. "Up the Dark Stairs—." *New Yorker* 1 (19 December 1925): 7–8.

Bent, Silas. *Ballyhoo: The Voice of the Press*. New York: Boni and Liveright, 1927.

Bierce, Ambrose. *Collected Works*. New York: Neale, 1909.

Blair, Walter. *Horse Sense in American Humor*. Chicago: University of Chicago Press, 1942.

———, and Hamlin Hill. *America's Humor*. New York: Oxford University Press, 1978.

Bode, Carl. *Mencken*. Carbondale: Southern Illinois University Press, 1969.

———, ed. *The Young Mencken*. New York: Dial, 1973.

Bowers, C. G. Review of *George Washington* by William E. Woodward. *International Book Review* (November 1926), p. 753.

Boyd, Ernest. *Portraits, Real and Imaginary*. New York: Doran, 1924.

Brooks, Van Wyck. *America's Coming of Age*. New York: Huebsch, 1915.

———. *On Literature Today*. New York: E. P. Dutton, 1941.

———. *Opinions of Oliver Allston*. New York: E. P. Dutton, 1941.

Broun, Heywood, et al. *Nonsenseorship.* New York: Putnam's, 1922.

Bruccoli, Matthew J. *Some Sort of Epic Grandeur.* New York: Harcourt Brace Jovanovich, 1981.

Burgess, Gelett. *Lark* (1 May 1895 to 1 April 1897) and *Epi-Lark* (1 May 1897).

Cabell, James Branch. *Jurgen.* New York: Grosset and Dunlap, 1919.

Calverton, V. F., and S. D. Schmalhausen, eds. *Sex in Civilization.* New York: Macaulay, 1929.

Chase, Stuart. *Tragedy of Waste.* New York: Macmillan, 1925.

————, and F. J. Schlinck. *Your Money's Worth.* New York: Macmillan, 1927.

Cohen, Sarah Blacher, ed. *Comic Relief: Humor in Contemporary American Literature.* Urbana: University of Illinois Press, 1978.

Cooke, Alistair. "The Public and Private Face." In *Six Men.* New York: Knopf, 1977.

Coolidge, Calvin. *Calvin Coolidge: Foundations of the Republic.* New York: Charles Scribner's Sons, 1926.

Cox, James M. "The Humor of the Old Southwest." In Louis D. Rubin, Jr., ed., *The Comic Imagination in American Literature.* New Brunswick, N.J.: Rutgers University Press, 1973.

————. "Mark Twain." In Louis D. Rubin, Jr., ed., *The Comic Imagination in American Literature.* New Brunswick, N.J.: Rutgers University Press, 1973.

Crichton, Kyle [Robert Forsythe]. *Redder than the Rose.* New York: Covici, Friede, 1935.

Curti, Merle. *The Roots of American Loyalty.* New York: Columbia University Press, 1946.

Davis, Elmer. "On the Banks of the Wabash." *New Yorker* 2 (26 June 1926): 13–14.

————. "Portrait of an American Author." *New Yorker* 1 (6 February 1926): 24.

Day, Donald. *Will Rogers: A Biography.* New York: D. McKay, 1962.

DeForest, John William. *Honest John Vane.* New Haven: Richmond and Patten, 1875.

Dell, Floyd. *Moon-Calf.* New York: Knopf, 1920.

————. *An Unmarried Father.* New York: Doran, 1927.

DeVoto, Bernard. *The Literary Fallacy.* Boston: Little, Brown, 1944.

Dolmetsch, Carl R. *The Smart Set: A History and Anthology.* New York: Dial, 1966.

Douglas, Ann. *The Feminization of American Culture.* New York: Knopf, 1977.

Editorial. "A New School of Satire." *Puck* 59 (5 February 1916): 3.

Editorial. "First Issue." *New Yorker* 1 (21 February 1925): 2.

Elder, Donald. *Ring Lardner.* New York: Doubleday, 1956.

Fatout, Paul. *Ambrose Bierce.* Norman: University of Oklahoma Press, 1951.

Fecher, Charles A. *Mencken: A Study of His Thought.* New York: Knopf, 1978.

Fiedler, Leslie. *Love and Death in the American Novel.* New York: Criterion Books, 1960.

Filler, Louis. *Crusaders for American Liberalism.* Yellow Springs, Ohio: Antioch Press, 1950.

Fitzgerald, F. Scott. *The Great Gatsby.* New York: Scribner's, 1925.

Flexner, Eleanor. *Century of Struggle.* New York: Atheneum, 1974.

Ford, Corey. *Coconut Oil: June Triplett's Amazing Book Out of Darkest Africa.* New York: Brewer, Warren, and Putnam, 1931.

———. "Creative Art in New York." *New Yorker* 1 (2 May 1925): 20; 1 (6 June 1925): 16.

———. *Meaning No Offense.* New York: John Day, 1928.

———. "A Parody Interview with Mr. Van Loon." *Vanity Fair* (November 1927): 90.

———. "The Pole at Last." *New Yorker* 2 (22 May 1926): 11–12.

———. *Salt Water Taffy.* New York: Putnam's, 1929.

Ford, Henry. Interview. *New York Times,* 20 May 1919, p. 14.

Forgue, Guy J. *H. L. Mencken.* Paris: Minard, 1967.

———. "Myths about Mencken." *Nation* 193 (16 September 1961): 163–65.

———, ed. *The Letters of H. L. Mencken.* New York: Knopf, 1961.

Frank, Waldo. *Our America.* New York: Boni and Liveright, 1919.

———, and James Oppenheim. Editorial. *Seven Arts* (November 1916): 52–53.

Frederic, Harold. *The Damnation of Theron Ware.* New York: Stone and Kimball, 1896.

Fussell, Paul. *The Great War and Modern Memory.* New York: Oxford University Press, 1976.

Gibbs, Wolcott. *Bird Life at the Pole.* New York: Morrow, 1931.

[Gilbert, Clinton W.] *The Mirrors of Washington.* New York: Putnam's, 1921.

———. *You Takes Your Choice.* New York: Putnam's, 1924.

Grosz, George. *A Little Yes and a Big No.* New York: Dial, 1946.

Gruening, Ernest, ed. *These United States,* first series. New York: Boni and Liveright, 1923.

Hanemann, H. W. *The Facts of Life.* New York: Farrar and Rinehart, 1930.

Harding, Warren G. *Our Common Country.* Indianapolis: Bobbs-Merrill, 1921.

Harrison, John M. and Harry H. Stein, eds. *Muckraking.* University Park: Pennsylvania State University Press, 1973.

Hauck, Richard Boyd. *A Cheerful Nihilism.* Bloomington: Indiana University Press, 1971.

Hecht, Ben. *A Child of the Century.* New York: Simon and Schuster, 1954.

———. *Eric Dorn.* New York: Putnam's, 1921.

Hemingway, Ernest. *Across the River and into the Trees.* New York: Scribner's, 1950.

———. *The Sun Also Rises.* New York: Scribner's, 1926.

———. *The Torrents of Spring.* New York: Scribner's, 1926.

Hobson, Fred C., Jr. *Serpent in Eden: H. L. Mencken and the South.* Chapel Hill: University of North Carolina Press, 1974.

Hoffman, Frederick J. *Freudianism and the Literary Mind.* Baton Rouge: Louisiana State University Press, 1957.

———, Charles Allen, and C. F. Ulrich. *The Little Magazine: A History and a Bibliography.* Princeton: Princeton University Press, 1947.

Hofstadter, Richard. *The Age of Reform.* New York: Knopf, 1950.

Kellner, Bruce. *Carl Van Vechten and the Irreverent Decades.* Norman: University of Oklahoma Press, 1968.

Kempton, Murray. "Saving a Whale." *New York Review of Books* 28 (11 June 1981): 8–14.

Kilpatrick, James K. "The Writer Mencken." *Menckeniana* 79 (Fall 1981): 4.

Kramer, Dale. *Ross and the New Yorker.* New York: Doubleday, 1951.

Lardner, Ring. *The Big Town.* New York: Scribner's, 1925.

———. *Gullible's Travels.* New York: Scribner's, 1925.

———. "Large Coffee." *New Yorker* 5 (28 September 1929): 26–27.

———. *My Four Weeks in France.* Indianapolis: Bobbs-Merrill, 1918.

———. "Over the Waves." *New Yorker* 8 (1 October 1932): 34–38; 8 (2 June 1932): 27; 8 (18 June 1932): 34; 8 (25 June 1932): 30; 8 (17 September 1932): 55; 8 (19 November 1932): 53–54; 9 (6 May 1933): 38; 9 (8 July 1933): 27.

———. "Profiles: Dante and ———." *New Yorker* 4 (7 July 1928): 27.

———. "Quadroon: A Play in Four Pelts Which May All Be Attended in One Day or Missed in a Group." *New Yorker* 7 (19 December 1931): 17–18.

———. "Ricordi to the Rescue: A Radio Play in One Endless Act." *New Yorker* 9 (5 August 1933): 43–44.

———. "Sit Still." *New Yorker* 6 (19 April 1930): 17–18.

———. "Sport and Play." In Harold Stearns, ed., *Civilization in the United States.* Connecticut: Greenwood Press Reprint, 1961.

———. *The Story of a Wonder Man.* New York: Scribner's, 1927.

———. *You Know Me Al.* New York: Doran, 1916.

———. *The Young Immigrunts.* Indianapolis: Bobbs-Merrill, 1920.

Leary, Lewis. "Benjamin Franklin." In Louis D. Rubin, Jr., ed., *The Comic Imagination in American Literature.* New Brunswick, N.J.: Rutgers University Press, 1973.

Leonard, J. N. *The Tragedy of Henry Ford.* New York: Putnam's, 1932.

Lewis, Sinclair. "The American Fear of Literature." *Why Sinclair Lewis Got the Nobel Prize: Address by Eric Axel Karlfeldt . . . and by Sinclair Lewis.* New York: Harcourt, Brace, 1931.

———. *Arrowsmith.* New York: Harcourt, Brace, 1925.

———. *Babbitt.* New York: Harcourt, Brace, 1922.

———. *Elmer Gantry.* New York: Harcourt, Brace, 1927.

———. *Main Street.* New York: Harcourt, Brace, 1920.

———. *The Man Who Knew Coolidge.* New York: Harcourt, Brace, 1928.

———. *Work of Art.* New York: Doubleday, Doran, 1934.

Lippman, Theo, Jr., ed. *A Gang of Pecksniffs.* New Rochelle: Arlington House, 1975.

Lippmann, Walter. *A Preface to Politics.* 1913; rpt. Ann Arbor, Mich.: Ann Arbor Paperback, 1962.

London, Jack. *The Iron Heel.* New York: Macmillan, 1907.

Loos, Anita. *A Girl like I.* New York: Viking, 1966.

MacLeish, Archibald. *The Irresponsibles.* New York: Duell, Sloane and Pearce, 1940.

Manchester, William. *Disturber of the Peace: The Life of H. L. Mencken.* New York: Harper, 1950.

Markey, Morris. "In the News." *New Yorker* 1 (12 September 1925): 17.

Marquis, Don. *The Almost Perfect State.* New York: Doubleday, Page, 1927.

———. *The Cruise of the Jasper B.* New York: D. Appleton, 1916.

———. *Danny's Own Story.* New York: Doubleday, Page, 1912.

———. *Hermione and Her Little Group of Serious Thinkers.* New York: D. Appleton, 1916.

———. *The Lives and Times of Archy and Mehitabel.* New York: Doubleday, 1950.

———. "Miss Higginbotham Declines." In *Chapters for the Orthodox.* New York: Doubleday, Doran, 1934.

———. *Off the Arm.* New York: Doubleday, Doran, 1930.

———. *The Old Soak and Hail and Farewell.* New York: Doubleday, Page, 1921.

———. *The Old Soak's History of the World.* New York: Doubleday, Page, 1924.

———. *Prefaces.* New York: D. Appleton, 1916.

———. *Sons of the Puritans.* New York: Doubleday, 1939.

Martin, Edward A. "H. L. Mencken and Equal Rights for Women." *Georgia Review* 35 (Spring 1981): 65–76.

———. "H. L. Mencken's Poetry." *Texas Studies in Literature and Language* 6 (Autumn 1964): 346–53.

———. "The Ordeal of H. L. Mencken." *South Atlantic Quarterly* 61 (Summer 1962): 326–38.

———. "A Puritan's Satanic Flight: Don Marquis, Archy, and Anarchy." *Sewanee Review* 83 (October to December 1975): 623–42.

Martin, Jay. "Ambrose Bierce." In Louis D. Rubin, Jr., ed., *The Comic Imagination in American Literature.* New Brunswick, N.J.: Rutgers University Press, 1973.

———. *Nathanael West: The Art of His Life.* New York: Farrar, Straus and Giroux, 1970.

May, Henry F. *The End of American Innocence.* Chicago: Quadrangle Books, 1964.

Mayfield, Sara. *The Constant Circle.* New York: Delacorte, 1968.

Mencken. H. L. "Ambrose Bierce." In *A Mencken Chrestomathy.* New York: Knopf, 1949.

———. "The American." *American Mercury* 29 (June 1933): 254–55.

———. "The American Language." In *Literary History of the United States,* 3 vols., edited by Robert E. Spiller et al. New York: Macmillan, 1948.

———. "Auroral." *New England Magazine* 22 (May 1900): 275. Reprinted in *Ventures into Verse.*

———. "Authors and Other Fauna." *New York Evening Mail,* 21 June 1918.

———. *The Bathtub Hoax and Other Blasts and Bravos from the Chicago Tribune.* New York: Knopf, 1958.

———. *A Book of Prefaces.* New York: Knopf, 1917.

———. "Books to Read and Books to Avoid." *Smart Set* 30 (February 1910): 153–54.

———. "On Breaking into Type" *Colophon* 1 (February 1930): 29–36. Reprinted in Elmer Adler, ed., *Breaking into Print.*

———. "A Counterblast to Buncombe." *Smart Set* 40 (August 1913): 154.

———. *Damn! A Book of Calumny.* New York: Goodman, 1918.

———. *The Days of H. L. Mencken.* New York: Knopf, 1947.

———. *In Defense of Women.* New York: Goodman, 1918; Knopf, 1922.

———. "A 'Doll's House'—with a Fourth Act." *Smart Set* 29 (December 1909): 153–54.

———. "On the Edge of Samar." *Criterion* 4 (July 1903): 17–18.

———. "Etymology of *bunk.*" *Smart Set* 67 (April 1922): 45.

———. "Fifteen Years." *Smart Set* 68 (December 1923). Reprinted in William H. Nolte, ed., *H. L. Mencken's Smart Set Criticism.* Ithaca: Cornell University Press, 1968.

———. "Free Lance" columns. *Baltimore Evening Sun,* 1, 3, 6 February 1912.

———. *George Bernard Shaw: His Plays.* Boston: Luce, 1905.

———. *Happy Days.* New York: Knopf, 1940.

———. "Hymn to the Truth." In *Prejudices: Sixth Series and The Bathtub Hoax and Other Blasts and Bravos from the Chicago Tribune.*

———. "The Leading American Novelist." *Smart Set* 33 (January 1911): 163–64.

———. Letter to Theodore Dreiser (1911). In Guy J. Forgue, ed., *The Letters of H. L. Mencken.*

———. *A Little Book in C-Major.* New York: Lane, 1916.

———. "Melancholy Reflections." *Chicago Tribune,* 25 July and 23 May 1926. Reprinted in *The Bathtub Hoax and Other Blasts and Bravos from the Chicago Tribune.*

———. *Minority Report.* New York: Knopf, 1956.

———. "A Neglected Anniversary." *New York Evening Mail,* 28 December 1917. Reprinted in *The Bathtub Hoax and Other Blasts and Bravos from the Chicago Tribune.*

———. *Newspaper Days.* New York: Knopf, 1941.

———. "Notes and Comments." *New Yorker* 9 (7 October 1933): 5.

———. "On Passing the Island of San Salvador." *New England Magazine* 33 (October 1905): 133.

———. *The Philosophy of Friedrich Nietzsche.* Boston: Luce, 1908.

———. "The Poet and His Art." In *Prejudices: Third Series.*

———. "Portraits of Americans." *A Book of Burlesques.* New York: Lane, 1916.

————. *Prejudices: First Series*. New York: Knopf, 1919.

————. *Prejudices: Second Series*. New York: Knopf, 1920.

————. *Prejudices: Third Series*. New York: Knopf, 1922.

————. *Prejudices: Fourth Series*. New York: Knopf, 1924.

————. *Prejudices: Fifth Series*. New York: Knopf, 1926.

————. *Prejudices: Sixth Series*. New York: Knopf, 1927.

————. "Puritanism as a Literary Force." In *A Book of Prefaces*.

————. Review with allusion to Conrad and Dreiser. *Smart Set* 50 (October 1916): 139.

————. Review of *A Far Country* by Winston Churchill. *Smart Set* 46 (August 1915): 150–55.

————. Review of *Jennie Gerhardt* by Theodore Dreiser. *Smart Set* 35 (November 1911): 153–55.

————. Review of *Love's Pilgrimage* by Upton Sinclair. *Smart Set* 34 (August 1911): 156.

————. Review of *Main Street* by Sinclair Lewis. *Smart Set* 64 (January 1921): 139.

————. Review of *A Preface to Politics* by Walter Lippmann. *Smart Set* 38 (December 1912): 154.

————. Review of *Women in Modern Society* by Earl Barnes. *Smart Set* 38 (December 1912): 154.

————. "Ring Lardner." In *A Mencken Chrestomathy*. New York: Knopf, 1949.

————. *Treatise on Right and Wrong*. New York: Knopf, 1934.

————. *Ventures into Verse*. Baltimore: Marshall, Beek and Gordon, 1903.

————, and Leo Drane. "The Passing of Sam Ching." *Criterion* 6 (September 1903): 18–22.

————, and George Jean Nathan. *The American Credo*. New York: Knopf, 1920.

————, George Jean Nathan, and Willard Huntington Wright. *Europe after 8:15*. New York: Lane, 1914.

————, and Robert Rives LaMonte. *Man versus the Man: A Correspondence between Robert Rives LaMonte, Socialist, and H. L. Mencken, Individualist*. Reprinted in Carl Bode, ed., *The Young Mencken*.

Morley, Christopher. "O Rare Don Marquis." *Saturday Review of Literature* 17 (8 January 1938): 14.

Nevins, Allan. Review of *George Washington* by William E. Woodward. *Saturday Review of Literature* 3 (11 December 1926): 415.

Nolte, William H. *H. L. Mencken: Literary Critic*. Middletown, Conn.: Wesleyan University Press, 1966.

Obituary. William E. Woodward. *New York Times*, 30 September 1950, p. 17.

Owens, Gwinn. "Mencken and the Jews, Revisited." *Menckeniana* 74 (Summer 1980): 6–10.

Perelman, S. J. *The Dream Department.* New York: Random House, 1943.

Podhoretz, Norman. "A Particular Kind of Joking." In Jay Martin, ed., *Nathanael West: A Collection of Critical Essays.*

Rascoe, Burton. "*Smart Set* History." In Burton Rascoe and Groff Conklin, eds., *The Smart Set Anthology of World Famous Authors.* New York: Reynal, 1934.

Ridgely, J. V. "Ambrose Bierce to H. L. Mencken." *Book Club of California Quarterly News Letter* 26 (Fall 1961): 27–33.

Roth, George M. "American Theory of Satire, 1790–1820." *American Literature* 29 (January 1958): 399–407.

Rourke, Constance. *American Humor.* New York: Harcourt, Brace, 1931.

Rubin, Louis D., Jr. "That Wayward Pressman Mencken." *Sewanee Review* 86 (Summer 1978): 474–80.

Rutledge. J. H., and P. B. Bart. "Urbanity Inc." *Wall Street Journal,* 30 June 1958, pp. 1, 6.

Santayana, George. "America's Young Radicals." *Forum* 67 (May 1922): 371–75.

Schlesinger, Arthur. *New Viewpoints in American History.* New York: Macmillan, 1922.

Schorer, Mark. *Sinclair Lewis: An American Life.* New York: McGraw-Hill, 1961.

Scruggs, Charles. *The Sage in Harlem.* Baltimore: Johns Hopkins University Press, 1984.

Sherman, Stuart. "H. L. Mencken and the Jeune Fille." *New York Times,* 7 December 1919, p. 718.

Simpson, Lewis P. "The Satiric Mode: The Early National Wits." In Louis D. Rubin, Jr., ed., *The Comic Imagination in American Literature.* New Brunswick, N.J.: Rutgers University Press, 1973.

Singleton, M. K. *H. L. Mencken and the American Mercury Adventure.* Durham, N.C.: Duke University Press, 1962.

Stefansson, Vilhjalmur. *Adventures in Error.* New York: McBride, 1936.

Stenerson, Douglas. *H. L. Mencken: Iconoclast from Baltimore.* Chicago: University of Chicago Press, 1971.

Stewart, Donald Ogden. *Aunt Polly's Story of Mankind.* New York: Doran, 1923.

———. *Mr. and Mrs. Haddock Abroad.* New York: Doran, 1924.

———. *Mr. and Mrs. Haddock in Paris, France.* New York: Doran, 1926.

———. *A Parody Outline of History.* New York: Doran, 1921.

Sullivan, Frank. *A Rock in Every Snowball.* Boston: Little, Brown, 1946.

———. *The Night the Old Nostalgia Burned Down.* Boston: Little, Brown, 1953.

Thompson, Vance. "Foreword." *M'lle New York* 1 (August 1895): 1.

———. "Leader." *M'lle New York* 1 (October 1895): 41–42.

———. "Leader." *M'lle New York* 2 (November 1898): 1.

————. "Polite Letters." *M'lle New York* 1 (August 1895): 14–15.

Thoreau, Henry David. *Walden,* edited by Walter Harding. New York: Washington Square, 1963.

Thurber, James. *The Years with Ross.* Boston: Little, Brown, 1959.

————, and E. B. White. *Is Sex Necessary?* New York: Harper,1929.

Toogood, Hector B. [Donald Ogden Stewart?] *The Outline of Everything.* Boston: Little, Brown, 1923.

Tunis, John R. *$port$: Heroics and Hysterics.* New York: John Day, 1928.

Tzara, Tristan. "Some Memoirs of Dadaism." *Vanity Fair* 28 (July 1922): 70, 92–94. Reprinted in Edmund Wilson, *Axel's Castle.* New York: Scribner's, 1931.

Van Doren, Carl. Review of *Bunk* by William E. Woodward. *Nation* 117 (October 1923): 398.

Van Vechten, Carl. *Spider Boy.* New York: Knopf, 1928.

Wagner, Philip. *H. L. Mencken.* Minneapolis: University of Minnesota Press, 1966.

Weber, Brom. "The Mispellers." In Louis D. Rubin, Jr., ed., *The Comic Imagination in American Literature.* New Brunswick, N.J.: Rutgers University Press, 1973.

Wells, H. G. *Outline of History.* New York: Macmillan, 1920.

West, Nathanael. *The Complete Works of Nathanael West.* New York: Farrar, Straus and Cudahy, 1957.

Wharton, Edith. *The House of Mirth.* New York: Scribner's, 1905.

White, E. B. "Alice through the Cellophane." *New Yorker* 9 (6 May 1933): 22–24.

————. *Quo Vadimus?* New York: Harper and Brothers, 1939.

Williams, W. H. A. *H. L. Mencken.* Boston: Twayne, 1977.

Wilson, Edmund. "The Boys in the Back Room." In *Classics and Commercials.* New York: Farrar, Straus and Giroux, 1950.

————. "Gilbert Seldes and the Popular Arts." In *The Shores of Light.* New York: Farrar, Straus and Young, 1952.

————. "H. L. Mencken." *New Republic* 27 (1 June 1921): 10–13.

Wolff, Geoffrey. *Black Sun.* New York: Random House, 1976.

Woodward, William E. *Bread and Circuses.* New York: Harper, 1925.

————. *Bunk.* New York and London: Harper, 1923.

————. *George Washington: The Image and the Man.* New York: Boni and Liveright, 1926.

————. *The Gift of Life.* New York: Dutton, 1947.

————. *Lottery.* New York: Harper, 1924.

————. *Meet General Grant.* New York: Liveright, 1928.

————. *Tom Paine: America's Godfather.* New York: Dutton, 1945.

————. "The World and Sauk Centre." *New Yorker* 10 (27 January 1934): 25.

Woollcott, Alexander. "Profile: George S. Kaufman." *New Yorker* 5 (18 May 1929): 29.

Wright, Louis B. "Human Comedy in Early America." In Louis D. Rubin, Jr., ed., *The Comic Imagination in American Literature.* New Brunswick, N.J.: Rutgers University Press, 1973.

Wylie, Philip. *Generation of Vipers.* New York: Farrar and Rinehart, 1942.

Yardley, Jonathan. *Ring: A Biography of Ring Lardner.* New York: Random House, 1977.

Yates, Norris. *The American Humorist.* Ames: Iowa State University Press, 1964.

Ziff, Larzer. *The American 1890s.* New York: Viking, 1966.

# Index